As a business leader, I have hungered for wisdom in many circumstances. Proverbs provides it. Dan and Drew bring to life this ageless guide and how you can lead conscientiously and courageously so that your company can flourish and perform. Take it with you to work!

Cheryl Bachelder
Former CEO of Popeyes Louisiana Kitchen, Board Member at Pier One, Chick-fil-A, and Procter & Gamble, and author of *Dare to Serve*

The book of Proverbs teaches us to cry out for wisdom. That truth should be no different for our businesses than our daily life. Drew and Dan help drive that point home in Sharpen.

David Green
CEO & Founder, Hobby Lobby, Inc.

I love this book. Two authors that have a deep understanding of both business and scripture write about my favorite topics: wisdom and successful living. If you want to learn timeless truths that relate to the challenges and opportunities in your life, read this book.

Mark Sanborn
Author of *The Fred Factor* and *The Potential Principle*

Timely. Powerful. Relevant! Dan & Drew offer powerful truth that impacts business because it impacts leaders. Trust matter more than ever and Sharpen offers deep and timeless insight to help you and your organization gain the greatest advantage of all time – Trust!

David Horsager
Bestselling author and CEO of the Trust Edge Leadership Institute

Sharpen is filled with refreshing, uncommon candor. Each chapter provides pragmatic applications to help Christian leaders tackle today's most common leadership challenges. I found as many applications for how I manage our home and family as I do in managing my company. Reading this book humbly reminds me of how to be a Kingdom Leader.

John Ramstead
Founder and Host of the Eternal Leadership Podcast
CEO, Beyond Influence

Any smart business person pursues wisdom. Whether one is a follower of scripture or not, the book of Proverbs offers direction. Add to it, tangible mental models that can be readily employed in day to day practice — Sharpen is a beneficial resource in your tool kit to help you heighten your impact.

Stacey M. Browning
President, Paycor

I was reluctant to read another book on leadership. As a former leadership consultant, I feel like I've already read them all! But Dan and Drew are proven business leaders and they've helped almost 100 other owners and CEOs be successful so I gave it a shot. I'm so glad I did! I found pearls of wisdom to immediately apply to running my organization. I'm confident you will, too.

Jeff Spadafora
Founder/President of The Way, Author of *The Joy Model:
A Step-by-Step Guide to Peace, Purpose, and Balance.*

Sharpen is one of those rare books that provides humor, insight and clarity around the application of scripture to the art of being a leader and running a business. I highly commend the work of Dan Cooper and Drew Hiss as they walk alongside of you in your journey to live with wisdom and grace.

Bill High
CEO, The Signatry

Adding value to the timeless wisdom of the book of Proverbs may seem like a fool's errand to some, but Dan and Drew pulled it off. Their combined business expertise, transparency, wit, and conversational style, all with an eye towards applying the wisdom practically, makes Sharpen a book from which every business leader can find value over and over again.

Rick Boxx
Founder and CEO of Unconventional Business
Network, www.UnconventionalBusiness.org

We all want clear direction in life. This book, and its mix of practical tools and deep introspection, will be a tremendous help for those seeking wisdom.

Dave Jewitt
Founder of www.YourOneDegree.com

While Dan and Drew have lots of both expertise and experience in leading and training business leaders, in Sharpen, they call upon a greater source of wisdom - the Proverbs of the Bible. The author of Proverbs is Solomon, one of the most successful business and life coaches of all time. Sharpen brings together these 31 chapters with practical applications and amazing case studies. Every business leader will be blessed by reading and applying this wisdom to their personal and business decision making.

Jerry Kirk
Founder of the Prayer Covenant

Sharpen is packed with practical, actionable and timeless insight to help leaders keep on course professionally and personally. Dan and Drew have done a great service for leaders who are looking for a go-to resource to maximize their impact business without losing their soul. What makes a book worth reading is when you know the authors actually live what it is they write, and Dan and Drew walk the talk. It will be a book that I will read and reference again and again.

Merle Mees
Lead Pastor, Pleasant Valley Baptist Church, Liberty, Missouri

So you want to dramatically improve your business and life... It's really quite simple – change your thinking. The wisdom of Solomon as framed by Dan and Drew, two extraordinary leaders, is a perfect place to start your transformation. Enjoy the journey.

Joe Calhoon
CSP, Author & Professional EOS Implementer™

Dan and Drew provide a reflection on wisdom that will meet any reader where they are today and help them to impact their leadership tomorrow. By combining biblical truths, personal experience, and contemporary reflection, this book demonstrates how wisdom can help today's business leaders breakthrough to greater success and significance. Each chapter includes practical examples and a call to action to actualize the concepts in the book. Dan and Drew clearly demonstrate how importance pursing wisdom is to any business leader become a better Servant Leader or People-Centric Leader.

Brian Wellinghoff
Partner, Barry-Wehmiller Leadership Institute

The ancient book of Proverbs is arguable the best business book for today's business leader. Dan and Drew have done a masterful job of teeing up these timeless principles for you so you can hit a homerun in your business. I predict adherents of these principles will wake up a year from now further down the road, then those who don't. Two Thumbs up!

Randy Frazee
Pastor & Author of *The Heart of the Story*

There's no better way to lead yourself well, and lead others, than with the wisdom found in Proverbs. This is a leader's field manual for true success!

Dr. Nathan Baxter
Founder of LeadSelfLeadOthers.com and RealCoachingSuccess.com

Businesspeople need wisdom, and entrepreneurial couples need wisdom to keep them on the same path. Dan and Drew have created a wonderful treasure that entrepreneurs and couples can use to grow in every area of life.

Kathy Rushing
Mentor to Entrepreneurial Couples at www.KathyRushing.com
and host of *Committed: A Podcast for Couples on the
(Sometimes) Crazy Entrepreneurial Journey*

If you're going to chase your dreams, you'll need wisdom. And plenty of it. This book not only breaks down Proverbs, Dan and Drew make it applicable to life and business.

Zech Newman
Speaker, coach, and author of *Chasing Dreams
in a Minivan. ZechariahNewman.com*

The path to the life you want—the life God has planned for you—is paved with wisdom. This book will help you trade confusion for wisdom, and move you forward.

Heather Turner
Coach, speaker, and author of *Dream Traders -
Discover and Pursue the Life You Want*

SHARPEN

*A Guidebook for Business Ownership
and Adventures in Leadership*

Dan Cooper & Drew Hiss

Sharpen:
A Guidebook for Business Ownership and Adventures in Leadership

Dan Cooper and Drew Hiss

Cover Design: MikeLoomis.CO

AcumenImpact.com
SharpenBook.com

Dedication

To the countless men and women seeking the entrepreneurial dream,
who aspire to succeed and thrive as leaders of impact.

We're honored to serve you at Acumen.

www.AcumenImpact.com

CONTENTS

INTRODUCTION: WHY

People don't buy what you do; they buy why you do it.
—Simon Sinek

Early in my (Dan) tenure as CEO of an online training company, we were a small but growing group and needed to fill a new position quickly. So we contracted with a placement firm. The contract terms stated that anyone we interviewed was under the agreement of the placement firm for six months. We spoke with six candidates with no good fit. We moved on without hiring anyone. About five and a half months into that six-month period, one of the candidates called back. "Hi, Dan, we talked a while ago and I've recently gotten some new certifications that make me more qualified for the position you had open. Have you hired anyone?"

"We haven't," I said. "Let's talk again, but I'll be busy for the next couple weeks. What does your schedule look like three weeks out?"

We meet three weeks later and had a good conversation. I made him an offer—outside the contract with the placement firm.

During his first week at our office, he answered an incoming phone call—which happened to be the head of the placement firm calling to check in. Of course, she recognized their previous candidate, now our employee, by his voice. She got transferred to me, and as soon as I picked up the phone, I realized she was putting on that fake happy salesperson voice with massive undertones of LIVID.

"Hi, Dan. Was that John who answered the phone?"

I believe I stammered out, "Uh . . . yes, it was."

"I thought he was a good candidate when we introduced him to you. When did you hire him?"

And from there she and I went into a thinly veiled argument about John, our agreement, the timeline, and our relationship.

By the letter of the contract, I was innocent. By the spirit of the agreement, I was guilty. And the relationship between our company and the placement firm? What relationship?

I remember thinking to myself, *How did I get here?* As a business owner, there are all kinds of pressures on you, and you are trying to make the best decisions for your company or organization. It's easy to get into justification mode. "I'm saving the company money. I'm frugal. The time on the contract was technically up, so ..."

But internally, I was convicted. I paid the commission on the hire. Our relationship was forever broken, and we now had an entire company who questioned our integrity and could impact our reputation.

Was that worth it? The commission was about $5,000. What do you think?

What happens when it is $50,000, or $500,000? Is that just "good business?" If I had been a student of Proverbs at that time in my career, my choice would have been easy. In fact, many decisions would have been easier.

Why Solomon?

It seems laughable, even ironic and verging on ridiculous, that in contemporary books written to business owners, CEOs, and executive leaders, there is rarely a reference made to history's wealthiest and most successful leader: King Solomon.

The world is quick to parade the likes of Bill Gates, Warren Buffett, Steve Jobs, Mark Zuckerberg, Jeff Bezos, Elon Musk, and so on as pillars of success, leadership, and business wisdom. Yet by comparison, Solomon amassed far greater wealth and success than any of them. And he left us a legacy gift. He and his scribes (he didn't author all of Proverbs by himself) gave us 31 chapters in a book called Proverbs that supplies incredible, practical, and timeless wisdom relative to success and leadership.

Maybe it's because he's not modern enough. Perhaps the gap of time between his existence and the current day makes him easily forgotten and overlooked. Or perhaps it's the fact that he spoke clearly and plainly about his affection for God that makes him "too religious" for our progressive, politically correct perspective. Whatever the case, it's unfortunate that the nuggets of wisdom and advice he left us are not given the same value as the writings and musings of the aforementioned allstars. It could also be that Solomon's style and approach to writing was random at best. Seriously random. Each chapter in Proverbs has about 30 verses. And although a few chapters have one main theme, most don't. So each chapter ends up being a commentary on many different topics. There is genius in this randomness because you can read a chapter on any day and get value from it. But it's also ADD.

In many ways, reading Proverbs is like reading a Twitter or Facebook feed—it's a listing of topics that you may or may not be interested in at the time. One proverb will be about integrity, and the next will be about anger, followed by a verse about wealth, leadership, and on and on. That which is the book's genius also makes it hard to act on. We can end up thinking, *What should I do with all these ideas?*

I (Drew) would argue that Solomon, like many successful business owners, CEOs, and executive leaders, had ADD. I also think he struggled with shiny object syndrome—that temptation to chase shiny objects and fuel the adrenaline rush—hence the randomness in his writing. Perhaps he simply captured thoughts in a very random sequence and journaled them sporadically. Frankly, Solomon probably had no clue that his writings would endure for centuries. His ideas and content resemble a box filled with puzzle pieces. You know a beautiful masterpiece awaits when everything is properly assembled, but getting there can be very frustrating. Even mind-numbing. The difficult thing about reading Solomon's wisdom is that his jigsaw puzzle box has no picture on the front. It's not always easy to figure out what he meant or how it applies to our lives today. Let's face it, by today's editorial standards, Solomon would have been flat-out rejected. Based upon our experience with publishers, here's some feedback we'd give ol' Sol.

Dear Sol,

To say that what you have accomplished and the manner in which you have led the kingdom of Israel during your reign has been nothing short of impressive. Your father would be proud. No doubt this will go down as Israel's "Golden Age" under your leadership in light of all of the progress, growth, and prosperity. By the way, the temple and palaces are exquisite and will be a defining exclamation point for your legacy.

About the book submission, Sol. We're for you. You've been a great king and have achieved many significant accomplishments. Here's the reality—while we wish we could provide you with equally flattering feedback about your book, we can't. A title we're playfully suggesting at this stage of the editorial process is Cryptic Chaos. Now, before you get upset and offended by that feedback, please understand that while this book is filled with deep spiritual insights, profound tidbits of knowledge, practical suggestions for effective living, and timeless wisdom for the ages, it's an editorial nightmare (to put it kindly).

There's some really good stuff here, Sol. So much so that maybe someday you'll be declared the wisest man ever to rule on the earth. You cover a wide range of topics with brevity and conciseness, but Sol, you're all over the board. One minute you're talking about the essential foundation of wisdom being the fear of the Lord, and the next minute you're talking about the adulterous woman. (Sort of ironic considering the number of wives and concubines you have, but who are we to judge?)

And there's really fantastic business leadership stuff in here. Concepts and principles that could impact business owners, CEOs, executives, pastors, politicians, and other leaders for centuries. Sol, the trick is moving the material you've submitted into a more linear and thematic arrangement versus the cryptic and journal-like topical randomness you've submitted in round one. Today it feels a bit ADD-ish. If we can get that done, I think this could be a much more useful periodical that will allow its readers to apply the content more practically to their everyday lives and leadership.

Sol, as mentioned earlier, we're for you! This is a grace and truth issue—and the truth is, in order for this to be a useful manuscript, it needs a lot of work.

Best regards to you and your ever-expanding family.

Warm regards,
Pub L. Isher
WWGD Literary House

PS. If you can get it to the next level, we might recommend a title such as "WisdoManifesto: King Sol's Manuscript for Wisdom and Better Living." Something a little catchier and trendier than "Proverbs" (seems a little understated and ordinary).

With all that in mind, what we have attempted to do with this book is assemble the puzzle for you in such a way that the topics and precepts are arranged together in a topically useful, meaningful, and practical way in order to reveal the leadership masterpiece that Solomon gave us. Our hope is that Solomon's centuries-old wisdom will become a foundation and resource that you can lean on as you lead and run your business or organization. We organized it in a way that will enhance your ability to engage in the wisdom He has given us through the lens of business and leadership.

Why Dan and Drew?

There are a lot of reasons why Drew and I have written this book, but the main one is that we love business. We've both owned companies and exited successfully. We've experienced the virtues of business as a commerce engine, a means to create wealth, and a way to serve others for the common good. We have a passion for exceptional leadership. We know firsthand how powerful the platform of business ownership can be relative to impacting the lives of other people: employees,

employees' families, customers, communities, vendors, suppliers, and more.

The power of the business platform is truly amazing. As an owner, you get to lead, serve, and shepherd people for 40-plus hours each week. You engage in their lives in various ways and have a microphone on the stage of life that allows you access to their minds and hearts. This can be good, neutral, or bad.

We believe that as Christ followers, we're called to a higher standard of impact and influence. We're called to a higher level of leadership excellence. We are ambassadors of God's Kingdom.

Sadly, even the most well-meaning Christian leaders fall short of being ambassadors who glorify God by the way they lead, serve, and shepherd their business. The question has to be asked: Am I helping people move closer to or further from God?

We also believe the stakes are higher and the battle is more challenging for those who attempt to lead with Christian values. The marketplace has no grace! It's dog-eat-dog, competitive, and ever-changing. Let's face it, the world and society today don't value the higher precepts and wisdom. Political correctness rules, and generational fads prevail. Many leaders see no value in a servant leadership model; they view it as too old-fashioned and out of touch.

Nothing could be further from the truth. Why? Because all things rise and fall on leadership! Look around your home, your neighborhood, your community, your country, and society in general, and tell us that's not true. High-impact leadership seems both rare and fleeting.

That's why we built Acumen.

After selling our businesses, we wanted to build something we wish we had as a high-stakes leader: community, sharpening, inspiration, safety, and accountability, all which would have made us higher performing leaders and our businesses more successful.

Acumen is an engaging community of CEOs and business owners who want more—personally and professionally. We use a proven framework to grow your business, challenge, and guide you as a leader.

In short, We Sharpen Your Edge.

Just like a **Swiss Army Knife**, you need:

- Tools & skills for a variety of leadership situations
- Wisdom on how to use and apply those tools effectively
- Techniques for sharpening the edge of each blade to optimize effectiveness
- A resource that can be readily available and accessible at any time
- Easy, light and compact to carry
- Simple to use and easy to understand
- Actionable and relevant in common, everyday situations

Because we lead a community of leaders, Drew and I have sat across the table from CEOs and business owners for thousands of hours over the past decade. One thing we love about Solomon is that there are many parallels between his shiny object syndrome and strategic whiplash and the challenges we've observed other very successful CEOs struggle with. It's quite natural for high-capacity leaders to be "all over the place." We resemble that. It's nothing to be ashamed of; in fact, it may even be a DNA marker for success.

Our aspiration for this book is to bring to life leadership principles written by history's most successful leader, and to help you amp your leadership effectiveness by making those ideas and principles simple to access and easier to apply. This book will help you be a better leader of yourself and others, and a better decision maker; it will also impact your business by showing you the fundamental truths in Proverbs and by helping you integrate Solomon's teaching with practical application so you can see blind spots, avoid pitfalls, and move forward with peace and confidence.

We are NOT theologians, pastors, priests, or divinity scholars. We are husbands, fathers, business owners, entrepreneurs, executive coaches, and growth catalysts. It is in that context that we deliver our interpretation, understanding, and filter of Proverbs in a way that will be insightful and meaningful for you.

This is NOT a commentary or an in-depth study into the meaning of each proverb, but a high-level look into the themes and tools derived from the book.

"So are you really wise or something?"

No. Not even close.

Wisdom is making wise decisions the first time, and Proverbs has been a lighthouse for us in that journey.

Yes, like most owners, we have learned many lessons the hard way. Wisdom is also for after you fail, are in the darkness where you can't see the light, and when you are faced with the toughest decisions of your life. Wisdom allows you to rectify, make peace, do better, react, shrug off, go after, and change in the face of these situations, challenges, and opportunities.

We will demystify Proverbs so that you can go farther faster. Becoming wise is an iterative process. You have to start somewhere sometime. Start now.

As noted in Proverbs 14:8, the wisdom of the wise is to give thought to their ways (they think about where they are going), but the folly of fools is deception (they keep lying to themselves).

Application, Tools, and Index

Because it's our desire for this book to be practical, in each chapter, we will call out mental models, application ideas, tools, and frameworks that match up with the truths we see in Proverbs. Our goal is to help you integrate the truth of Proverbs with modern models and applications that will cement what you are learning for easy recall and use in your daily life.

We've also created an **index** of Solomon's wisdom at the back of this book. The goal there is to let you read a group of key verses connected with specific topics discussed in this book so that you get the main point without having to read a sea of verses. Going to the index will help you go deeper on a subject and be used on an as-needed basis when you want to go right to verses on that topic.

As we prepare to dive in, let's talk about the Lindy Effect, a mental model. Farnam Street's Shane Parrish defines it this way:

> "The Lindy Effect refers to the life expectancy of a non-perishable object or idea being related to its current lifespan. If an idea or object has lasted for X number of years, it would be expected (on average) to last another X years. Although a human being who is 90 and lives to 95 does not add 5 years to his or her life expectancy, non-perishables lengthen their life expectancy as they continually survive. A classic text is a prime example."

Let's use *How to Win Friends and Influence People* by Dale Carnegie. It was published in 1936 and has been in print for over 75 years. Why? Because the concepts have stood the test of time. They just work. Who can argue with, "A great man shows his greatness . . . by how he treats little men"? If it's been true for 75 years, you can project that the ideas will still be true 75 years from now.

That is how we see Proverbs. The book was written between 200 and 1,000 years before Christ. According to the Lindy Effect, it's likely that the ideas will last another 3,000 years. Now that's some history and truth!

PART 1

GETTING WISDOM

"If any of you lacks wisdom, he should ask God, who gives generously to all without finding fault, and it will be given to him."
James 1:5

Are you the type of reader that skips the introduction? Don't do that with this book! You'll get key insights to start you off on the right foot including how the chapters are arranged and formatted so you get the most out of your time. It's also short. Seriously, go back and read it.

We are all professional researchers. We can "know" anything in less than 10 seconds with Google on any device anywhere in the world. As long as you are somewhat discerning, the content you retrieve will most likely be correct.

That means information isn't a problem in the modern world. Instead, it's your actions based upon the available information that is the real challenge.

In a similar way, wisdom is different from information. Knowing something doesn't make you wise. It just gives you the information you need. Your attitudes, beliefs, values, morals, and discipline are what give you the context that, when paired with knowledge, inform your actions. The doing. If you come to a situation with those systems out of whack, you'll make foolish decisions.

So how can we get our hands on wisdom? How can we find it? Develop it? Grow it? Use it? Those are the questions and concepts we'll explore in the following chapters.

Chapter 1

Wisdom's Origin and Birth

But the wisdom that comes from heaven is first of all pure; then peace-loving,
considerate, submissive, full of mercy and good fruit, impartial, and sincere.
James 3:17

Do you find it difficult to wrap your mind around the meaning or importance of wisdom? I do. I (Dan) have prayed for it. I've prayed that others may be given wisdom. But often it seems so nebulous, so unattainable, so idealistic that perhaps it's out of my reach.

Where did wisdom come from? What is its origin? And is it really a what? A how? A when? Perhaps it's all of that. One thing you discover from Solomon is that wisdom predates the very existence of our planet. That's because wisdom is part of who God is and how He operates.

Think of it this way: wisdom is God's operating system. We think Windows or iOS. He thinks *wisdom*. All of creation was built upon and is sustained by a wisdom operating system.

And in the book of Proverbs, God personifies His OS, speaking of wisdom as a "her."

If you're not familiar with that term, personification is attributing human characteristics to something not human, such as wisdom. In Proverbs, the personification of wisdom allows for wonderful metaphors, details, story, and descriptions that otherwise wouldn't work if it were just a defined word. As such, like any person, Wisdom had to be born.

Proverbs 8:22–31

[22] The LORD brought me forth as the first of his works, before his deeds of old; [23] I was formed long ages ago, at the very beginning, when the world came to be. [24] When there were no watery depths, I was given birth, when there were no springs overflowing with water; [25] before the mountains were settled in place, before the hills, I was given birth, [26] before he made the world or its fields or any of the dust of the earth. [27] I was there when he set the heavens in place, when he marked out the horizon on the face of the deep, [28] when he established the clouds above and fixed securely the fountains of the deep, [29] when he gave the sea its boundary so the waters would not overstep his command, and when he marked out the foundations of the earth. [30] Then I was constantly at his side. I was filled with delight day after day, rejoicing always in his presence, [31] rejoicing in his whole world and delighting in mankind.

The verses that jump out at me are 30–31, when Wisdom says, "I was filled with delight day after day, rejoicing always in his presence, rejoicing in his whole world and delighting in mankind." Now *that* is how I imagine heaven—being filled with delight day after day, rejoicing always in God's presence.

What jumped out at you when you read the verses above?

Imagine if you could talk to Wisdom. What would you ask her?

Application: How to Read Proverbs – Say, Mean, Me?

We've structured this book to include commentary from the authors as well as key Scripture passages that reveal important truths for each chapter. As you read, feel free to take notes right on the page. We want this to be a practical book, so get practical as you read.

Also, you might be tempted to blow through the Scripture passages and get back to the commentary as you read each chapter. Don't do that. You will diminish the value you get from this book.

Speaking of reading Scripture, here's a tried-and-true process for engaging the Bible—and this is an excellent framework to use with Proverbs especially. As you read a Scripture passage, answer these three questions.

1. *What is it saying?* This is simple. You need to read the text and understand what it says. It's okay to read it multiple times.
2. *What does it mean?* How do you interpret what you just read? What is the context? Who is involved? Is there anything to pull apart, such as a metaphor or comparison?
3. *What does it mean to me?* Finally, it's time for application. What jumped out as you read? What one thing can you do today to integrate this into your life? Perhaps you could even finish this sentence: "Today, I will..."

By making what you read actionable, you will be able to hold yourself accountable. Coming up with a desired action without real account-ability is a waste of time. For example:

- I will ... not be the first person to talk during all meetings and interactions.
- I will ... say something positive to every person on my staff.
- I will ... call Eric.

Your "I will . . ." needs to be specific so that you can measure it at the end of the day. Did you talk first? Did you find something positive to say to everyone? Did you call Eric?

What doesn't work are "I wills" that are generic:

- I will . . . be nice.
- I will . . . love people.
- I will . . . be grateful.

How do you know if you were nice or grateful all day? How do you know if your measure of nice or love is the correct amount?

Using these three questions can multiply the impact of Scripture in your life and leadership—especially when it comes to integrating Proverbs into your life.

Chapter 2

THE CASE FOR WISDOM

How long will you who are simple love your simple ways? How long
will mockers delight in mockery and fools hate knowledge?
Proverbs 1:22

Ever had that moment when you thought, "I wish I wouldn't have done that, said that, gone that direction, made that decision, reacted in that manner, made that investment, started that division, hired that person, bought that second home, had that extra glass of wine, and so on?"

To make matters worse, you had that bad gut feeling, tap on the shoulder from your conscience, voice from your spouse, advice from counsel that informed you otherwise—yet, you went there anyway. You even prayed about it and just knew that God was affirming your decision (though somewhere in your soul you also knew you were rationalizing).

Were you really listening?

I (Drew) remember expanding our outsourced payroll and HR tech business into the St. Louis market. Prior to launch, I sought advice from various sources. One common theme I heard was this: "The moment you expand into new geography, your business will become exponentially more complex. The challenges will more than double, and it will be very difficult to replicate the culture and success you achieve in your current region. It will cost more money and require far more time than you currently anticipate, and it will produce new business at a much slower rate."

Really? That sounded more like a double dog dare to my competitive, bring on the fight, macho man, I'll prove you wrong personality. "If I can be successful here, look out, St. Louis! I'll really knock the cover off the ball over there."

Wham. They showed me who the baseball city was!

The only thing I did right was find an office suite to call home base. Virtually everything else bloodied and bruised my ego (and pocketbook). The sales team never produced enough to break even. Leadership was challenging to identify and equip. Recruiting was ineffective at best. What worked in Kansas City didn't work in St. Louis. The competition was stiffer and more entrenched in the culture. The story and recipe that brought us success in KC did not translate.

It was as if I had opened for business on the moon, even though it was just a four-hour drive across the state between offices.

I realized that in order to create success, I was going to have to rethink the whole strategy. More importantly, I would need to invest much more time, financial resources, and training/development to achieve a successful formula.

Wisdom had raised her voice through the people I spoke with. Yet I ignored her when she shared the obstacles before us. I flat-out was not listening. I thought we were an exception. My ego got in the way and muzzled our ears. I thought our talent and success formula would allow us to skip over the speed bumps and realities of expansion. I was a fool. I was a mocker. I was simple. I was not wise because I didn't heed wisdom's voice.

Proverbs outlines three types of people that are not wise:

- *The Simple.* These people are just plain ignorant. They don't know and don't want to know.
- *The Mockers.* These are prideful know-it-alls who can't be taught.
- *The Fools.* These people want everything the world can offer (money, power, sex, etc.) without thinking about the impact and consequences of blindly chasing those things.

Proverbs 1:20–33

20 Out in the open wisdom calls aloud, she raises her voice in the public square; 21 on top of the wall she cries out, at the city gate she makes her speech: 22 How long will you who are simple love your simple ways? How long will mockers delight in mockery and fools hate knowledge? 23 Repent at my rebuke! Then I will pour out my thoughts to you, I will make known to you my teachings. 24 But since you refuse to listen when I call and no one pays attention when I stretch out my hand, 25 since you disregard all my advice and do not accept my rebuke, 26 I in turn will laugh when disaster strikes you; I will mock when calamity overtakes you—27 when calamity overtakes you like a storm, when disaster sweeps over you like a whirlwind, when distress and trouble overwhelm you. 28 Then they will call to me but I will not answer; they will look for me but will not find me, 29 since they hated knowledge and did not choose to fear the LORD. 30 Since they would not accept my advice and spurned my rebuke, 31 they will eat the fruit of their ways and be filled with the fruit of their schemes. 32 For the waywardness of the simple will kill them, and the complacency of fools will destroy them; 33 but whoever listens to me will live in safety and be at ease, without fear of harm."

Wisdom is harsh, isn't she? "Repent at my rebuke!" she says (verse 23). Wow ... okay, but how? Although certain leaders have big pride issues or treat people poorly, I find that most leaders are ignorant. They just don't know what they don't know, or their team won't tell them the truth out of fear or safety.

Me too. I (Dan) was extremely ignorant for the early portions of my leadership career. I either thought I knew what was going on at the front lines, or by just looking at numbers on a spreadsheet, I created stories that matched. That got me in trouble during times where I trusted things that looked or sounded funny instead of removing my ignorance.

In fact, my pride helped me remain ignorant because I didn't want to look stupid in front of my team. "Of course I know that, I started this place! I know all, as I'm the great and powerful Oz!"

Application: The "Am I Really Listening?" Checklist

At times we have all been ignorant, prideful, or gone chasing after something to the detriment of others. So, when in doubt, ask yourself these three questions:

1. Am I ignorant anywhere in this situation?
   - What else do I need to know?
   - Where am I biased?
   - Am I choosing to ignore information?

2. Where is my ego in this decision? Is my pride getting in the way?
3. Am I chasing something to the detriment, damage, or harm to others? This one is hard. We can all justify our actions. Asking others on your team or list of mentors and advisors this question about your situation may reveal more light than your answer.

It's also incredibly important that we ask "Why?"

What is a three-year-old child's favorite question? Why. Why, Daddy? Why, Mommy? Have you ever answered the first four whys only to be asked a fifth and then yell in frustration? Me too. Being curious and asking why peels the onion on a situation and allows you to identify root causes, sacred cows, and "We've always done it that way."

If you can humble yourself and listen to your team, experience, and intuition, you can overcome ignorance. Be curious. Ask questions. You'll learn a lot.

Chapter 3

THE BEGINNING
OF WISDOM:
DO I (REALLY) BELIEVE?

The fear of the LORD is the beginning of knowledge,
but fools despise wisdom and instruction.
Proverbs 1:7

Why read Proverbs? Solomon tells you why below. It's the feature part of the sales call. You'll gain all types of wisdom: insight, instruction, understanding, discretion, the ability to tell right from wrong, knowledge, and learning. Who wouldn't want those?

The key verse is Proverbs 1:7. The beginning of knowledge is "the fear of the LORD." It all starts there.

In August of 2017, there was a solar eclipse. It seemed like the entire country just stopped to stare at something that happens very rarely. We (Dan and family) were lucky enough to be at a large farmstead in the path of the eclipse, and we were able to see totality—when the moon was directly in front of the sun. We experienced a brief episode of "nighttime" darkness even though it was early afternoon. It was maybe a couple of minutes, but the feeling from everyone in attendance was that of awe and wonder. My favorite part was when, just as the sky was breaking back into daylight, the farm's rooster crowed. It had to wake everyone up—after two minutes of sleep!

Imagine what transpired thousands of years before you were born when people encountered a natural phenomenon such as an eclipse. Moments like that wipe out thoughts of coincidence, happenstance, and luck.

The fear of the Lord is not about His wrath or being afraid of what He can do to us. It's about our relationship with Him. It's about understanding that He is the creator, our Father, and respecting His authority. It's about the wonder that comes through contemplation of those things. There should be genuine fear too, or another word may be respect. Ever been caught in a riptide or been buzzed by an electric outlet? That's a teeny tiny sliver of Him.

Where in your life have you felt the awe and wonder of God and His blessings?

Proverbs 1:1–7

[1] The proverbs of Solomon son of David, king of Israel: [2] for gaining wisdom and instruction; for understanding words of insight; [3] for receiving instruction in prudent behavior, doing what is right and just and fair; [4] for giving prudence to those who are simple, knowledge and discretion to the young—[5] let the wise listen and add to their learning, and let the discerning get guidance—[6] for understanding proverbs and parables, the sayings and riddles of the wise. [7] The fear of the LORD is the beginning of knowledge, but fools despise wisdom and instruction.

Proverbs 8:13

To fear the LORD is to hate evil; I hate pride and arrogance, evil behavior, and perverse speech.

Proverbs 14:26–27

[26] Whoever fears the LORD has a secure fortress, and for their children it will be a refuge. [27] The fear of the LORD is a fountain of life, turning a person from the snares of death.

Proverbs 28:14

Blessed is the one who always trembles before God, but whoever hardens their heart falls into trouble.

Proverbs 30:1–6

[1] The sayings of Agur son of Jakeh—an inspired utterance. This man's utterance to Ithiel: I am weary, God, but I can prevail. [2] Surely I am only a brute, not a man; I do not have human understanding. [3] I have not learned wisdom, nor have I attained to the knowledge of the Holy One. [4] Who has gone up to heaven and come down? Whose hands have gathered up the wind? Who has wrapped up the waters in a cloak? Who has established all the ends of the earth? What is his name, and what is the name of his son? Surely you know! [5] Every word of God is flawless; he is a shield to those who take refuge in him. [6] Do not add to his words, or he will rebuke you and prove you a liar.

"Fear the Lord." I've always struggled with that reference and terminology. What does that really mean? As I've (Drew) grown in my faith, I've learned that "fear" has much to do with respect, reverence, understanding (who He is and who I'm not), power, Lordship, control, and authority. I've learned it's when I genuinely revere and submit to God that I'm able to reap the fruit, abundance, knowledge, wisdom, and insight that He desires and wishes to freely and generously share with me.

Most days, I try to grab the firehose of life, tightly grip the joystick, and be the master controller. The results usually aren't optimal.

Such was the case again at the onset and launch of my payroll business. I was new to this faith journey thing. I still had my hands fully engaged in managing all of the controls and turning all the dials. No surrender or submission, just full throttle in control of my own destiny.

Things didn't go so well. The business plan was flawed from day one. I blew through our capital at Mach speed, and ultimately we ran out. The company wasn't even at 50 percent of our business plan. And then I discovered I had made a grave error in selecting our technology partner. We were hitched to the wrong wagon and would never be able to scale in a profitable manner. Plus they were dishonest! Talk about adding insult to injury.

I really hadn't invited God into this business-planning-start-up equation either. I hadn't asked for His help in this endeavor (you're shocked, right?). It was all being done out of my own might and will. Still, He brought some people into my life who willingly offered up advice (things like you'll need twice as much capital and twice as much time—hmmm . . . imagine that!). Of course, I wasn't listening (there's a pattern here) because I knew we could muscle through it. I'd be rich in a matter of months. A self-made business tycoon. Once again, wrong!

My wife's company had gone out of business soon after our launch. We went from Dual Income No Kids (DINK) to No Income Two Kids (NITK) in an eighteen-month window. I can't pronounce NITK, but it was without question a four-letter word and felt a lot like "nada." Were we going to lose our house? Eat peanut butter for the rest of our lives?

Desperate, depressed, discouraged, and drained both emotionally and fiscally, I sat in my car, parked in front of our home, and literally held the keys to my car up and uttered these words:

"Lord, you take control. Every time I try to take control, things get ugly, messed up, and broken. I'm done. You drive. I'll be the copilot."

Amazing what the four "Ds" will do to you. I was ashamed and embarrassed. We were on thin ice and in desperate need of cash to survive. I had given up my corporate career to start this stupid money-sucking, flawed-technology, life-draining business.

In that moment, God seemed like a logical place to turn.

Why do we do that? Why do we turn to Him when things are at their deepest darkest stages?

By His grace, this misfit business I launched somehow became successful. I reengineered and engaged a new technology partner, brought on "friendly" (but expensive) capital, rebranded, and refocused.

Success didn't happen overnight. The sky didn't suddenly become clear and blue. Stress and anxiety didn't disappear. But it was very clear that God forged a purpose for this entrepreneurial business hack. He had a purpose for this rags-to-riches-to-reverence story that has taken place in the context of ordinary commerce. It has been a formative experience that has shaped my view and belief structure of how impactful and influential a business platform can be for Kingdom impact. It has been the heartbeat of my life work.

And it all began by acknowledging and surrendering to a genuine, call it desperate, fear and reverence for the Lord.

So I'll ask you: where in your life do you need to hand Him the keys?

Application: Ask for Wisdom

Do you desire Wisdom?

Follow James' advice and *ask* God for it. Stop and do it right now!

In Don Whitney's book, *Praying the Bible*, he discusses how in prayer, there are times when you don't know what to say or are saying the same things over and over. He suggests that you can use the Bible in your prayer as a way to get closer to God by using the words of God. Ask God to show you how to apply this in your life, your business, key decisions, and difficult challenges.

For example, let's use the verse from the beginning of the section, James 1:5. Read the verse again, and then use the words to form your prayer about seeking wisdom.

If any of you lacks wisdom, he should ask God, who gives generously to all without finding fault, and it will be given to him.

Your prayer might look like below. Feel free to use this prayer to get you started.

Lord Jesus, thank you for my mind that can think critically and reason and my heart that can feel. I am grateful for all that I have. I am seeking wisdom in this world. Can you give me the wisdom that helps me live my life, my family, and my work in a way that gives you glory? Especially when it comes to . . .

Listen. What is Jesus saying to you?
What else would you like to say to Jesus?
Amen!

Chapter 4

THE VALUE OF WISDOM

I don't want features; I want value. I don't want benefits; I want value.
—David Karp

Highlight or circle any place where you see value in the Scripture passages below. Seriously, do it.

Proverbs 3:1–2
[1] My son, do not forget my teaching, but keep my commands in your heart, [2] for they will prolong your life many years and bring you peace and prosperity.

Proverbs 3:13–24
[13] Blessed are those who find wisdom, those who gain understanding, [14] for she is more profitable than silver and yields better returns than gold. [15] She is more precious than rubies; nothing you desire can compare with her. [16] Long life is in her right hand; in her left hand are riches and honor. [17] Her ways are pleasant ways, and all her paths are peace. [18] She is a tree of life to those who take hold of her; those who hold her fast will be blessed. [19] By wisdom the LORD laid the earth's foundations, by understanding he set the heavens in place; [20] by his knowledge the watery depths were divided, and the clouds let drop the dew. [21] My son, do not let wisdom and understanding out of your sight, preserve sound judgment and discretion; [22] they will be

life for you, an ornament to grace your neck. [23] Then you will go on your way in safety, and your foot will not stumble. [24] When you lie down, you will not be afraid; when you lie down, your sleep will be sweet.

Proverbs 9:10–12
[10] The fear of the LORD is the beginning of wisdom, and knowledge of the Holy One is understanding. [11] For through wisdom your days will be many, and years will be added to your life. [12] If you are wise, your wisdom will reward you; if you are a mocker, you alone will suffer.

Proverbs 12:8
A person is praised according to their wisdom, and one with a warped mind is despised.

Proverbs 24:3–4, 13–14
[3] By wisdom a house is built, and through understanding it is established; [4] through knowledge its rooms are filled with rare and beautiful treasures.
[13] Eat honey, my son, for it is good; honey from the comb is sweet to your taste. [14] Know also that wisdom is like honey for you: If you find it, there is a future hope for you, and your hope will not be cut off.

What did you circle that intrigued you most? Was it prolonged life, peace, prosperity, foundation, blessings, honor, strong roots, safety, lack of fear, praise, or hope? And why? God "gave birth" to wisdom before He created the rest of the universe. God is wisdom. Wisdom has more value than anything God created (rubies, gold, or silver from the verses above). Why wouldn't we seek wisdom with the same tenacity that a miner searches for gold or a businessman searches for opportunity, profitability, cash flow, and riches?

I know . . . I didn't mention riches in the values list. Although there are earthly riches to be gained with wisdom, and Solomon was the richest person in the world for his time, if increasing wealth is your sole goal in acquiring wisdom, then you are a fool (as defined in chapter 1).

The search for wealth alone is an intellectual and time-bound earthly exercise. As Ben Franklin said in *Poor Richard's Almanac*, "If you desire many things, many things will seem but a few." Wisdom does not guarantee earthly riches. But it does put you in the place to take advantage of the opportunity along with everything else in the list above.

Application: How Much is Enough?

It's an age-old question, but is it a trap question? I think so. Our minds immediately race toward financial resources. As if the net worth figure in your personal balance sheet is an indicator of "enough." Enough can take on a lot of different aspects and characteristics.

The book of Ecclesiastes is a key on this topic.

> 10 *Whoever loves money never has enough; whoever loves wealth is never satisfied with their income. This too is meaningless.* 11 *As goods increase, so do those who consume them. And what benefit are they to the owners except to feast their eyes on them?* 12 *The sleep of a laborer is sweet, whether they eat little or much, but as for the rich, their abundance permits them no sleep.*
>
> **Ecclesiastes 5:10–12**

If happiness were totally based on money and the balance in your bank account, then why aren't more Americans happy and joyful? We live in the wealthiest country on the planet, and yet the happiness factor could be categorized as sketchy at best. Having traveled to Haiti,

Guatemala, and other very impoverished countries, it's mind-blowing to see just how happy people can be with nothing but the clothes on their back.

Solomon had everything he could possibly fathom. Yet, he was quick to dismiss wealth as something that created happiness. He had enough by all accounts. Yet he cited wisdom as more valuable than anything and the only thing that we should set our eyes on and try to obtain.

Personally, I (Drew) feel as though I fell into the "enough" trap. Upon selling my payroll business, on paper, I had enough. The transaction was a reverse triangular merger of two firms, and as a result, was a stock and cash deal that was eight-figures in scope. I chose to roll a significant percentage of the value in stock while cashing out the balance. Pay Uncle Sam and a couple of partners and investors, and shazam, look what's left over in cash. That number (especially in comparison with the rest of the world) looked a lot like it was enough. The financial planning experts even affirmed this idea.

After the transaction and liquidity dust had settled, I didn't expect to experience the subtle scarcity mentality, comparison conundrum, hoarding behavior, dullness of my edge, fear not to blow it, boredom and isolation, and erosion of trust in God. But I experienced all of those, believe it or not.

My mentality before that point had been to seize the moment, go for it, just do it, take the hill, and whatever other motivational cliché you can conjure. Then the "enough" dichotomy crept into my inner competitive motor system. I took my foot off the gas. Instead of climbing the mountain, I found myself in more of a camping or maintenance mode, slipping into a preservation and don't-blow-it mentality.

I had observed peers who had liquidity events with their businesses and immediately went out, sprinkled their magic dust, invested wads of cash on the next "big thing," and blew it all. They thought their secret sauce from the first successful recipe would automatically create success in the next opportunity. They learned the hard way that not all businesses succeed just because you show up at the door with a success badge on your sleeve. I didn't want to be that guy. I wanted to avoid that hardship. I don't think that was necessarily a bad strategy. However, it triggered the preservation, timidity, and camping dynamic.

Fortunately, I found the Halftime organization and specifically the book *Halftime* by Bob Buford. The Halftime Institute exists to coach, teach, and connect high-capacity leaders to discern and engage in their life purpose. As Bob stated it, going "from success to significance." During my journey with The Halftime Institute, I learned that I am inherently a builder. Builders don't do well with camping, timidity, and status quo. I thrive when in build mode.

I'm guessing that's what Solomon struggled with as well. He was likely a builder and creator, not a maintainer. Maintaining and camping is boring to builders. I hear that often when engaging with other CEOs and business owners. Growth and building are where it's at. I suppose at some level, most leaders are wired that way. Hunter and provider by God's very design.

By understanding that I am a builder, I had direction and motive. My focus moved from maintaining me to stewarding my strengths for others. The inward understanding transitioned to an outward action based upon wisdom I searched for and received.

The value of wisdom is about trust and stewardship versus how much is enough. If you're wired to be a builder, then build. Just do it with the right motive, aspiration, and desire to glorify Jesus along the journey.

Chapter 5

WALKING WITH WISDOM

The good life is a process, not a state of being.
It is a direction not a destination.
—Carl Rogers

My (Dan) son Ben started kindergarten last year. About a week before school started, we did the standard "haircut and new shoes" Saturday since his shoes were blown out and his hair was too long.

A funny thing happened when we got to the shoe store. Ben was all about shoes with laces. He wanted shoes like his older brother and sister had, not his childish Velcro shoes. He wanted to learn to tie his shoes before school since he was in "real school" now. Honestly, I was a little hesitant. I just saw myself tying his shoes for the next six months. But he was sooooo sure that he could do it, so I relented.

When we got home, Ben asked if my wife would help him learn. After two to three tries, he got frustrated, saying, "I'll never get it!" My wife continued to prod gently to keep on trying. "Bunny ear . . . bunny ear, loop, and through."

Over the next couple of days, Ben practiced. He must have tried to tie his shoes 50 times. Before we left for dinner later in the week, Ben tied one of his shoes perfectly. We all clapped. He was very proud and enjoyed all the attention.

Then he tried to put his shoe on. He was still working on the order of operations. "Small steps forward," we reminded him.

The next morning, he completed the entire process and in the right order. The confidence in knowing he could tie his shoes allowed him to concentrate on the order in which to do it.

It's funny what your kids teach you. From Ben, I learned patience, to keep on trying, that there is progress in action, and that you get better with practice and time.

Wisdom is the same way. You don't become wise overnight. Sometimes you get the process wrong and forget the put the shoe on first.

Proverbs 2: 1–22

[1] My son, if you accept my words and store up my commands within you, [2] turning your ear to wisdom and applying your heart to understanding—[3] indeed, if you call out for insight and cry aloud for understanding, [4] and if you look for it as for silver and search for it as for hidden treasure, [5] then you will understand the fear of the LORD and find the knowledge of God. [6] For the LORD gives wisdom; from his mouth come knowledge and understanding. [7] He holds success in store for the upright, he is a shield to those whose walk is blameless, [8] for he guards the course of the just and protects the way of his faithful ones. [9] Then you will understand what is right and just and fair—every good path. [10] For wisdom will enter your heart, and knowledge will be pleasant to your soul. [11] Discretion will protect you, and understanding will guard you. [12] Wisdom will save you from the ways of wicked men, from men whose words are perverse, [13] who have left the straight paths to walk in dark ways, [14] who delight in doing wrong and rejoice in the perverseness of evil, [15] whose paths are crooked and who are devious in their ways. [16] Wisdom will save you also from the adulterous woman, from the wayward woman with her seductive words, [17] who has left the partner of her youth and ignored the covenant she made before God. [18] Surely her house leads down to death and her paths to the spirits of the dead. [19] None who go to her return or attain the

paths of life. [20] Thus you will walk in the ways of the good and keep to the paths of the righteous. [21] For the upright will live in the land, and the blameless will remain in it; [22] but the wicked will be cut off from the land, and the unfaithful will be torn from it.

Seeking wisdom is like seeking a relationship with Jesus Christ. It's a lifelong journey of growing and change. Jesus' words in Matthew 7:7–8 (below) are about pursuing God, and they are reflected above in the proverbs about pursuing wisdom.

"Ask and it will be given to you; seek and you will find; knock and the door will be opened to you. For everyone who asks receives; he who seeks finds; and to him who knocks, the door will be opened."

If you seek wisdom earnestly and energetically, then God will give it to you.

The humbler we become before God, the more we have His mind and make wise choices.

So, what are you seeking? What would you ask God for regarding wisdom and character as you earnestly seek it?

Application: The Expanding A

How do we get from point A to point B? The question has been posed hundreds of times in my (Drew's) life to map out a journey, goal, strategy, a problem to solve, a mountain to climb, etc. It's no doubt a fantastic way to map out a systematic process to achieve an outcome.

You need goals and outcomes to achieve, right? Ten-year, five-year, one-year, quarterly, monthly, daily goals.

For some people and organizations, point Bs become rigid milestones that spin off thick strategy manuals and countless action steps. Point Bs set an important course toward a desired future. The statistics support the validity and value that a clear point B and supporting action steps improve your business. High achievers are goal setters.

Is this really a problem?

When you near the successful completion of one point B, you are ready to immediately create another point B. If you are like me, you rarely celebrate. You don't relish the moment. If you're like me, you immediately set another point B. What I often forget to do is just truly enjoy the journey. I'm so busy striving to check off the action steps that I am an unable to enjoy the ride. My team can't either.

A friend and former NFL veteran of 10 years named Jon McGraw has devoted his life on the other side of football to the professional field of performance science. He states that his ability to perform on the field was more a function of managing his mental and emotional health than it was his physical body. Don't get me wrong; his physical training was essential to compete at a world class level, but the mental and emotional swings that accompanied the pressure of competing at the NFL level were more consequential.

As a result, through his company, Vision Pursue (visionpursue.com), he's developed and refined a performance mindset process over the years that he credits to extending his NFL career.

One of the concepts that McGraw provides in his Performance Mindset training system is related to the idea of an "expanding A." It's a process and framework that places less emphasis on the result or outcome (the B) and greater emphasis on the process and journey.

He argues that B inherently causes us to focus only on striving toward the end goal. He argues that since when has buying something or achieving an outcome provided us with lasting happiness? It's fleeting at best, and then we are on to a new B that we think will provide us with greater pleasure, more status, or higher achievement.

Constantly striving and rarely enjoying the journey and process to get there leads to a lifelong pursuit of dissatisfaction. Instead of that path, McGraw suggests we focus with great energy, passion, and enthusiasm on the process that helps us be successful at the things we value most in life, thus constantly expanding our A rather than striving for the next B.

John Wooden, Hall of Fame basketball coach for the UCLA Bruins and 10-time NCAA Champion (over a 12-year period), said, "Success is peace of mind knowing you made the effort to do the best with which you were capable. I never mentioned winning. You can lose when you outscore an opponent and you can win when you are outscored. I told my players if people see you after a game, they should not be able to know the outcome of the game based on your actions."

All too often, I've placed all my self-worth and mental energy on my next outcome or milestone. My occupation. My role. The car I drive and the house I live in. My family. Comparing myself to others. I've forgotten to enjoy the process and journey.

Take a moment to consider these questions:

- What Bs have your currently set for yourself?
- What Bs have your currently set for your company?
- What As could you expand to enjoy the journey letting the process and joy in it dictate your success?

Chapter 6

KEEPING WISDOM

"Do not let this Book of the Law depart from your mouth; meditate
on it day and night, so that you may be careful to do everything
written in it. Then you will be prosperous and successful."
Joshua 1:8

I (Dan) have always liked boxing. Growing up in the Mike Tyson era made everyone love boxing. Video games like Mike Tyson's Punchout didn't hurt either. Then, there was MMA (Mixed Martial Arts). If I liked boxing, I loved MMA. I remember the very beginning of the sport when Royce Gracie won three of the first four UFCs (Ultimate Fighting Championships) against fighters of all styles such as boxing, Karate, Kung Fu, and Savate. We fans were watching the worlds martial arts styles literally fight it out to see which one was best.

I dreamed of getting in the ring. I always wanted to learn Jujitsu and get into the octagon or a ring for real. Unfortunately, there were only Tae Kwon Do schools around at that time. And although I get the art of it, I'm not a belt-progression guy.

My junior year of college, a Brazilian Jujitsu place opened up close to my house. Over the next three months, I was there three times a week and getting the crap kicked out of me. I was one big ball of purple bruises. It was awesome. I went back to school too quickly to make any real progress, but I promised myself that I needed to get into the ring. I had dabbled in some other training from time to time but never put in a serious effort to reach the goal of a ring experience.

Time was running out. At the age of 31, I joined a boxing club to be able to check the box for getting into the ring. It took me three months of solid training before the trainers finally relented and let me fight. They didn't want to do it, but I was so annoying I think they let me in the ring to shut me up.

I ended up "winning" my first unofficial three rounds against another amateur who was at the club as well. It was a ton of fun to experience the sweet science from a first-person point of view. I did take a couple of shots to the head, and even with headgear on, I knew that as quickly as it started, my boxing career should end. A worried wife and three kids at home helped too.

Any sport is about habits. But boxing/fighting is really about habits. There isn't a team to lean on in the ring. That one moment where you swing for victory has to come from you, and the time you put inside and outside the gym has a direct correlation to your sharpness, stamina, and game plan to achieve your goal.

I accomplished my goal of getting in the ring, and that journey reminds me of a lot of my faith walk. Intense fire followed by spotty attendance and some dedication here and there. Only when I put together a consistent effort do I reach the aptitude to participate at the lowest level. What could I have accomplished in the ring if I put in the hard work over a long period of time?

More importantly, what can you achieve in your life when you put in the hard work to grow wiser and closer to God over a long period of time?

Proverbs 4: 5–13
[5] Get wisdom, get understanding; do not forget my words or turn away from them. [6] Do not forsake wisdom, and she will protect you; love her, and she will watch over you. [7] The beginning of wisdom is this: Get wisdom. Though it cost all you have, get understanding. [8] Cherish her, and she will exalt you; embrace her, and she will honor you. [9] She will give you a garland to grace

your head and present you with a glorious crown. [10] Listen, my son, accept what I say, and the years of your life will be many.

[11] I instruct you in the way of wisdom and lead you along straight paths. [12] When you walk, your steps will not be hampered; when you run, you will not stumble. [13] Hold on to instruction, do not let it go; guard it well, for it is your life.

Proverbs 8:1–21

[1] Does not wisdom call out? Does not understanding raise her voice? [2] At the highest point along the way, where the paths meet, she takes her stand; [3] beside the gate leading into the city, at the entrance, she cries aloud: [4] To you, O people, I call out; I raise my voice to all mankind. [5] You who are simple, gain prudence; you who are foolish, set your hearts on it. [6] Listen, for I have trustworthy things to say; I open my lips to speak what is right. [7] My mouth speaks what is true, for my lips detest wickedness. [8] All the words of my mouth are just; none of them is crooked or perverse. [9] To the discerning all of them are right; they are upright to those who have found knowledge. [10] Choose my instruction instead of silver, knowledge rather than choice gold, [11] for wisdom is more precious than rubies, and nothing you desire can compare with her. [12] I, wisdom, dwell together with prudence; I possess knowledge and discretion. [13] To fear the LORD is to hate evil; I hate pride and arrogance, evil behavior, and perverse speech. [14] Counsel and sound judgment are mine; I have insight, I have power. [15] By me kings reign and rulers issue decrees that are just; [16] by me princes govern, and nobles—all who rule on earth. [17] I love those who love me, and those who seek me find me. [18] With me are riches and honor, enduring wealth and prosperity. [19] My fruit is better than fine gold; what I yield surpasses choice silver. [20] I walk in the way of righteousness, along the paths of justice, [21] bestowing a rich inheritance on those who love me and making their treasuries full.

Proverbs 16:16

How much better to get wisdom than gold, to get insight rather than silver!

Proverbs 19:8

The one who gets wisdom loves his own soul; the one who cherishes understanding prospers.

I could not get into the ring without three months of training and being persistent in practice. Showing up and putting in the work gave me the opportunity. Keeping wisdom is like that. It is continually showing up to the gym and putting in the work. Does the gym come to you? No. If you stop putting in the work, you get out of shape. Just like working on your body takes intent, keeping wisdom takes intent.

If you stop reading and learning more about God, Jesus, and His Word, you are going to forget what's in it. We forget too much too fast. Once you start this journey, study should become an intentional, lifelong, and frequent habit.

Application: Building a Wisdom Habit

What kind of habits do you have? I bet you went straight to the negative ones. Those are so easy to name and so hard to stop. But what about your good habits?

Here are some of my good habits: daily teeth brushing (twice!), working out, eating a small healthy breakfast, asking each kid a what or how question at dinner, and morning prayer/reading time.

If you want to make seeking wisdom a lifelong journey, you need to create the habit to do it. But how?

Here's a system I (Dan) used to build my Wisdom Habit.

1. *Location and time.* Where and when will you start your habit?
   First thing in the morning on my couch or at our Church is how
   I have grown this habit. The silence at these locations is what
   I like. My mind is the least cluttered first thing as well. What
   about you?

2. *Bite-size chunks.* When I first started reading the Bible, I
   thought I had to read a full chapter or even an entire book to get
   something out of it. I've since found out that often a single verse
   rises to the top and becomes a beacon for the day. If you are just
   starting out, give yourself permission to read one Proverb per
   day. That's fifteen seconds to read and perhaps thirty seconds
   to think about what it means to you. As you begin to build this
   habit you can increase the time and depth as it makes sense.
   Start small, and God will meet you there.

3. *Write something down, anything.* Document it. Write it down.
   Journal. Text yourself. This has been a game changer for me.
   When I started to write what I was taking from my reading along
   with my action for the day, it took something that was foreign
   and far away and integrated it into my life. Recording your
   thoughts doesn't have to be a work of genius. Be honest about
   how you feel—a story you thought of when reading the proverb,
   an action you should do today, and so on. Short, personal, real,
   simple. I look back at all my notes on a monthly basis and it is
   amazing to see the trends, learning, and wisdom in what I've
   written. Sometimes it is so inspired I wonder if I even wrote it!

4. *Find a buddy.* Nothing motivates you to keep an activity going like
   accountability. When you ask someone to come along with you
   or ask you how you are doing your consistency will skyrocket.
   Who should join you in this journey? Your spouse, a friend,
   your kids?

Seeking wisdom (and the Christian walk) is a lifelong journey. We
are never perfect, and there is always more to learn, more to understand,
and a deeper relationship to build with Christ. In time, what we learned

previously will deepen and there will be newer learning with different situations, seasons, and perspectives. Build a habit, be consistent, and be persistent.

PART 2

LEADERS LEAD.
GET ON WITH IT.

Everything rises and falls on leadership.
—John C. Maxwell

If you are a leadership nerd like me (Dan), you've read lots of leadership books. These books talk about leaders who are:

- People leaders
- Culture leaders
- Wartime leaders
- Peacetime leaders
- Product leaders
- Maximizers
- Achievers
- Calm and quiet
- Cheerleaders

- Strategists
- Competitive
- Talk to think leaders
- Think to talk
- Big room leaders
- 1-on-1 leaders

And this list can go on and on.

There are a lot of those types of leaders in the Bible as well. Leaders such as: King David, the warrior poet. Solomon, the philosopher and builder. Peter, the faithful leader. Paul, the teacher. And Jesus, the servant.

One thing I've learned is that it takes all kinds of leaders to run a successful business, and no one kind, style, philosophy, or method of leadership is perfect in all companies, in all situations, in all times, or all generations.

What you need to know is that you *are* a leader—and that God has put you in that position for a reason. He's given you strengths, talents, and even weaknesses that are perfect for where you are right now. Your past challenges, opportunities, and situations have made you ready for whatever is coming next.

I am a leader. So are you. Leaders lead. Get on with it.

Chapter 7

THE KING, THE SHEPHERD, AND THE RULER

Everyone who has been given much, much will be demanded; and from the one who has been entrusted with much, much more will be asked.
Luke 12:48

Most people who read the above Scripture relate it to money. I (Dan) would like to offer an alternative. If you are given the mantle of leadership, you have been given much and entrusted with God's most precious and highest valued resource: people. People are eternal; everything else fades. As a leader, your influence and impact are enormous. The power you hold is more than the paycheck you provide. You are a shepherd of your flock and the driver of your bus.

The bus I'm referring to is of course the employment bus—a bus I've driven and in which I've experienced many fails.

I'm convinced after decades of business ownership and mentoring other owners that 85 to 90 percent of all challenges, opportunities, and problems in business can be attributed to people and leadership. People are the key resources to the success of any organization. And those who lead are the catalysts that bring out the best performance in people—assuming of course that "the right people are in the right seats on the bus," a metaphor from Jim Collins and his best-seller *Good to Great.*

Filling the seats on the bus with the right occupants is tricky at best. Which of these statements is true for your organization?

- Sometimes the passengers occupy the exact seat in which they were intended to be.
- Sometimes they occupy a seat, and then it becomes clear it's the wrong seat, and thus they need help finding a more suitable seat.
- Sometimes finding that new seat is difficult. Perhaps they are willing to move, and you would like to keep them on the bus, but there are no more open seats in other areas or no other seats are suitable for their skill set.
- Sometimes it's impossible to make changes because they are related to the bus driver or (an)other passenger(s) on the bus.
- Sometimes you are afraid to ask them to move because they might throw a fit or they know too much about the current seat, and if you move them from the current seat, the bus might suffer irreversible damage.
- Sometimes you just ignore the disruptive or toxic behavior of the passenger hoping it will not have an adverse effect on other passengers around them.
- Sometimes you just tolerate poor performance of the passenger and apply a deep level of hope that they will someday perform.
- Sometimes your sunk cost bias is just too heavy, and you would rather continue to have the passenger on the bus even though they will never help the bus go farther or faster.
- Sometimes the driver attempts to change their ability to perform only to find the effort futile.
- Sometimes they exit the bus without notice or warning, sometimes through the window, out the front door, or even out the back.
- Sometimes the driver is forced to finally muster up enough courage to request an occupant to depart from the bus, and more often than not, he rhetorically mutters to himself, "Why did I wait that long?"

I'm (Drew) personally guilty of tolerating C– players and poor performers. At one company, a key leader of my customer service team had a long history in our industry, was very competent, had a professional industry designation, and had worked with top, high credibility firms in our region. However, she was a C− player at best. She had terrible communication and leadership skills, and her attitude was repelling. Despite complaints from her subordinates and peers, I allowed her to continue to lead this key customer service group. I think I had gotten lazy and didn't want to go through the pain and cost of recruiting someone new. *If we just stick with her, she will change*, I thought. I don't understand my thinking on that last one as there was nothing being done that would effect some form of magical transformation.

Eventually, we ripped the Band-Aid off and reintroduced her to industry. After some short-term pain during the transition, it became very apparent that we should have done this months and months and months earlier. Why did I wait this long?

A business owner I was mentoring had an individual that was managing a team three or four levels deep in his manufacturing organization. That individual had been caught making lewd and inappropriate sexual comments to females in that area of the firm. Despite numerous warnings, the individual continued his behavior. His COO requested that they terminate this individual not only for his inappropriate and potentially costly commentary, but also because of his toxic attitude.

The individual in question was a personal friend of the owner and a long-time employee. The owner was very loyal to him and would not allow the COO to take necessary action. Not only did the owner essentially place an anointing halo on the toxic employee, he also zapped the COOs authority. The COO left the company shortly thereafter, citing an inability to effect change that upheld the company values and a lack of genuine empowerment and authority. Sadly, the CEO cut off all outside counsel (present company included). He closed the shutters to the world, jumped into a foxhole with his company, and returned to a micromanagement style of leadership. The company began to spiral and was ultimately sold.

All business rises and falls with leadership and people. As a leader, you can have an enormous impact.

Proverbs 16:14
A king's wrath is a messenger of death, but the wise will appease it.

Proverbs 19:12
A king's rage is like the roar of a lion, but his favor is like dew on the grass.

Proverbs 20:2
A king's wrath strikes terror like the roar of a lion; those who anger him forfeit their lives.

Proverbs 20:28
Love and faithfulness keep a king safe; through love his throne is made secure.

Proverbs: 28:2
When a country is rebellious, it has many rulers, but a ruler with discernment and knowledge maintains order.

Proverbs: 28:3
A ruler who oppresses the poor is like a driving rain that leaves no crops.

Proverbs: 28:15
Like a roaring lion or a charging bear is a wicked ruler over a helpless people.

Proverbs 29: 2
When the righteous thrive, the people rejoice; when the wicked rule, the people groan.

Proverbs 29:12
If a ruler listens to lies, all his officials become wicked.

What great imagery in these proverbs!
As a leader you can:
- Bring wrath
- Strike terror
- Be a messenger of death
- Forfeit people's lives
- Be like a charging bear or roaring lion
- Create a company culture that is
  ~ Rebellious
  ~ Sends people into hiding
  ~ Groans

As a leader you can also:
- Bring justice
- Give favor
- Winnow out the wicked
- Bring love and faithfulness
- Have discernment and knowledge
- Create a company that rejoices
  ~ Like dew on grass
  ~ Rainclouds in the spring

Who you are as a leader affects how people come to work, go home to their families, use their resources, and change lives. You will never have a better chance to impact the world than you do right now. The number of people you put on your impact circle will only be eclipsed as your company and influence grow. You must decide what kind of leader you want to be and what kind of company you want to build—because you have been given much and much is expected.

How many people do you impact? Let's find out.

Application: The Impact Circle

Take out a sheet of paper and draw a small circle. Title this circle "Family" and list the names of your immediate family and extended family that you impact. Draw a second, bigger circle around the first one. Title it "Company." Then list all the people in your company. If you have a large company, list your direct reports and the total number of employees under your leadership. Then draw a third circle around that called "Network." List partners, vendors, resellers, customers, and clients. Draw another circle around that and write "Community." List your tribes, community groups, church, sports teams—anything outside home and work. Next, add up the total number of people. Finally, multiply that number by three because all of those people have families.

How many people do you personally impact?

Was that number larger than you thought?

You have been given much; therefore, much has been demanded. And if you use your leadership mantle in a way that honors God, more will be entrusted, and more will be asked.

Application: Four Big Questions

Once a quarter, our entire community of CEOs and owners gets together for connection and sharpening. Bestselling business book author Mark Sanborn came and spoke to our community shortly after publishing *The Potential Principle*. One of the activities he shared was to ask four big questions about why you lead. Often, we are thrust into leadership without intentionality. The pace of business also keeps us from being very specific in our leadership journeys.

Here is a great way to stop and take stock of who you are, why you lead, and where you want to go. (And Mark's book is an excellent resource if you want to go deeper into these four questions.)

- *Why do you lead?* Are you a born, developed, or reluctant leader? Why have you accepted the mantle of leadership? What vision will sustain you as a leader? For me (Dan), I lead to develop others. I've been made to come alongside others to help them grow. This definition of my "why" helps me keep motivated and focused on my strengths.

- *What kind of leader do you want to be?* What does that look like on a daily, weekly, and monthly basis? Once you know why, you can start to structure the types of activities, messaging, and strategy to make you the best you of a leader. A quick exercise to help you brainstorm is to list three leaders that inspire you. What about them inspires you? What would you like to emulate?

- *How will you get better?* What do you need and want to learn or improve? What is the most important future for you and your company?

- *How will you last?* What does your legacy look like? What will you start that can't be finished in your lifetime?

Answer these questions, and share them with someone else in your company, at your next executive team meeting, or with another leadership group—heck, even your spouse. Talking about it will cement the ideas and hold you accountable. It will also help to hone your answers so they aren't wishy-washy.

Don't be wishy-washy. Put a stake in the ground.

Chapter 8

WHO ARE YOUR PROPHETS?

He that is taught only by himself has a fool for a master.
—Hunter S. Thompson

The fellowship of true friends who can hear you out, share your joys, help carry your burdens, and correctly counsel you is priceless.
—Ezra Taft Benson

Having prophets in your life is very near and dear to my (Dan's) heart. I believe in it so much I've decided to do it for a living. Through Acumen, I am a mastermind facilitator, a certified executive business coach, and thrice a business owner. I've experienced it myself and heard over and over how isolated you feel, how information coming to you is biased, and how easy it is to get lulled into thinking you are in control, know it all, or can figure it out by sheer will. I wish I had a community of trusted advisors back when I was CEO.

For these reasons, you need truth tellers around you to help you see blind spots and get sharp, inspired, and challenged to increase your leadership effectiveness and organizational performance—all so you can clearly see yourself and your company.

Who is one person who you should listen to right now?

Who is speaking truth to you that you are having trouble hearing?

Proverbs 11:14

For lack of guidance a nation falls, but victory is won through many advisers.

Proverbs 12:15

The way of fools seems right to them, but the wise listen to advice.

Proverbs 15:28

Plans fail for lack of counsel, but with many advisers they succeed

Proverbs 19:20

Listen to advice and accept instruction, and at the end you will be counted among the wise.

Proverbs 20:5

The purposes of a person's heart are deep waters, but a man of understanding draws them out.

Proverbs 20:18

Make plans by seeking advice; if you wage war, obtain guidance.

Proverbs 27:17

As iron sharpens iron, so one person sharpens another.

We had just endured a heated debate about where we were putting our resources for the following year. The topic was a project that should have been killed a *long* time ago. I (Dan) was feeling some six-figure sunk cost bias and saw a teeny tiny light at the end of the tunnel.

After that meeting, our COO came into my office and told me the hard truth about what I was doing to the company. He said I was stealing. Can you believe that? What was I stealing?

- Employee time from our core business
- Profitability

- Energy
- Our culture

All because of my pet project. My initial reaction was anger: What?!? "You don't have all the information. I have a vision for this company!" He let me run my course and did an amazing thing. He let the silence and his stare hold his words.

Sigh ... He was right.

When you hear the word *prophet*, what do you think? Is it this otherworldly person who tells the future and it's usually doom and gloom? Although prophets have been that (see the Old Testament), prophets were first and foremost advisors and teachers intended to serve the king. They worked for him, yet they told the truth and gave honest feedback. Many prophets lost their lives because of the truth.

In Ken Blanchard and Phil Hodges *The Servant Leader*, they told some truth of their own:

> "If you can't name any active truth tellers in your life or if you have avoided or undervalued the ones you have, it's time for a change. Having truth tellers in your life is important. It is probably your greatest opportunity for growth. There are two main ways that growth takes place: when one is open to feedback from other people and when one is willing to disclose vulnerabilities to others."

Answer these two questions for yourself.

1. *Are you teachable?* I'm amazed by the number of leaders who know it all, have a perceived understanding of all facets of their company, and are still "Command and Direct" leaders. They come from an "Only the strong survive" and "Never let them see you sweat" culture. If the above scenario happened to you, how would you have reacted? Can you change your mind, position, and perspective when the facts change?

2. *Can you name your prophets?* Name three to five people in your life that speak truth to you. Truth is both positive and negative, celebratory and critical. If you can't name any such people, see below. If you can, do they know that they are your prophets? Are they safe from your wrath when they do tell the truth? How do you engage them to get the feedback you need?

Having both internal and external prophets allows you to make better decisions and have a greater understanding of yourself inside and outside the office; it also helps you grow, which is something I see leaders stop doing at the top quite often. It's not because you don't want to. It's because you don't take the time, or you don't have a community to join.

Having a few trusted truth tellers in your life can help with your organizational and personal performance. Who are your prophets? They need to be specific names. It comes down to relationships with individual people where you get the juiciest fruit. Bible study is great, but coffee with Tim is awesome.

Make a list of your prophets. Where do you need people in your company and life to help you in these areas?

- *Faith: Who do you go to for spiritual guidance?*
- *Family, Marriage, and Kids: This is not your spouse.* This is someone whom you can honestly share the good and bad of your family at whatever stage of life.
- *Internal Company: Who is your trusted advisor on your executive team who will tell you the truth or call you out when and where appropriate?*
- *External Company: Who do you turn to get overall perspective when you need direction, can't see the forest for the trees, or just make sure you aren't crazy?*

The ceiling of a company's growth is only as high as the growth potential of its leader. When you stop growing and listening, so does your company.

Mental Model: WW_D?

I know the first name that came to mind when you saw the above: Jesus. I like that sentiment, but I feel it's an unattainable standard. What would Jesus do? I don't know—see into the depths of someone's soul, know their true self, motive, intent, and ask them a simple and deep question to change the course of that person's life forever. (I would have also accepted "heal them" or "perform a miracle"). Yeah, I got none of that.

What I do have is a list of people throughout my career that have shaped my ideas, values, experiences, and actions. Some of them are in the Bible. I dig Paul and Peter. They teach me a lot about how I want to be and give me direction when I ask myself that question. What would Paul do?

Many modern leaders ask this question as well, especially when they are the next generation of leadership. What would the founder do? What would the person who was larger than life whose role I now fill do? What would my mentor for my past company do?

I love this model because it makes you get out of your own head and think from another point of view. There is a ton of value in changing the angle of a situation or challenge. This is one way to do that. You can scroll through different people like you were playing *Mortal Kombat* and pick the warrior who is best for the job. Maybe even have several of them debate each other.

The danger of this is when you then go and do exactly what you think that person would do. Quick tip: don't do that. This is a filter only. Here's why. What you think they would do isn't what they would actually do. It's a version of it. You have different circumstances, experience, background, culture, strengths, weaknesses, time in history, stage in the company, leadership style, and whatever else you are thinking. You still need to make the decision.

The WW_D? filter helps brainstorm options that you wouldn't immediately come up with on your own. It can also help you hold onto specific values, process, ideas, or outcomes that you would like to keep top of mind in the decision.

As a dad, I (Dan) do this all the time. Although I am much better caregiver now than early in my dad career, I often ask myself, "What would Ali (my wife) do?" I found by putting on her hat my decision was fifty to sixty percent better than what I would do alone, which usually trends toward efficiency with no empathy. It is still never what she would have done. And there are good things about efficiency and how I see the world that can benefit the kids. So, my strengths with her filter create a lot of better experiences for the kids and me.

What about in business?

Have you ever thought or heard someone say, "It's a mini Berkshire Hathaway," or, "I want to create the next Berkshire Hathaway." Don't we all.

There are more books, quotes, interviews, and discussions about Warren Buffett and partner Charlie Munger than almost any other investor duo on the planet. Their annual meetings are legendary and along the lines of a Grateful Dead show for finance nerds. Many people look up to them, and with good reason. They do things the right way, for the right reason, and over a long period of time.

If you wanted to create the next "Berkshire Hathaway," you couldn't do it the same way they did. What, how, and when they did it worked for who they were, the time period, the market, the opportunities, and challenges they were presented with.

You can't do that. What you can do is take their principles or concepts, make them your own, and choose the direction you want to take.

WW_D? is a powerful model, but it's used best as a filter to help make better decisions that are right for now—for where you are and who you are.

Chapter 9

PLANNING: USELESS AND INDISPENSABLE

In preparing for battle I have always found that plans
are useless, but planning is indispensable.
—Dwight D. Eisenhower

If you are a leader, you are a planner. You have to be. Strategic plans, weekly plans, daily plans, contingency plans, plan B, and so on. Yet, look what God's Word has to say about plans and planning:

> *Now listen, you who say, "Today or tomorrow we will go to this or that city, spend a year there, carry on business and make money." Why, you do not even know what will happen tomorrow. What is your life? You are a mist that appears for a little while and then vanishes. Instead, you ought to say, "If it is the Lord's will, we will live and do this or that." As it is, you boast in your arrogant schemes. All such boasting is evil.*
> **James 4: 13–17**

How should we understand these words? Is planning useless? In the Proverbs below, Solomon stated that the Lord "establishes your plans." That creates tension. How am I supposed to plan if He establishes my plan? Am I just supposed to sit in my office and wait for divine intervention? What does all that even mean?

Proverbs 16:1–3

[1] To humans belong the plans of the heart, but from the LORD comes the proper answer of the tongue. [2] All a person's ways seem pure to them, but motives are weighed by the LORD. [3] Commit to the LORD whatever you do, and he will establish your plans.

Proverbs 16:9

In their hearts, humans plan their course, but the LORD establishes their steps.

Proverbs 19:21

Many are the plans in a person's heart, but it is the LORD's purpose that prevails.

Proverbs 21: 31

The horse is made ready for the day of battle, but victory rests with the LORD.

Proverbs 24:27

Put your outdoor work in order and get your fields ready; after that, build your house.

Proverbs 27:23–27

[23] Be sure you know the condition of your flocks, give careful attention to your herds; [24] for riches do not endure forever, and a crown is not secure for all generations. [25] When the hay is removed and new growth appears and the grass from the hills is gathered in, [26] the lambs will provide you with clothing, and the goats with the price of a field. [27] You will have plenty of goats' milk to feed your family and to nourish your female servants.

No, you are not supposed to wait in your office until you get struck with divine intervention. You need to live in the tension of waiting on the Lord and doing what you need to do.

Application: The Four Questions for Pre-Planning

Let's break this down by focusing on Proverbs 16.

16:1—To humans belong the plans of the heart, but from the LORD comes the proper answer of the tongue.

You have plans that are in your heart. You want to grow the company, retire by a certain age, transition the company, buy a building, whatever. Those plans are there for a reason. You need to honor those thoughts, pray on them, think them through, and plan accordingly.

16:2—All a person's ways seem pure to them, but motives are weighed by the LORD.

Because these are thoughts and plans you have, you believe they are pure and correct. Why wouldn't they be? You thought them up. But motives are weighed by the Lord. How many times have I thought my motives were pure, and yet somewhere in the back of my head I was plotting something not so pure? We're often focused on money, pride, deception, or any other reason we do what we do. Weigh your motives. Pray and ask God to reveal your motives and that they are pure. And in your executive meetings, ask what your company motives are.

16:3—Commit to the LORD whatever you do, and He will establish your plans.

In what order do you plan? Plan then pray? Pray then plan? Plan then ask God for approval? How do you engage God in your planning? The biggest mistake I see is that businesses put a plan together and then take it to God for approval. "You agree with me, right Lord? Please bless it. Amen." That's backward. You need to commit to the Lord whatever your next steps are going to be. Pray on it. Pray about it. Then, you can start planning.

This doesn't have to be weeks of prayer and preparation, although there are decisions big enough for that to make sense. You can simply say a prayer before your meeting that honors the Lord and ask for His will to be done, and ask the Holy Spirit to guide your conversations.

16:9—In their hearts, humans plan their course, but the LORD establishes their steps.

Once you have a plan, how do you get confirmation of the next steps? If you've done a good job in planning, there should be an obvious first step. Start moving. This is where walking the plan out with the Lord becomes key. Don't just rubber stamp a plan and run as fast as you can. You need to check in with the Lord about your steps. This is constant communication, not one and done.

In my experience, there are four big questions you need to answer before you start planning:

1. What plans are in your heart?
2. What are your motives?
3. How will you involve God in your planning? What does commitment to Him look like?
4. Based on the above, what is the first step?

There are so many ways to do strategic planning. I'm of the opinion that you should use the one you like and are comfortable with. I only really like three things: a long-term vision (five to ten years), annual goals and metrics, and quarterly initiatives or rocks. You can use Traction's V/TO, or Scaling Up's One Page Strategic Plan, or The Advantage from the Table Group.

The key, though, comes before you start planning. You as a leader and as an executive team need to work through and keep in mind the four questions above before, during, and after developing your plan.

Then God controls the outcomes. Sometimes the best plans miss, blow up, scuttle, or are just plain wrong. You learn from those experiences and become better planners. I know it seems counterintuitive, but we cannot be tied to the outcomes as long as we bring Him into the process.

Work like it's all on you. Pray like it's all on Him. Live in the tension.

Confirmation In the Doing

Have you ever been stuck in transition? You need to make a decision to move forward but are hung up with feelings of uncertainty and uneasiness. Risk is everywhere, and the next step will change everything going forward.

Wouldn't it be great if you could feel more at peace about your decision and have more clarity and confidence?

Let me share one truth that I have learned by watching many leaders make these kinds of decisions: There is confirmation in the doing.

I know ... mind blowing, right?

Quick example: An executive wants to make a career change or has recently sold their business. They set out to find "what's next." What's an achiever like this to do? They research, analyze, read, think about, and perhaps hope that an answer will appear. They categorize their passions, skills, experience, expertise and try to match those to a job or market.

When this is done in the "research and decide" vacuum, one of two things can happen. First, they do nothing ... paralysis of analysis. Second, they pull the trigger and figure out in ninety days that it's the wrong decision.

Both suck.

There is confirmation in the doing. By getting out of the office and doing, you'll get the green, yellow, or red light with opportunities and challenges. Move forward. Proceed with caution. Stop. Take a left turn. Yield.

But you need to *do* in a way that will move you forward and provide clarity informing your next steps.

Transition specialist from The Halftime Institute, Jeff Spadafora, suggests low-cost probes. *The Lean Startup* author, Eric Ries, suggests using a minimum viable product (or in this case process) and the scientific method: using a hypothesis, getting out of the office to test, receive feedback, learn, and iterate.

Both concepts have the same basic idea. You don't know a final answer until you go try something. When you get out of the office you get feedback, learn, and can make a more informed decision about what to do or not do next.

The key in both is to start with small, easy-to-execute tests.

Be careful: Where this process goes wonky is when you really, really want your test to go a certain way or you have decided on the outcomes before you start the test. This creates a considerable amount of bias with yourself, the data, information, feedback, and results. In order to truly receive confirmation, you must remain open, objective, and unattached.

The other kicker is time. This is a slower process than most people like. In big decisions like this, time is your friend. Slower is better.

Life is about transitions: going from one state to another.

To get clear on the right path, stop thinking about, researching, analyzing, or assuming. Instead, get out there and see what works, what doors open and close, and what the next step will be.

Chapter 10

MAKING BIG DECISIONS

One of the benefits of our CEO community is the value of discernment. When there are situations, opportunities, or challenges that are big or small, CEOs have a place to receive the benefit from 300 years of combined experience in a very short period of time.

One of things I've noticed is that even though there are similar situations in the problems we assess, the intent, action, and outcomes are different based upon many factors—such as the individual leader, perspective, type of business, current market conditions, and so on.

As Solomon says in Ecclesiastes, there is a time for everything:

[1] *There is a time for everything, and a season for every activity under the heavens:*

[2] *a time to be born and a time to die,*
 a time to plant and a time to uproot,

[3] *a time to kill and a time to heal,*
 a time to tear down and a time to build,

[4] *a time to weep and a time to laugh,*
 a time to mourn and a time to dance,

[5] *a time to scatter stones and a time to gather them,*
 a time to embrace and a time to refrain from embracing,

[6] *a time to search and a time to give up,*
 a time to keep and a time to throw away,

[7] *a time to tear and a time to mend,*

a time to be silent and a time to speak,
8 a time to love and a time to hate,
a time for war and a time for peace.

Ecclesiastes 3: 1–8

In our communities, there have been times where the council has advised leaders to:

- Be as shrewd as snakes and as innocent as doves (Matthew 10:16).
- Turn the other cheek (Matthew 5:39).
- Be like David vs Goliath and fight (1 Samuel 17:32–51).
- Love your neighbor (Matthew 22:34–40).

These are vastly different approaches that all could be applied to the same situation. So, how do you know when it's appropriate to go to battle and when it's time to be the peacemaker? When to save and when to spend? Where should you focus your generosity? Do you focus on high growth? Enter that new market?

Answering those questions take discernment. Are you discerning? Do you have good judgment? How do you try to understand situations or get direction when you are standing at a fork in the road? How do you involve your faith, your team, and your spouse?

Discernment is a key skill of a leader. It takes humility and patience. Discernment is simple, but not easy.

Proverbs 10: 13
Wisdom is found on the lips of the discerning, but a rod is for the back of one who has no sense.

Proverbs 15:14
The discerning heart seeks knowledge, but the mouth of a fool feeds on folly.

Proverbs 15:21

Folly brings joy to one who has no sense, but whoever has understanding keeps a straight course.

Proverbs 16:21

The wise in heart are called discerning, and gracious words promote instruction.

Proverbs 17:10

A rebuke impresses a discerning person more than a hundred lashes a fool.

Proverbs 28:5

Evildoers do not understand what is right, but those who seek the LORD understand it fully.

Proverbs 28:11

The rich are wise in their own eyes; one who is poor and discerning sees how deluded they are.

I'll (Drew) never forget the time when one of the CEOs in our community was faced with a really big decision regarding the future strategy of his company. He was stuck and was mired in so much detail and so close to the situation that he had a difficult time seeing the best path. I suggested he share the situation with his fellow cohorts and seek the wise counsel of experienced business owners who had dealt with challenges of this nature. Additionally, I encouraged him to prepare for that discussion and present his situation with some forethought.

The tool I commonly recommend is something we call the Situation Briefing tool. The framework helps the presenter take their thoughts, realities, and dynamics and put them on paper in a linear fashion. Further it forces the individual to describe the situation and clearly define how the team can specifically be most helpful.

I have found that unless you define the situation, opportunity, or challenge *specifically*, the group may naturally migrate their line of questioning and solutions toward an unrelated or undesired situation or problem. By defining what advice the individual would like from their fellow counselors, it helps keep the desired outcome forefront.

Further, the Situation Briefing form forces the presenter to specify background information about the situation and define its current impact on him personally, the organization's culture, employees, customers, and other related areas such as profitability, cash flow, values, stewardship, and so on.

I love these two questions from the form most:

1. If nothing changes, what might be the single most positive or negative long-term impact?
2. What is your spouse's feedback?

Not every issue or challenge needs a spouse's perspective, but I'm always blown away when it seems obvious that the spouse should be included, and he or she hasn't been confided in at all. Back to the story. I knew this particular individual was the classic CEO who commonly made many decisions based on gut feel and instinct born out of experience. He rarely writes anything down, and his mind is a constant whirl of motion. You can practically see the gears grinding when you toss a question his way.

When he showed up to present his issue that day during our mastermind session, I recall him saying that "Filling this form out actually helped me think through the matter at hand in a linear fashion. While I still want to share this with the fellow members of my team and get their feedback, I think this really helped me answer the question I was having such a difficult time wrestling with." He did actually go ahead and present it to the team and got some additional feedback and valuable advice. But just the exercise of putting thoughts on paper reminded me how valuable and important this process is.

Application: Discernment Through the Situation Briefing Process

How do you know the Lord's purpose? That takes discernment. Discernment is a process. It is simple but not always easy, and it usually takes more time than you would like. What I've described below isn't the only way to discern decisions, but it is a framework for understanding your business situations, opportunities, and challenges in a way that gives you a higher standard approach to the best possible outcome.

There are seven steps in this process that I recommend:

Step One is prayer. This is probably starting to sound like a broken record but if you aren't connecting with God on a regular basis through Scripture and prayer, it's going to be tough to make good decisions. So start with prayer. In the still silence is when you can hear God's voice the clearest.

Step Two is to understand the situation.

Specifically, you need to identify answers to these questions:

- What is the opportunity, challenge, or situation you want to discern?

  Be specific. What question are you trying to answer?

- What background information is important to understand?

  This is key background information. I continuously see that too much detail and "understanding" confuses good decision making. These are big events and milestones not he said, she said.

- How are you and the business being impacted?

  Personally, organizationally, culturally, profitability, cash flow, customers, brand, credibility, suppliers, values, stewardship, etc.

- If nothing changes, what could be the long-term impact?
- What role have you played in the situation?

    This is where you look in the mirror and give an honest assessment of your part.

- If applicable, what is your spouse's feedback?

    It's amazing the number of times a spouse's feedback is a version of the go-forward strategy. They know you (and your company) better than anyone; why wouldn't you include them?

- What is your ideal outcome?

    If there were rainbows and unicorns in the sky, what would have happened?

- What is the potential dollar value on the situation?

    We're not looking for an enterprise accounting firm estimate compiled by expensive consultants, but rather a guesstimate of the impact. And it may not be dollars—in some cases it's an impact on people's lives and the greater good.

> These questions come from the Situation Briefing form that Acumen uses at monthly councils.
>
> You can download this form at:
> www.acumenimpact.com/resources.

Step Three is to bring the situation to your advisors. Take the information you wrote down above, and discuss it with your advisors. This could be your executive team, family, mentors, coach, and so on. Make sure that a segment of advisors has no direct or emotional connection to the outcome of your decision. This is key to getting honest and direct feedback.

Step Four is to ask for biblical wisdom. By exploring Scripture, parables, stories, and experiences through faith, you prioritize godly values and principles before worldly ones. Trust this process. The Holy Spirit can work through others to guide you. Here are some important questions to spark your ideas during this step:

- Does the Bible offer anything on the subject?
- Did anyone in the Bible ever face a situation like this?
- What wisdom do we get from Scripture as we engage this issue?
- How did God's people respond when something similar happened?
- Does this remind you of anything that happened in the Bible?
- What counsel might we draw from Scripture?
- How does the Bible address this?
- Does Jesus have anything to say about this?
- Calling upon what we know from the Bible, who's perspective might we gain?
- What do you think your favorite Bible character might have done?

Step Five is explore possible solutions and advice. What shared experiences, realities, or blind spots do your advisors see? It's not always a total consensus, but when you start hearing the same thing over and over on steps 4 and 5, that's the time to focus on the solution.

Step Six is to ask these questions: What did you hear? What are you going to go do?

And Step Seven is another round of prayer. Remember, only you and Jesus know all of the details. At this point, you may have multiple options you believe are the right path. You may also have conflicting advice. Lay these out and anything else on your heart to Jesus and ask for the next step.

But what if I don't hear anything in prayer? How am I supposed to know the direction I should take? This isn't always the case, but when you hear nothing, you should move forward with your best discerned course of action. Then get confirmation in the doing. Frequently, the next step is revealed more directly as you move forward with action.

Chapter 11

PRUDENCE IS SEXY

Prudence is what makes someone a great commodities trader—the capacity to face reality squarely in the eye without allowing emotion or ego to get in the way. It's what is needed by every quarterback or battlefield general.
—John Ortberg

Prudence is not a sexy word. The face people make when asked about prudence is the same one they make after eating a large piece of grapefruit—sour. Maybe that's because most people connect the idea of "prudence" with being a "prude." In high school, a prude was not someone you'd want to hang out with. "Yeah, you are really proper and modest . . . let's hang out!"

And yet, that connection couldn't be further from the truth. Being prudent may not be trendy or written about—but when you see a leader who is prudent, you respect them a lot more.

According to *Merriam-Webster,* prudence is the ability to govern and discipline oneself by the use of reason, shrewdness in the management of affairs, the skill of good judgment in the use of resources, and cautionary as to danger or risk.

Based on that definition, would you like to be a prudent leader?

Proverbs 12:16
Fools show their annoyance at once, but the prudent overlook an insult.

Proverbs 14:8

The wisdom of the prudent is to give thought to their ways, but the folly of fools is deception.

Proverbs 14:15

The simple believe anything, but the prudent give thought to their steps.

Proverbs 16:22

Prudence is a fountain of life to those who have it, but folly brings punishment to fools.

Proverbs 27:12

The prudent see danger and take refuge, but the simple keep going and pay the penalty.

A prudent person overlooks insults, listens, has emotional intelligence, gives thought to their ways and steps, sees danger, and takes refuge when necessary. Fools are annoyed, quick to talk, show their ignorance, believe anything, disregard risk, and pay the penalty.

Personally, I'd rather be prudent. What about you?

Leaders Take Big Swings

Some companies need tweaking. Improve customer service, decrease cost of goods, add a key player, and they experience growth and prosper.

But what happens when you what got you here won't get you there? When you see a shift in the market that gives you enough pause that you know you need to take a big swing?

As an owner or CEO, it's likely you'll have to make one big decision in the next two years that will change the course of your company for the next decade.

I (Dan) led an e-learning company for ten years. For the first four, we were a custom shop. Everything was personalized, branded, and storied for you, the client. Around that same time, we took a big swing: that we would become an off-the-shelf (generic content) provider first, then add custom when needed.

The problem was that we were creating the same course over and over again. It cost a fortune, and we could only sell enterprise level clients due to the need for big budgets. The courses took forever to sell, and the account management was expensive due to heavy hand-holding. Our revenue was stagnant, and we were bumping into the same challenges again and again. Adding people or process wouldn't fix the issues.

So, we decided to take a big swing. Changing our model would put us in a position to grow with larger target markets, multiple price points, and leverage our internal intellectual property.

It was against everything we had created up to that point. Process, people, messaging, philosophy—all had to change. It was an idea we chewed on for six months. What if we missed? What if people weren't on board? How would it affect our current customer base? Revenue? Cash flow?

After the first year, we saw an increase in purchases with our current clients (more bang for their buck and serving multiple departments), we created a reseller strategy, which allowed others to sell our products and increased our sales without investing in new sales talent, and we increased our offering from 50 courses to 250.

The decision paid off and set us up for the next five years of growth.

What about you? How do you know you need to take a big swing?

It's usually starts in your gut. You can just see the market changing. But you've always done it this way, and it starts to become your biggest worry.

Your current path might become the elephant in the room at your executive meetings. Everyone knows it's there, but no one wants to be the one to bring it up because of politics, change, and how much hard work it will take. It's easier to sit in the foxhole and hope no one throws in a grenade.

Trust your team and put it on the table. Allow the conversation to challenge your bias and thesis. Be able to argue all sides. Then, make your decision—keep tweaking or take the big swing.

Once you decide, you'll need to hold on to the idea and recast the vision. For many leaders, this is where it goes off the rails. It's not a shiny object anymore, so they move on to new things and people. Taking your eye off the ball will ruin the company. If it took 2–3 years to get your business off the ground, it will take at least that long to change the direction.

You might only take one or two big swings in your company over a decade, but they are what will take you into the future with confidence.

So check your gut. What do you need to swing at? Then run it through the Discernment Filter.

But wait ... what does this have to do with prudence? Wasn't that about minimizing risk, looking before you leap, and going slow? Yes, prudence is all of those things, but as the leader of your company, you need to have a wider lens than that.

Prudence can be seeing the market and sensing danger. Prudence can be contrarian because it's not doing what everyone else would do. Prudence is not putting your head in the sand and hoping it all turns out well. It's a deliberate, honest, calculating, and risk-management mindset in all facets of your business. And it's just flat-out sexy.

Mental Model: 10-10-10 and 10-100-1000

Do you remember that scene in *The Matrix* where Morpheus and Neo meet for the first time? They are in a dark room sitting on Victorian furniture, and Morpheus tells Neo what the matrix is and that he is a slave in it. Then he gives Neo a fork-in-the-road decision to make. "This is your last chance. After this, there is no turning back. You take the blue pill, the story ends. You wake up in your bed and believe whatever you want to believe. You take the red pill, and you stay in Wonderland, and I show you how deep the rabbit hole goes. (long dramatic pause) Remember, all I'm offering is the truth, nothing more." (Eerie music playing...)

Have you ever been in this situation? Red pill, blue pill, decide right now. Uncertain future. You know enough to be dangerous, but there is unknown risk. Or, you know the risk, but you can't measure if it's a good decision or bad one. Been there?

This could be signing a large contract with a new vendor, buying a new building, or taking on a new partner. It could be staring sin in the face. Heads I go up to the hotel room with her/him, tails I turn and run away. No matter the situation, there is a great mental model that can help you quickly get out of your emotional state of "now" and instead look toward the future.

In Suze Welch's book *10-10-10*, she outlines how, when faced with a challenge, you can ask yourself questions using these three 10s to help process and understand consequences.

"The name of the process is just a totem meant to directionally suggest time frames along the lines of: in the heat of the moment, somewhat later, and when all is said and done."

The first 10 is now, so it could be 10 minutes or 10 hours. The second 10 is later, so perhaps 10 days or 10 months. The third 10 is long term, so perhaps 10 years.

By looking at the situation in different time frames, you get an immediate perspective change, and you engage your logical mind and step out of the here-and-now emotional state.

I think there is also a "values multiplier" you can add to the timeframe. You may only be making this decision once. That is dangerous because you can get really creative justifying that decision. Multiply by 10 each time to see if the decision is in line with your why, your values, and your mission.

Meaning, would you make that same decision 10 times? 100 times? 1000 times?

Decisions we make carry consequences—both good and bad. By thinking about potential outcomes, time, and values, you can quickly decipher if you want to move forward with those consequences.

Chapter 12

RECOGNITION AND CELEBRATION

"For it is in giving that we receive."
—Francis of Assisi, Peace Prayer

You complete a project, overcome an obstacle, close a big deal—great! And then it's on to the next project, obstacle, or big deal. You just don't think about it. It's not on your radar. "It" is recognition and celebration.

What I've (Drew) found in leaders is that what goes on in your head is *ahead* of your team. You have already completed the project and have in your sights the next hill to climb. Your people don't. They are living out work in real time. This causes a disconnect that, if left alone, can leave your teams tired and uninspired. What's the point of all the hustle if you don't stop and see what all that hard work accomplished? A great friend and mentor named Merle Mees, a mega church pastor in our community, posed a thought-provoking question to me regarding the value of recognition. He asked, "What is the universal sign that an individual needs recognition?"

I have always been one who loves to recognize and celebrate people, victories, and wins, but I was stumped by his question. Clearly by the smirk on his face it was of those "The answer ought to be obvious" trick questions, but I remained dumbfounded.

"Breathing." He chuckled.

Of course. Yet, obvious as that answer sounds, I've been amazed at how often I gloss over opportunities to celebrate and recognize people, milestones, and achievements. I see this all too frequently with the CEO community I serve as well. We live in a world of "What have you done for me lately," which ties into the content discussed earlier in the book about "A to B" versus "expanding A" mindset. We are always quick to establish another B to go out and conquer.

Such is not the case for Acumen partner who is the CEO of one of the country's top roofing, guttering, and siding firms— an Ernst and Young Award winner and on the Inc. 5000 list and growing, going from one location in 2010 to seventeen locations in 2019. Their team is spread throughout the US and is composed of a very diverse collection of employees and staff. The strength of their organization lies in their sales, marketing, and business development units. Diversity would be a great way to describe the sales team related to the eclectic mix of background, experience, skills sets, and education.

He invited my wife and me to attend his annual sales celebration. He had verbally shared with me some of their creative approaches to celebration. I'd seen a few pictures as well. But holy cow, I was blown away! I've been involved with a number of organizations and seen a variety of sales team celebrations. We were big on celebrating at our company as well. I actually thought we did a great job until I attended his celebration. I suddenly had a healthy case of celebration envy!

Our evening started with the typical cocktail hour preceding dinner. The banquet hall was on lockdown so that no one could sneak a peek. Once they flung open the doors and let everyone in, I could see why. As we took our seats to a chorus of upbeat, get-your-blood-pumping tunes, I was amazed by the massive showcase of trophies and awards. It was dazzling. It looked as though royalty was to be bestowed upon the entire team. The entire back side of the stage was a trophy case that was at least four terraces high, with each terrace holding 30 glimmering trophies. Some were made of glass, some of shiny gold. The room was dark, but the stage was lit up with Hollywood-esque lighting to illuminate the hard-earned recognition soon to be lavished upon the team. I was just a casual observer, but I was jacked up to see the ceremony unfold.

The dinner, celebration, and recognition program lasted for several hours. It was nonstop, high energy, and fun. A variety of leaders and performers were recognized for their various achievements. It wasn't just limited to sales people. It extended deep into their service support and operations teams as well. I'd never seen anything so fantastic. At one point prior to the meal, he even shared a brief but poignant viewpoint on his faith and how he aspired to integrate it into the culture, leadership fabric, and DNA of his firm, publicly acknowledging he wasn't perfect but aspiring to be held to a higher standard of accountability.

Just when I thought the party was over, an announcement was made to the entire crowd that they needed to assemble in the lower level of the hotel lobby. As we descended the escalator into the lobby, you couldn't help but hear a small but loud and mighty jazz band as they blared their brass and percussion instruments. The entire assembly then proceeded out the front door of the hotel and down a very busy street in New Orleans, escorted by a team of policeman complete with sirens and bright flashing lights. We were now officially a parade—a parade marching down very busy nighttime streets of New Orleans.

In a couple of blocks, we made a turn that pointed us directly down Bourbon Street. Have you ever been to Bourbon Street in New Orleans at 11:00 at night? It's a literal circus! I was at a loss trying to figure out how our band of 250-plus people was going to actually get down the street. Led by our triumphant jazz band and a police escort, the sea of people on Bourbon Street seemed to happily part, allowing our entire procession to advance to one of the French Quarter's most popular watering holes.

Holy cow, wow! What an off-the-charts night! Not only a celebration banquet with recognitions galore, but also a lifetime memory and experience that will not be soon forgotten.

Oh, by the way, for those who thought this was over—wait, there's more! For employees who hit the elite thresholds of production and performance, a seven-day, all-expenses-paid Caribbean cruise awaited the next morning, not only for the individual but for their spouse as well. Recognition done well—exceedingly well!

Huge expense . . . or a huge investment?

You answer that question. I know firsthand the impact that event had on motivation, morale, retention, and recruiting.

Here's what I love most, though. He is allowing God to work through him as he leads this organization and leverages his platform of impact to influence the lives of those he serves for Kingdom impact. He's intentional, willing to be vulnerable with those he leads, and unafraid to allow God to use him and work through him as a vocational steward. He understands the eternal implications of the skills, leadership gifts, and business platform he's been entrusted with by his creator and is quick to share his story and point people to Jesus—and not just point but lead them to an eternal relationship with Christ.

Cheers to breathing!

Proverbs 22:29
Do you see someone skilled in their work? They will serve before kings; they will not serve before officials of low rank.

Proverbs 25:13
Like a snow-cooled drink at harvest time is a trustworthy messenger to the one who sends him; he refreshes the spirit of his master.

Proverbs 27:18
The one who guards a fig tree will eat its fruit, and whoever protects their master will be honored.

How awesome would it be to have a "snow-cooled drink at harvest time"? The original outdoor cooler. I just love that simile. Refreshing! That's what a valued servant does for his master. He refreshes his master's spirit.

Do your people refresh you? If so, how so? If not, why not?

In Bob Chapman and Raj Sisodia's book *Everybody Matters*, there is a wonderful chapter on recognition and celebration. They make the case that when you recognize and celebrate, your employees will know they matter to you and to the company.

When you genuinely and meaningfully appreciate your people, they get reinforcement about who they are and what they do for and with you. This isn't always about money. Recognizing and celebrating the "fire lighting" and "firefighting" of your organization is tied to your culture, your values, and performance. It also helps create a culture of people doing the things you want to see happen often.

What do you want to see happen? When you achieve something significant, how do you recognize teams and individuals? "Our most important asset is our people." We all say it, but if that's true, how do you show it? Do they know it? How?

In our CEO mastermind community, we wanted to recognize and celebrate our partners (what we call the members in a team) in a way that truly honored them and also reinforced behaviors that create the most engaging and beneficial time together at a council meeting. One of our fire-lighting activities is based on Proverbs 27:17: as iron sharpens iron, so one person sharpens another. So we created an award to recognize the partner that most exemplifies this action during the year; it's called the Sharper Edge. This award is for the partner who is quick to challenge and call others, who isn't reluctant to ask tough questions and bring attention to blind spots, who is unafraid to challenge the status quo or sacred cows, and who is willing to scrutinize to help sharpen fellow partners.

The team voted on which partner in the group most exemplified these behaviors. Then, at our all community event, we announced each partner publicly and gave them a short sword with their name, date, and the name of the award engraved on it.

The feedback was interesting. There were partners who didn't know that's how their team felt about them. It was a validation of actions they didn't know were there. It was a special enough award that it went home and to the office with them.

"You got what for what?"

"I sharpen my team, like iron, so I got this sword."

The next time we met as a team, that Sharper Edge was all around the room as people leaned into the role. It was a ton of fun to be able to give those awards, to honor our partners, and to reinforce behaviors that makes everyone better. It was refreshing.

When you recognize and celebrate with your team, you will be refreshed. What should you celebrate and recognize? When do you do it? How should you do it? Who should be involved?

Application: How to Implement a Recognition Program That You Can Sustain as a Busy Leader

It was the first time I (Dan) was recognized publicly. I had just joined a technology company as an inside salesperson. Part of onboarding was to work for a week in tech support. Answering phones made me learn the product quickly and have real conversations with customers learning their needs and challenges.

Tech support is a gold mine for sales. Solve a problem or offer a solution to a problem. Toward the end of my week, I received a call and set up the sales team to close a $20,000 deal in a short time frame.

In an all-hands meeting, the CEO called me out in front of the everyone. The high fives, handshakes, and meeting people I hadn't met yet was extraordinary, so much so, that I always thought I would be the type of person to recognize others when I got into a leadership role.

I must have forgotten. By the time I was running a company, I had too much to do with too little time. Recognition was an afterthought. I knew I should do it and that the impact could be huge, but it was a low priority.

I have had frequent conversations about this challenge—prioritizing and executing a personal recognition program. Here are five simple ways to get started making an impact through recognition.

1. **Make it handwritten: high value, old school.**

   Hands down, the handwritten note is still one of the most impactful ways to recognize an employee and let them know you appreciate their efforts. It's must be written by you and call out precisely what you are recognizing. Many a note ends up getting shown to family or hung up in their office. The time it takes to craft the message and drop it off pales in comparison to the impact of a handwritten note.

2. **Make it personal.**

   If your company celebrates important dates, make the gift personal; birthdays, work anniversaries, company milestones. When you are singling out an individual, make the gift individual. Nothing says I almost care like the token gift that everyone gets. One particular leader would always know what the hobbies of the individual were and get something associated with it, like a crochet set (no lie, people do this) or mountain biking accessory.

3. **Get the family involved.**

   Many employees don't talk about work with their spouses once they are home. One construction company asked for the emails of all spouses and included them on the monthly internal company newsletter. In that communication, the CEO would call out and affirm specific people and projects. Many spouses never knew what a job site looked like or that their significant other was part of constructing that building going up down the street. The feedback was overwhelmingly positive and created a new sense of community within the company.

4. **Schedule it.**

If you want to be intentional about recognition, then you have to schedule it. Put it on your calendar, and make it habit weekly or monthly to write that note, send that email, make that phone call, buy that gift. Make it a habit. How many people can you touch in 30 minutes or an hour of intentional focused time?

5. **Delegate the management.**

Assign someone in your office the management and reminders for the events. Birthdays and anniversaries can all be scheduled in advance. Designate someone to create and manage the schedule so you and the team never miss that important date. This person can also hold you accountable, which is what you need.

Recognition will have a meaningful impact on your company and with a plan comes momentum. What do you need to start doing to recognize and engage your employees more?

PART 3

BUILDING KEY RELATIONSHIPS

Business is a cobweb of human relationships.
—Ross Perot

What's really important in the world? People. Why? Because people are eternal. All of our stuff will pass away, but with Christ, we have eternity before us. Why not spend eternity with the people that are close to you?

We are called to know God and give Him glory though our thoughts, words, and actions. Once you have decided that Christ is King, you can bring His light to your spouse, your kids, and if you're lucky, your grandkids.

Have you ever known anyone whose house burned down? It's a huge loss that all their stuff is gone, but all they really care about is that everyone is safe. That's true for your business as well. It's all about people and the impact you can and will have on their lives. Within your business you can create ripple effects that can last for generations.

How do you look at your work? Do you look at your people eternally? Your employees, partners, clients, vendors, and industry. They are eternal as your family is eternal. You have the opportunity to help others know who Christ is through you and your company. Your company is a platform for influence and impact, and that's huge!

Your company can be looked at as a family. Just as Jesus is our shepherd and we are His flock, you are the shepherd of your company, and those under your care are your flock.

What's the status of your flock? What is the status of you, the shepherd?

Chapter 13

Your Business Marriage

"Let us not give up meeting together, as some are in the habit of doing, but let us encourage one another—and all the more as you see the day approaching."
Hebrews 11:25

What kind of ship always sinks?

A partnership.

A bad joke, but all too often true. They say partnerships are like marriages ... and they are right. If you talk to most entrepreneurs, they all have a partnership break-up story. I do too. Yes, this section is about marriage, so where is your marriage in your business? What relationships are so important that you need to continue to work on them like you would with your spouse?

You say, "But I don't have a partner." Yes, you do. Owned by private equity? Your partner is the board. You own the whole thing? Your partner is the second in command. (You know, the person who keeps your "crazy" from the rest of the company).

As you read below, replace the words *wife, husband,* and *spouse* with the word *partner* and see what you learn.

How do you think about your partner in these verses?

How would your partner read them as they thought of you?

Proverbs 11:22

Like a gold ring in a pig's snout is a beautiful woman who shows no discretion.

Proverbs 12:4

A wife of noble character is her husband's crown, but a disgraceful wife is like decay in his bones.

Proverbs 19:14

Houses and wealth are inherited from parents, but a prudent wife is from the LORD.

Proverbs 21:19

Better to live in a desert than with a quarrelsome and nagging wife.

Proverbs 31:10–31

[10] A wife of noble character who can find? She is worth far more than rubies. [11] Her husband has full confidence in her and lacks nothing of value. [12] She brings him good, not harm, all the days of her life. [13] She selects wool and flax and works with eager hands. [14] She is like the merchant ships, bringing her food from afar. [15] She gets up while it is still night; she provides food for her family and portions for her female servants. [16] She considers a field and buys it; out of her earnings she plants a vineyard. [17] She sets about her work vigorously; her arms are strong for her tasks. [18] She sees that her trading is profitable, and her lamp does not go out at night. [19] In her hand she holds the distaff and grasps the spindle with her fingers. [20] She opens her arms to the poor and extends her hands to the needy. [21] When it snows, she has no fear for her household; for all of them are clothed in scarlet. [22] She makes coverings for her bed; she is clothed in fine linen and purple. [23] Her husband is respected at the city gate, where he takes his seat among the elders of the

land. [24] She makes linen garments and sells them, and supplies the merchants with sashes. [25] She is clothed with strength and dignity; she can laugh at the days to come. [26] She speaks with wisdom, and faithful instruction is on her tongue. [27] She watches over the affairs of her household and does not eat the bread of idleness. [28] Her children arise and call her blessed; her husband also, and he praises her: [29] "Many women do noble things, but you surpass them all." [30] Charm is deceptive, and beauty is fleeting; but a woman who fears the LORD is to be praised. [31] Honor her for all that her hands have done, and let her works bring her praise at the city gate.

Wow. Proverbs 31 is like what a partner should truly be. Imagine that you and your partner thought of each other in this way.

When I (Dan) jumped into my first partnership, the three of us were all on the same page and had the same vision. I had been downsized and outsourced in my last two companies. The other two were changing their business model and needed another income stream. Together, we all played an integral role in getting the company off the ground and then moving forward. We'd talk on the phone daily, meet weekly, and have email updates flying all over the place. A lot of the time we spent together was quality relationship-building time.

As the company grew, the partner meetings grew less frequent. We were less likely to call each other, share wins/losses. We were working harder, so we canceled more meetings with each other thinking time was better spent with clients or employees, or out playing.

Toward the end, we were meeting quarterly to really just rubber stamp the update I put together and discuss how we would distribute profits, and if we needed to bump it for taxes. It became transactional when it used to be relational.

We had all drifted apart without ever knowing how. None of us were on the same page strategically, and after 10 years, I didn't share the same vision. The cracks in the foundation formed and, through years of non-communication, became holes—and those holes lead ultimately to divorce.

I think it happens that way in a lot of actual marriages. Why not our business marriages?

Now having seen many, many partnership relationships ebb, flow, start, and end, I've discovered there is one big thing you can do to help keep the train on the tracks. It's like the verse at the start of the chapter (Hebrews 11:25): *Don't stop meeting together.*

But we do. We stop meeting, communicating, caring, trying. We're just too busy. Just like a marriage can't sustain a lack of communication and hard conversations, neither can business relationships.

You need to stay on the same page. Here's how: whatever cadence got you here is what you should keep. Remember when you first started dating...I mean working together? You need to get back to that. I would suggest weekly or biweekly meetings for between two and four hours in length. Make them offsite, and make the goal for you to reconnect. Yes, this is over and above the weekly meeting you have because it's about relationship and big picture, not the daily, monthly, quarterly objectives—although you may discuss some of those challenges and opportunities if it makes sense. At the very least, it should be once a month. If you cancel twice in a row, that should be a red flag. This doesn't have to be formal either. Feel free to go to breakfast or lunch, play golf, happy hour. Make it something you look forward to, not dread.

Here are some topic suggestions for this get together:

1. *General check in: How are you doing?* Spouse, kids, a fun story or event recap. You are human. Start with talking about human things and remember that life is more than winning at achieving. This includes the good and bad, ups and downs of life. Share those. The more open you are the stronger your relationship will become.

2. *Work wins and good news: So much time is dedicated to solving problems and fighting fires that you forget to share good news.* What great interactions or wins did you have with employees, customers, partners, and each other?

3. *Situations/Challenges/Opportunities: What big items need to be discussed where you as partners need to be on the same page?* These could be from succession planning to hiring for a specific position. Because you have different communication patterns within the organization, you'll be able to share alternative viewpoints that make you more aware of what is going on. If you can move forward on something that's great, but there isn't always anything to solve. Like GI Joe said, "Knowing is half the battle." Yet, if you end up talking about the same topic for three meetings in a row, that is a clear sign that you need to dig deeper and solve it.

So, since I and many others have the partnership scars ... lots of people will tell you they will never get involved in partnership again. I don't blame them. I get it. But I don't think that's the right answer for everyone. Why create a partnership in the first place? Because you can get farther, faster, better with others.

In Ecclesiastes 4:9–10, Solomon writes: Two are better than one, because they have a good return for their work: If one falls down, his friend can help him up, but pity a man who falls and has no one to help him up!

I know a partnership is scary because you have to trust someone else with your livelihood. That's why it's like a marriage, and it takes wisdom and discernment to pick the best partner you can. If you have had a failed partnership, you understand what got you there and are a much better partner in the next one.

I know. I am in one again.

Application: The Arrows

This is a simple question partners can ask each other, or you can ask yourself about the partnership, that will tell you where you are.

Start by drawing an arrow on a piece of paper. Hand your partner the pen and ask him to draw a second arrow symbolizing your relationship. (Another option is for you both to draw arrows signifying your relationship and then compare/discuss).

What does this look like? Here are the common themes:

Same direction:

When your arrows are going the same direction, there will still be issues and challenges, but you are striving to get there together. This is where everyone starts. When the business begins, there is a battle for everything, so you have to be totally aligned to accomplish the goal. You are more open to ideas, have less ego, and can let slights and imperfections go. There just isn't time or energy to deal with it. So, this is a great place in a partnership, but it is also really hard to stay here.

Different direction:

This is the warning territory. Going in different directions is natural as businesses grow and change and people grow and change. The key is to recognize it and then discuss why.

Opposite direction:

Take the relationship up a notch. This happens when partners are totally doing their own thing. This will create passive-aggressive behavior and a company that isn't sure which partner to follow. Another version of this is when the company becomes two companies under one roof. Factions form as people start to take sides or decide which mini company and partner they want to work for. This can work for a while but ultimately falls down due to an unequal fairness chart. Someone is almost always carrying the load with one part of the organization and will feel like he's being taken advantage of.

Against:

Red warning sirens are going off. A storm is rolling through. It might already be too late without intervention and a lot of humility on both sides. Employees are picking which partner they think will win and coming alongside, looking for new employment, or putting their heads down to see who wins. This one will kill the golden goose, and everyone can go home a loser if you aren't careful.

The point of this simple exercise is to create a way to honestly assess and talk about your relationship. As you go deeper in this conversation, you'll find it's less about business and more about life.

This is one of those times that what got you here will get you there. How you started your relationship is what is going to keep you both engaged and heading the same direction. If you both head in a different direction, it's okay. You get to discuss it and come up with alternatives that are good for the company and for the partnership. If it's time for one of you to sell, leave, divest, etc., do it in a healthy way, and do it early. The day you take out your swords and call the lawyers, everyone loses.

Application: Sharing Your User Manual

How will your partner and your team work well together unless you know how to work together? There are many personality tests and profiles that have helped companies become more focused on treating each other differently, which work wonders. Another way to open up communication and run more smoothly is to share who you are, what you value, and how you work.

This idea is like learning a new piece of technology. You can either figure out how to use your new phone by playing with it, or you can spend a little time reading the manual and hit the ground running more productively. The same is true with your staff. They can spend years figuring you out, or you can tell them how to work with you on day one. I've often found that executive teams don't understand (or care?) about each other's drive and motivation, and they end up with conflict.

This idea and framework of a user manual came from two LinkedIn articles by Adam Bryant and Abby Falik.

Your assignment is for you (and your team if applicable) to answer the following questions below in 30–60 minutes. Keep it simple and high level. Then share your answers with each other. Revise if needed. Then share with your subordinates.

Hint: Start your answers with "I." I am, I will, I prefer, I don't. Another option is to create a general rule or phrase that has sticking power with a one-sentence explanation: the Golden Rule, *Good to Great*, etc.

1. What is your leadership style?
2. What do you value in work and relationships?
3. How do you make decisions?

4. What is the best way to communicate with you?
5. What is your philosophy on coach give and get feedback?
6. How are you misunderstood or confusing to others (idiosyncrasies, habits, personality)?
7. How do you prefer to coach and solicit feedback?

Chapter 14

ADULTERY

"Man is basically as faithful as his options."
—Chris Rock

How easy it is for us to get ensnared in situations and opportunities that invite adultery.

There's a scene in the movie The Big Sick where the dad (Ray Romano) is talking about how he made a huge mistake and had an affair at a convention. He's walking through how he got there: depression, opportunity, attraction, and then activity. Not some five seconds afterward, he's screaming inside his head: "What did you just do? What did you do?"

I think he captured what a lot of people have felt.

The readings here from Proverbs warn about how adultery (both live and online) affects your life and how to guard against it.

Proverbs 5:1–10

[1] My son, pay attention to my wisdom, turn your ear to my words of insight, [2] that you may maintain discretion and your lips may preserve knowledge. [3] For the lips of the adulterous woman drip honey, and her speech is smoother than oil; [4] but in the end she is bitter as gall, sharp as a double-edged sword. [5] Her feet go down to death; her steps lead straight to the grave. [6] She gives no thought to the way of life; her paths wander aimlessly, but she does not know it. [7] Now then, my sons, listen to me; do not turn

aside from what I say. [8] Keep to a path far from her, do not go near the door of her house, [9] lest you lose your honor to others and your dignity to one who is cruel, [10] lest strangers feast on your wealth and your toil enrich the house of another.

Proverbs 5:15–20

[15] Drink water from your own cistern, running water from your own well. [16] Should your springs overflow in the streets, your streams of water in the public squares? [17] Let them be yours alone, never to be shared with strangers. [18] May your fountain be blessed, and may you rejoice in the wife of your youth. [19] A loving doe, a graceful deer—may her breasts satisfy you always, may you ever be intoxicated with her love. [20] Why, my son, be intoxicated with another man's wife? Why embrace the bosom of a wayward woman?

Proverbs 6:23–28

[23] For this command is a lamp, this teaching is a light, and correction and instruction are the way to life, [24] keeping you from your neighbor's wife, from the smooth talk of a wayward woman. [25] Do not lust in your heart after her beauty or let her captivate you with her eyes. [26] For a prostitute can be had for a loaf of bread, but another man's wife preys on your very life. [27] Can a man scoop fire into his lap without his clothes being burned? [28] Can a man walk on hot coals without his feet being scorched?

Proverbs 23:26–28

[26] My son, give me your heart and let your eyes delight in my ways, [27] for an adulterous woman is a deep pit, and a wayward wife is a narrow well. [28] Like a bandit she lies in wait and multiplies the unfaithful among men.

Proverbs 30:20

This is the way of an adulterous woman: She eats and wipes her mouth and says, "I've done nothing wrong."

I (Drew) very vividly recall a steamy and potentially disastrous incident a fellow CEO and business owner shared with me. He was attending a national industry event with some of the high rollers in his space. As was typically the case, a happy-hour event was scheduled at the conclusion of the busy day of meetings and best-practice discussions. He found himself with the other CEOs in a lounge area of the event space, enjoying a customary glass of wine or other frosty adult beverage.

He said he didn't think much about it, but ... "Suddenly I found myself engaged in conversation with a woman whom I hadn't seen at the event until now. She had been introduced to me by one of my peers. In my naivety, I thought she was an attendee and was part of someone's team from another part of the country. She was strikingly attractive and seemed to have taken an unusually special interest in me and the success of my company. As was the case with many of my travels of this nature, I was at the event by myself—my wife hadn't joined me for the rather short event.

"Strangely, I found myself thinking those thoughts I remember from in college. Did I still have it? Was I still attractive to other women? Don't get me wrong, I am very happily married and had no interest in carousing. But I couldn't get these thoughts out of my head. And here she was. Salivating over every word I said. There were, without question, sparks flying and fireworks soaring. Then I started thinking those horrible thoughts like, My wife will never know. *I'm 500 miles from home. I see other guys in the room hooking up with women, too, I might as well as join them. In fact, I know George across the room has a routine of cheating on his wife—he's gotten away with it, why can't I?*"

He went on to say, "I couldn't believe I was thinking all these things. And no doubt Susie Q was there to do precisely what she was doing. Seize the moment. Perhaps I was a great sugar daddy target.

Whatever the case, her intentions were not good. I finally had a very convicting thought and realization: *This is not going to end well. There is nothing positive that can come from this.* Perhaps it was the Holy Spirit. Perhaps it was the moral red lights flashing that were engrained from an understanding of the ugly path this could take. Flashes of scorched-earth, a furious wife, and deeply scarred children. Whatever the case, I chose to cordially say no thanks and end our conversation."

"The experience will never leave my mind," he explained. "Such a close call! It was such a thin thread and fine line that I could have crossed. And the consequences could have been eternally disastrous."

What saved the day? Perhaps it was "discretion and understanding" as outlined in this segment of Proverbs.

Comedian Chris Rock's line that we're only as faithful as our opportunities is funny . . . until it isn't. So what's your plan when that opportunity presents itself?

This sounds odd, but I think the best way to deal with this temptation is to act like Monty Python's Knights of the Holy Grail. "Run away! Run away!"

Paul agrees with that strategy:

> [18] **Flee** *from sexual immorality. All other sins a person commits are outside the body, but whoever sins sexually, sins against their own body.* [19] *Do you not know that your bodies are temples of the Holy Spirit, who is in you, whom you have received from God? You are not your own;* [20] *you were bought at a price. Therefore honor God with your bodies.*
>
> **1 Corinthians 6:18**

Seriously, just run away. It's too hard to be nice. Just disappear when the option or opportunity arises and your first thought isn't pity or disgust . . . run. If you get that "Huh, interesting . . ." or "How flattering" feeling, then run. You aren't going to win if you stay and fight.

Now, this isn't an excuse to stop having meetings with the opposite sex. Seriously, people, that's just stupid. You can have a business meeting with a man or woman, alone, and not have crazy feelings of lust and desire. If you do have those feelings all the time, there is something else you need to look into further.

Now, should you go to dinner alone together while at the Annual Conference in Vegas and split a bottle of wine at a cozy upscale restaurant at a table for two? No. But should you be able to grab a bite at the buffet and debrief the day? Yes. Please, people. Use common sense. Be reasonable. Don't put yourself in situations that give opportunity to temptation.

Application: The Priority Waterfall

Are you cheating on your life? There are many articles, blogs, and videos about creating balance in your life. Heck, I've even written some of them. The biggest constraint within all those articles is time. And time is the biggest objection when we are talking to an owner about joining an Acumen team. It's the most valuable asset you have. It's also the easiest thing to cheat on because we get our priorities screwed up.

There are lots of ways to manage your time, and different tactics, systems, and structures work for different people. The one thing that should be the same, though, is the framework. Everyone's framework should be the same. It's like the neighborhood with a bunch of houses that are the same style, layout, and guts but different paint color, brick, porch, landscapes, fixtures, and flooring.

So, what should the guts of your house look like? Here's the priority waterfall from Kyle, one of our Acumen partners, that should inform whatever system you create. I've seen other versions of this but liked this one the best because it informs what you do when what you are currently doing (trying harder) doesn't work.

A waterfall's flow of energy always starts from the top and fills up the source below. This is a key we'll break down in a bit.

Put these words in priority order for your life right now: Work, God, Kids, Spouse, Community

Were you honest? Did you do what you know should be true or what is actually true? What did you learn as you did that? What should the order be?

The greatest commandment Jesus laid out is the catalyst for the waterfall:

> [30] *Love the Lord your God with all your heart and with all your soul and with all your mind and with all your strength.' [31] The second is this: 'Love your neighbor as yourself.' There is no commandment greater than these"*
> **Mark 12:30–31**

So, your highest priority is God.

When God is first, it's amazing how much more in tune with yourself and the world you are. Yes, things still go wrong (it's the world and full of humans), but God is with you. You'll spend most of your life figuring out how to practice the presence of God. It's a great adventure.

Everyone always agrees God should be first.

But then we get to the second part. This is where the nodding momentum stops and heads start to tilt sideways. You're supposed to love your neighbor as yourself.

Who is your neighbor? How do I prioritize my neighbor? The parable people look toward is the Good Samaritan (Luke 10:25–37). I am not against that message at all. You still need to prioritize, and the priority isn't an excuse to not help those in need or that everyone is your neighbor.

Your first neighbor is your spouse, which is the next important connection in your life. Just like a business partner, the person who is the partner in your life is key. The time you spend together can make or break everything that comes under it in the waterfall.

Next are your kids. If you or someone you know has recently become an empty nester, you may have heard the couple needs to date each other again. We spend so much time focusing on our children that it causes problems when they go away. So much so that people need to be reintroduced to each other. What if you don't like the person on the other side anymore? If you've ever said your kids are your everything, you may want to reassess. Your kids are very important, but not more important than your spouse.

Next is work. Yes, it's way down here. When I was running my first company, I had this all screwed up. I had work, community, kids, wife. (Sports might have been between kids and wife.) A lot of us fall into the trap of the world's view of priorities. See how it's all jumbled up?

Why do we put work first?

Work can give us identity. We get instant gratification, kudos, power, prestige, time to think, winning, and teamwork. Work is good. Adam and Eve were put in the Garden of Eden to work. But work is not ultimate or eternal. Only people are eternal. And the people that are most important to you and that are eternal are more important than work.

There will always be more work than you can accomplish. Always one more email or text to send, idea to research, phone call to make. When we put work first, we give up so much of our life.

I can hear people asking, "So I'm just supposed to hang out with my wife and kids and not work? I have to provide for my family."

Yes, please provide for your family. Please do that well. Yet, when work becomes sprinting a marathon, when work becomes your identity, when work is where you go to get away from your family, when you are chasing the world through work—then it's out of priority in your life.

This has happened to me throughout my career, especially when I'm killing it at work and getting a lot of satisfaction from growing something. Every time, I've looked back and thought of ways I could have worked less and accomplished the same goal or close—this includes those family dinners where I was at the table but not present.

I know we all have to sprint sometimes and allow family to take a back seat, but you know what I'm talking about. This is the sustained focus on work.

Last on the list is community.

Community is last because this is everyone else. These are all the opportunities and requests that come and can take time from your top priorities. A lot of times, these are good opportunities. They just are not best. Knowing when to say yes and no requires discernment.

Okay, so you get the waterfall. Here's what it looks like:

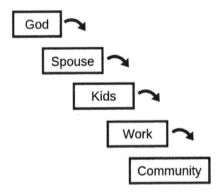

The cool thing about the waterfall is that when you have a problem with one of the levels on the waterfall, you just need to move up a level and focus on it until it flows over. A level below cannot fire on all cylinders until the level above is full and then overflows into it. Thus the waterfall.

Are you and your spouse in a doldrum? After fifteen years of marriage, are you spent and tired and the kids running you ragged? Spend more time on your relationship with Christ, and you'll be amazed at how He will direct your time with your spouse.

Are the kids driving you nuts and you can't seem to find one good thing to say to them? All you do is yell at them from one event to the next. You and your daughter aren't talking anymore? Walk back up the waterfall and concentrate on time with your spouse. Inevitably, you'll work out some strategies together to work on your relationships.

Here's a fun one. Does work suck? Can't catch a break? Focus on your kids. I can't tell you how many times their joy, perseverance, and teaching has helped me find gratitude in life and a new spirit to tackle work problems I didn't want to face.

Still questioning the wisdom of the waterfall? Let's use another filter from Matthew, a disciple of Jesus. He wrote, "What good will it be for someone to gain the whole world, yet forfeit their soul?" (Matthew 16:26)

Let's flow down the waterfall and replace a couple of words each time – "whole world" and "soul."

What good will it be for someone to gain the best marriage, yet forfeit their soul?

What good will it be for someone to gain the best kids, yet forfeit their marriage?

What good will it be for someone to gain the most successful company, yet forfeit their kids?

What good will it be for someone to gain honor in the community, yet forfeit their business?

Get the idea? This is a simple framework that will help you build your house. What your house looks like and how you manage it is up to you, but the guts need to be built on God. This is a weird concept. Trust me and try it. You'll be surprised at how well it works. Like all things, this takes work and time. Put in the hard work, and you'll be rewarded.

Chapter 15

DO WHAT YOU SAY

When I was a boy of 14, my father was so ignorant I could hardly stand to have the old man around. But when I got to be 21, I was astonished at how much the old man had learned in seven years."
—Mark Twain

Man, if that Mark Twain quote isn't the truth something fierce . . . I (Dan) remember really revering my mom and dad until I was about sixteen. At some point, they lost their wisdom and became static noise. Not that I wasn't obedient, I just didn't see value in it, or they just didn't "get it" for me. Fast forward to when I was twenty-three years old and looking to buy a house, and all of a sudden, my parents became geniuses again. Funny how that works.

Fast forward fifteen more years, and now with my kids, I find myself saying things my parents told me that helped me through life. My "father's commands" and my "mother's teaching" as written in Proverbs 6:20–22 below.

Proverbs 4:1–4
[1] Listen, my sons, to a father's instruction; pay attention and gain understanding. [2] I give you sound learning, so do not forsake my teaching. [3] For I too was a son to my father, still tender, and cherished by my mother. [4] Then he taught me, and he said to me, "Take hold of my words with all your heart; keep my commands, and you will live."

Proverbs 6:20–22

20 My son, keep your father's command and do not forsake your mother's teaching. 21 Bind them always on your heart; fasten them around your neck. 22 When you walk, they will guide you; when you sleep, they will watch over you; when you awake, they will speak to you.

Proverbs 20:29

The glory of young men is their strength, gray hair the splendor of the old.

What happens if and when the commands and teachings aren't connected to actions? Do what I say, not as I do. That's a lesson fraught with peril because kids always do as you do, not as you say.

So do employees.

Caught, Not Taught

My ten-year-old son has a bad habit of saying "I know" to almost everything. Even after he's asked you a question and you give him an answer, he'll belt out "I know." After he did this to some of our friends, he and I had one of those father/son conversations about respect. I promised to raise his awareness to help him curb the habit.

Fast forward two days, and I'm working out in a class of about twenty people and the instructor comes by to tell me that I need to watch my knee so it doesn't go over my ankle during an exercise. My response? "I know." Boo. Now both my son and I have been given the authority to help each other get out of the habit.

So what does that have to do with business? Everything. My son caught how I acted and emulated it.

In the same way, your employees catch the culture, values, rules, service levels, and work ethic from you and your executive team. Your customers do too.

Do you have an "open door policy" yet stay in your office with the door closed all day and avoid all other conversations except meetings? Do you expect on time attendance yet arrive 30 minutes after everyone else and leave by 4:00 every day? Do you say you are looking for new ideas, risk takers, and innovation, but people who try anything outside the norm get a frank discussion and put on a performance plan?

(Note: all of the above examples are real.)

Your employees are catching all that, and it effects every decision they make, their loyalty, their attitude and much more.

"But I'm the boss," you say. "That's why I started the company. So I can do what I want, when I want." That's true. Just know that your employees *and your customers* understand that too.

Application: Analyze Another Business

It's hard to see what your culture is from the inside. A way to reframe how you look at your business is to look at someone else. The next time you go into a client, partner, or vendor's business, stop and take in the immediate impression you get. Were you greeted? Was that person friendly? Is the place clean? Bright? Are the employees happy or do they look bored or fearful? What was the interaction like during the meeting? How was the follow up?

Now think about your employees and customers coming into your business and interacting day to day.

What are they catching?

Just like kids catch how to act from their parents, your employees catch how to act from you and your team. So before you trot out the next round of vision, mission, and values, make sure you are living them first.

Chapter 16

THE FAMILY BUSINESS

You have to respect your parents. They are giving you an
at-bat. Respect the other party ... My dad and I pulled
it off because we really respected each other.
—Gary Vaynerchuk

I (Dan) was an SOB—Son of Boss—until I took over as CEO. I wanted to make sure that no person ever saw me as profiting because of my last name, so I wanted to outwork everyone, stay later, arrive earlier, and have more ideas. Even then I still think our relationship caused issues.

There are two types of family members in the business when it comes to respect. The first is the hard worker because of the last name. Those are kids and relatives that want to be respected for what they do, so they work with a chip on their shoulder to make sure they are pulling their weight. The second is the one who is working for a paycheck and uses who they are to their advantage and everyone else's detriment. Heck, sometimes they aren't even there ... and still get the paycheck. "Wouldn't say I've been missing work, Bob." Beware of this second kind.

The "Who I am kids" (as in "Do you know who I am?") are culture wreckers and undermine everything the older generation has built. A lot of times family leadership doesn't know it has a problem until the damage is done. Who wants to tell on the boss' kid? Or family leadership knows that their kid is a terrible employee, but who wants to fire their son/daughter/brother/aunt/cousin?

This message is to the kids and other family under leadership. Don't be a "Who I am" kid. Most family owned companies don't make it past the second generation. "Who I am" kids are a major reason. They take the golden goose for granted and in doing so, kill it.

Proverbs 17:2
A wise servant will rule over a disgraceful son and will share the inheritance as one of the family.

Proverbs 23:22–25
[22] Listen to your father, who gave you life, and do not despise your mother when she is old. [23] Buy the truth and do not sell it—wisdom, instruction and insight as well. [24] The father of a righteous child has great joy; a man who fathers a wise son rejoices in him. [25] May your father and mother rejoice; may she who gave you birth be joyful!

Proverbs 27:11
Be wise, my son, and bring joy to my heart; then I can answer anyone who treats me with contempt.

Proverbs 28:24
Whoever robs their father or mother and says, "It's not wrong," is partner to one who destroys.

As Proverbs 28:24 says, *who* kids rob their family and destroy the company. Confronting a *who* is hard. It sets a course for improvement, stagnation in career path, or leaving the company. This conversation can challenge even the healthiest of relationships. Not doing it challenges the health and future of your company.

Parents, if you have a "who kid," read the chapter on discipline. There are ways to move your kid along or out of the company that will make everyone better in the long term and still allow all to hug each other.

Application: To Know Them
Is To Love Them

One challenge I often see with what kids is that when they are in the wrong seat, they become *who* kids. I see family members with the right attitude and work ethic but in the wrong positions or underachieve due to a skill set mismatch. They have strengths, but it's not in the role they have been given.

"You should start in sales. That's a great place to learn the business."

"But Dad, my background is in finance."

"I know. It's just for a little while, we just need to fill this hole for now."

Two years later, the finance-minded person is a poor performer and unengaged. Wonder why.

It is up to you to figure out what the kid is good at *before* they jump into roles at the company. One family makes their kids work outside the business for three to five years before considering employment. Others do extensive assessments like Gallup Strengthsfinder, Kolbe, and Culture Index. The key is to not just find an open hole and plug it. Finding the right seat on the bus is important for everyone, but especially when it comes to family because the ramifications of a miss carry more collateral damage.

What's the point of working together if it ruins family dinners and Christmas forever?

What's your policy for family working in the business? What's the hiring process like? Do they have the same criteria as everyone else? If not, how do you make sure that they earn what they receive?

Having a plan and doing due diligence on family before they ever show up will help set the right expectations and conversations so you minimize the risk for relationship termination.

Chapter 17

The Value of Your Network (and Real Friends)

I have no friends and no enemies—only competitors.
—Aristotle Onassis

I (Dan) had an interesting exit as CEO. One day I was the CEO, and because of an ownership transition, the next day I wasn't. When the change is that drastic, you find out very quickly who are real friends and who aren't. It turns out that most of my network of "friends" were only that way because of my title and status and what I could do for them. Man, did that suck.

On top of that, we were a national company, so my network was around the country. I couldn't even grab coffee or connect on another level. The phone makes you easy to forget.

So basically, I had nothing in terms of authentic relationships. No "call that guy when it got tough" friends locally. I did have family (which is different) . . . but not friends beyond chit chat at kids' games and school functions. I spent so much time heads down at work that when I finally had time to take a breath and look up, I found out that there wasn't any fruit on the vine in terms of relationships. I had a dead branch, and it was dry. It was also sad. I had what the world thought was awesome (company, title, wife, kids, house, etc.) but only a giant hole when it came to friends, network, and community.

I have found that this is common with men. We're just terrible at it. Women are better. But in general, if you are an achiever, the higher you go in an organization, the less time and energy you spend on friendships of any kind.

Sometimes a client will say to me, "My spouse is my best friend." Great! Yet, you need a network and friends that are the same sex going through the same life stages as you (kids, work, sex, faith).

What's your story? How would you define your network and friendship vine currently?

Proverbs 17:17
A friend loves at all times, and a brother is born for a time of adversity.

Proverbs 18:24
One who has unreliable friends soon comes to ruin, but there is a friend who sticks closer than a brother.

Proverbs 27:6
Wounds from a friend can be trusted, but an enemy multiplies kisses.

Proverbs 27:9
Perfume and incense bring joy to the heart, and the pleasantness of a friend springs from their heartfelt advice.

Friends will tell you hard truths, see blind spots, create clarity, and help with the feeling of being alone. That's often because they are going through the same thing as you.

After my transition, I rebuilt my network by having coffee and lunch nonstop with anything that fogged a mirror. As long as you were breathing, I'd meet. Didn't care for what or why, I just wanted to hear that person's story and see if there was any value I could add, even if it was just listening. It took a long time. It turned out to be fun. I got good at understanding who I would click with and common things that drew people closer. It was also awkward at times. Not all people should hang out together.

That's okay too.

Hopefully, you aren't in the situation I was in needing to spend that kind of time rebuilding. But making friends is important, so how do you start to develop friendships and a local network when you are busy?

Application: The Circle Approach

Find some circles! Circles are a way to kickstart a friend process as it has a built-in network, cadence, and connection.

1. **Find circles.** Once I found some common bonds, it turns out a circle would form, or I would find a circle that existed that I could fit into. Where are your circles? I have a soccer circle, a Bible study circle, a work/network circle, and a couples circle. The fun really begins when you can comingle circles. Finding circles helps to maintain closer relationships because the circle helps keep it going, and it's not on any one person.

2. **It takes effort.** Once you find some people you want to continue hanging out with, you have to keep the connection alive. A random text doesn't do it. How will you do that? Weekly, monthly, quarterly?

3. **Listen first.** The other person should always talk first. Ask questions leading with "what" and "how." Most people fail at this. The best question you can ask at the end of a new conversation is, "What can I do for you?" If they are not professional networkers, then this question will make them sit back and say, "Huh, I don't know"—and you've just started to get deeper into your relationship, which is what friendships are about.

4. **It takes time.** This isn't just a project that lasts a quarter. This is lifelong. People become friends over a common bond that grows into something else. That doesn't happen overnight and sometimes it's not the people who you thought you would be friends with. Friends can come and go with certain seasons in life. As one fades away, there are new opportunities to connect.

I went from nothing and dry to, five years later, having multiple groups of people from different walks of life that I can lean into and vice versa. That might be the most enlightening part: helping others, which in turn helps me.

PART 4

LOVE PEOPLE, USE MONEY

Earning a lot of money is not the key to prosperity. How you handle it is.
—Dave Ramsey

If there is a key theme about finances in all of Proverbs, I think it is this:

> [8] *Keep falsehood and lies far from me; give me neither poverty nor riches, but give me only my daily bread.* [9] *Otherwise, I may have too much and disown you and say, 'Who is the LORD?' Or I may become poor and steal, and so dishonor the name of my God.*
>
> **Proverbs 30:8–9**

Let me be satisfied with what you have given me, and not have too much that I forget who you are, or not have enough and become a thief. That's powerful. And that's different than how the world looks at wealth.

How does the world look at wealth? How much is enough in the world's opinion? Just a little bit more.

If you own the company, are a partner in one, or are a highly paid executive, this is hard. You have the ability to create enough wealth to be your own god, getting what you want, going where you want, whenever you want, however you want.

The other side of this coin is when your financial picture looks bleak. When cash flow has gotten tight from several surprises or you've had two to three weak quarters in a row. Will you still hold on to all your values then, or might you be more open to "dishonoring the name of God" in order to make payroll that month?

If there were a second underlying financial theme in Proverbs (or in Scripture), it's to love people and use money. Once again, the world gets this backward: Loving money, using people. We can't. If what we believe is true, then our financial outlook and prowess need to be different. Money is a tool. You need to discern how to use what has been given to you and what your financial philosophy is when it comes to accumulating wealth, risk, debt, and generosity.

No one can serve two masters. Either you will hate the one and love the other, or you will be devoted to the one and despise the other. You cannot serve both God and money. (Matthew 6:24).

Chapter 18

BETTER A LITTLE— THE DECEITFULNESS OF WEALTH

I wish everyone could get rich and famous and do everything
they ever dreamed of so they can see that it's not the answer.
—Jim Carrey

If you are reading this, you are most likely rich. If not by your own standards, then the standards of the world. In the US, the average annual wage is $44,952. In the world, the average annual wage is $20,328. Mind boggling, right? If you make $100,000 per year, you are earning over 200–400 percent more than the national and global average of annual income.

Yes, you are rich.

In Jesus' time, and I would argue even today, people associate wealth with being blessed. God must be favoring you if you have wealth. This wasn't true back then, and it's not true now. The opportunity to have and create riches is tied to so much more than what you control. Location in the world, time in history, parents/family, intelligence, and luck are all drivers that have nothing to do with what you did; they are a product of your environment, not some divine intervention.

Remember what Jesus said? "It is easier for a camel to go through the eye of a needle than for someone who is rich to enter the kingdom of God" (Mark 10:25).

Why is this? It needs to be said again. When you are rich, you can be your own god. You can decide when, where, how, with what, and with whom you are going to spend your life. When you think you alone are the one who created and maintains your wealth, there is danger. The quest for wealth alone uses people and loves money. The love of money can become your "fortified city" on which you rely.

How you accumulate, think about, and use your wealth is vitally important. It's also really hard to do it well, like trying to place a camel through the eye of a needle.

Proverbs 15:16–17
16 Better a little with the fear of the LORD than great wealth with turmoil. 17 Better a small serving of vegetables with love than a fattened calf with hatred.

Proverbs 16:8
Better a little with righteousness than much gain with injustice.

Proverbs 17:1
Better a dry crust with peace and quiet than a house full of feasting, with strife.

Proverbs 18:11
The wealth of the rich is their fortified city; they imagine it a wall too high to scale.

Proverbs 23:4–5
4 Do not wear yourself out to get rich; do not trust your own cleverness. 5 Cast but a glance at riches, and they are gone, for they will surely sprout wings and fly off to the sky like an eagle.

Proverbs 28:6
Better the poor whose walk is blameless than the rich whose ways are perverse.

Proverbs 30:7–9

⁷ Two things I ask of you, LORD; do not refuse me before I die: ⁸ Keep falsehood and lies far from me; give me neither poverty nor riches, but give me only my daily bread. ⁹ Otherwise, I may have too much and disown you and say, 'Who is the LORD?' Or I may become poor and steal, and so dishonor the name of my God.

My (Dan) youngest son is the best eater we have. He'll eat anything. The downside to that is the volume he eats. When he was young, he would often complain about a stomachache after a meal. Just because it was in front of him, he'd eat it. In time, he learned how to measure the right amount to be full but not ache.

For much of the first world, our belly aches. What is enough? Do you know your "right amount?" How might you define "neither poverty nor riches" as said in Proverbs 30:8? No, I'm not saying it's bad to have wealth. But what's the point of all that wealth if it comes with turmoil, hatred, injustice, strife, perversion, and lies?

Where does your belly ache? Make a list right now, where does your life have too much, or where is the excess causing you stress?

I'll say it again. It's okay to plan for, create, and have wealth. It's not okay for the stress be a catalyst to the detriment of yourself, your family, or your community. When you can tie the search for wealth back to turmoil, strife, perversity, hatred, and injustice—there's a belly ache that needs attention.

Yes, this is about money, but it can also be tied to everything in the world. Where does your belly ache in terms of time, activities, friends, keeping up with joneses, and so on? Too much golf, booze, travel, working out, spending, kids' activities, parent activities, and the list can go on and on. Better a little.

Mental Model: Essentialism

In C.S. Lewis' 1942 book *The Screwtape Letters*, a senior demon of Hell, Screwtape, writes to his nephew, Wormwood, who has just joined "the company" where they try to get and keep souls for Hell. In the letters, Screwtape explains the ways and means to go about keeping humans from being saved, doing good, and connecting with God. One of the main themes is the busyness of man. Keep you busy and focused on the wrong things, and you won't have any room left for growth and depth. Busyness clouds the mind and leaves no room for deep thought or a life pondered.

That book was written over 75 years ago, and if it was bad then, it's an epidemic now (or each generation experiences its own version). The speed of life, constant connectivity and communication, personal, business, and experiential opportunities have all increased during that time span. If you are successful, add even more options to that list.

So what can we do for today's day and age?

Enter Greg McKeown with his book *Essentialism: The disciplined pursuit of less as the antidote for the undisciplined pursuit of more*. In the book, McKeown touts "less, but better" to push us to focus on what is essential and to cut our clutter and busyness.

Although there are many strategies and tactics in the book, two big ideas really stuck out to me as game-changers for busy executives.

1. *Create more space and time to think.*

   With information coming with higher frequency and volume every day, we need more space to think, not less. How much time have you set aside in your week to think about the important and not urgent things in and of your business? Most CEOs I know want to spend 25–50 percent, yet say between five and 10 percent. In a 50-hour work week, that's between 2.5 and five hours. Check your calendar. Do you have two to five hours of unscheduled think time built in? In a row? For working on the stuff you always want to get to? Even the 5–10 percenters are usually lying. They just don't want to say 0 percent because it feels bad.

Thinking produces clarity and vision. Doing more thinking helps you and your company. The only way to test of the value of think time is to schedule it on your calendar. Right now, pick a day next week and block out two to four hours with yourself without an agenda. You'll know what to think about when you get there.

Then you need to protect that time. I guarantee the minute you schedule it, there will be a request for that time by someone important that you just "have to" talk with or meet. Or, you'll try to do it at the office. You won't close your door. You won't turn off the phone. So you'll end up answering questions and texting/emailing and wonder where all the time went. Trust me: if you are going to do this . . . do this. One CEO I know was so adamant about it that he booked a flight across the country because he was alone and unplugged on the plane.

Seriously, protect it! Think time is only as important as you make it. The next step is to do this weekly/monthly. Schedule all the days this year right now. You'll be amazed by the momentum you'll create doing less but better.

2. *Know how and when to say "No."*

Greg McKeown states, "Saying no is like any other skill . . . It may be the most useful skill you ever develop. Because it's only by saying no to things that aren't really meaningful that we have the space and energy to concentrate on the things that are."

Boom! Saying no allows you margin and time to say yes to things that you define as essential. So, what event would have the biggest implications and most pressured, stressful, ask/decision event we have in our lives? A Marriage proposal.

YouTube has videos of marriage proposals and unfortunately too many failed marriage proposals. One particular video caught my attention.

The proposer is waiting at the center court of a live televised broadcast of a Houston Rockets game. The presumed girlfriend is walked up to him by some staff. Guy gets on his knee and . . . She says no. Right then, right there. Then she swiftly runs off the court leaving the proposer standing there stunned. Even the broadcasters aren't sure what to say.

She had options. Say yes, then walk off court and break the news later. Wait till they got home and then say no. Sleep on it and then say no.

She took the hardest road, but it probably had the best long-term impact. For the rest of her life, she'll be happy for making that decision. Very hard, short, sweet, and final.

What about him? I'm sure it hurt like a son of a gun and was humbling at the time, but how much better now than six months into planning the wedding. Or at the altar. Or one year into marriage.

A hard no may have saved both of them months and years of problems and heartache.

What does this have to do with business? I can't guarantee it, but I'm pretty sure almost every business decision in your life will not be as hard as the one Center-Court Woman made. If she can say no in that situation, you can say no to things that won't be good for you: You can say no to shiny objects that will move your company away from its core focus. You can say no to coffees, meetings, opportunities, boards, and everything else that takes you away from maximizing your time and effort with focus and purpose. It's not to say that those opportunities aren't good. But are they best? You can decide to focus on three big rocks for the year and say no to the other five good (but not best) ideas.

What do you need to say no to today?

What does that allow you to say "Yes" to?

Chapter 19

JUST RIGHT

*Timing, perseverance, and ten years of trying will
eventually make you look like an overnight success.*
—**Biz Stone**

Looking at a billboard of a billion-dollar Powerball number made me
think, *Man what good I could do for the world with that wealth.* Then I
wondered, *Could I handle it?*

It would throw your life into a crazy direction. One day you are a
working man, and the next day you don't have to work ever again. Every
relationship you have in the world changes. There are expectations to
share the winnings, opportunities to invest, the good life to live, and it
all comes at you at 1,000 miles an hour. What chaos that creates.

Then there's this statistic: According to the National Endowment
for Financial Education, about 70 percent of lottery winners end up in
bankruptcy. Too much, too fast, too gone.

Too much too fast isn't natural. Too much rain too fast can turn into
a flood. Too much fire burning too quickly can light up a forest. Too
much snow too fast can create an avalanche.

Thus it's the same with our companies, our leadership, our power,
and our lives. Most overnight sensations are 10–20 years in the making.
The owners and employees slogged through many ups and downs to get
there. They are confident in how to move forward.

A flood soon recedes, fires burn out, and avalanches stop at the bottom of the mountain. The quicker something is gained, the more likely it is to quickly disappear.

Proverb 13:11
Dishonest money dwindles away, but whoever gathers money little by little makes it grow.

Proverbs 20:21
An inheritance quickly gained at the beginning will not be blessed at the end.

Proverbs 21:20
The wise store up choice food and olive oil, but fools gulp theirs down.

What does just right mean to you? One industry's growth is another's down year. What are you pushing too hard too fast? Where do you see danger signs of a possible catastrophe? Exponential growth isn't bad, but most of the time, steady growth creates returns for the long term.

Mental Model: The Goldilocks Principle

This simple model is recognizable by the name. You remember Goldilocks? She didn't like her porridge too hot or too cold, but just right. Amazingly simple, this model can be used as a guideline for all sorts of topics—including your money. If you are being honest with yourself, what's "just right" when it comes to wealth? What's just right when it comes to revenue? What's just right when it comes to salaries?

When it comes to your company, this principle can be used all over the place.

- Revenue: Just because you can grow doesn't mean you should. Have you ever experienced lower profit with higher revenues or seen a company grow themselves broke?
- Titles: Three "C-level execs" in a four-person company . . . really?
- Hiring
- Salaries
- Vacation time
- Insurance
- What else can you add to this list?

This isn't to say explosive growth and aiming for a huge goal isn't the right strategy or the one that you should take. But it does make you sit back and think before you go. The market wants you to grow, scale, acquire, ramp up, scale up, and IPO. That's great, and I want the same for you—but only in the context of what is right for you, your industry, your company, and the vision God has given you.

Let's take hiring as an example. I've (Dan) worked with several ad agencies, and I've noticed they have quite the conundrum when it comes to hiring. Their work can spike or dip at any time. Giant projects are followed by lulls, and it's a huge challenge to create recurring revenue streams across a diverse client portfolio. If you staff up to support a huge project or client, you have to either find more work to use those people on the next gig or let the team go when the project ends or the client leaves. This is stressful for all involved.

How might you "Goldilocks" this?

Here's a high-level example. Agencies sell time and expertise for money. Once a resource (person) is at capacity, there is a need to work more or add capacity. One agency set a threshold of 115 percent of work capacity for 30 days consecutively before hiring on a new person. Not new project work, but a new normal in work product with clients under contract. The thought is that everyone can sprint for 30 days. Beyond that, people will start to burn out.

Obviously, this is a simple version, as they took into account retainers/projects/clients/relationship, etc. But the point is that everyone on the team knew the threshold at which hiring someone made sense. This helped keep staffing levels "just right" and allowed for dips and bumps as well. If production dipped below 100 percent, they also weren't overstaffed so much as to burden the company or let a large number of people go.

What's too hot or too cold in your business right now? How can you use the Goldilocks principle to make it just right?

Chapter 20

Debt Philosophy

The Golden Rule of Lending Money: He who has the gold makes the rules.
—Alf Griffin

One of the valued covenants of our community is that we focus on healthy and growing businesses. This is not to say that we are not interested in serving CEOs and owners who have and experience an occasional glitch and deep challenge. In fact, I would say that is the greatest value that we offer those who commit to the shoulder-to-shoulder counsel of this nature. However, there's a difference between the rhythmic ups and downs that business owners encounter and a chronic lack of health.

Think of it in a medical context. If you had a chronic issue, you would seek out a specialist to resolve the matter. If it were a normal, everyday challenge or issue that was a blip on the screen of an otherwise healthy person, you would go to a practitioner that served a broader set of circumstances and challenges.

It's the same with our community. If you are chronically sick, you need a specialist (consultant).

Sadly, I (Drew) recall an individual who showed up every month at our executive session and brought with him the same old gloom-and-doom chronic problem each time. He had built a fascinating business that centered around the acquisition of commercial property, infusion of equity and debt to renovate, remodel, and dress it up; property management, and a long-term hold strategy that on paper generated a handsome ROI to his investors. But he was heavily burdened by encumbering debt.

The challenge was that, operationally, there wasn't much cash flow, and the amount of debt became exceedingly cumbersome—so much so that an immense amount of energy and time was spent "shuffling" and leveraging assets of one entity against another in order to break cash loose. As I observed, it was a constant shell game, and moreover was a huge distraction and emotionally stressful dynamic to the owner.

Our team and I attempted a triage session to give pointed advice toward a better future. We formulated a walkaway plan and were confident this would help alleviate the difficulties he consistently encountered. Unfortunately, this particular individual had a difficult time making tough decisions relative to the recommended strategy. And I get that. It's very difficult to let go or say no to things we hold dear. It was classic sunk-cost bias, which is the inability to let go of something because we've already made an investment in it or emotionally can't let go.

This particular entrepreneur consistently brought his chronic matter to our team. It became apparent that we needed to go different directions, and that frankly he needed to pursue help from a "surgical specialist" relative to his debt predicament. It was a great reminder to all of us about the biblical truths that warn us about debt, becoming "slave to the master." We all witnessed the impact it had on his emotions, his soul, his family, his investors, his peers, and his ability to pivot in healthier strategic directions.

Debt also had an adverse effect on his culture and ability to retain top A players. Constant drama. Constant strife. Constant crisis.

All debt is not bad. Debt is a tool. But debt can be bad when not used correctly, when you overextend, or when you leverage too much of yourself and your company.

Although there are a group of Proverbs about debt, I've included only three as they state the picture best.

Proverbs 17:18

One who has no sense shakes hands in pledge and puts up security for a neighbor.

Proverbs 22:7

The rich rule over the poor, and the borrower is slave to the lender.

Proverbs 22:26–27

26 Do not be one who shakes hands in pledge or puts up security for debts; 27 if you lack the means to pay, your very bed will be snatched from under you.

Proverbs 22:7 says it all. The borrower is slave to the lender. How much freedom you have as an individual and company is directly tied to how much debt you have and what bank covenants you have agreed on.

I (Dan) had a client that was moving office spaces. It was a big decision as the team was growing, and this space would need to be bigger than they currently needed in order to accommodate growth for the next five years.

He found several spaces that fit the bill but was apprehensive and uncomfortable with the price and contract. This was a new level for the company. As we started talking about debt, he realized he needed to create a view of what was comfortable and uncomfortable for him and the company.

Doing so allowed him to say no to several active opportunities and look for space within the new guidelines he set for the company. After much deliberation and several false starts, he signed a contract for a space that fit his needs and was acceptable to the new philosophy.

Application: What is Your Debt Philosophy?

Do you have a debt philosophy? Your banker does, and they live by it vigorously.

If you don't think you do, you do. Think about all your business and personal debt. What does it look like? Are there themes? Does your financial plan fit your philosophy? Are you outside your comfort zone anywhere? Stretched too thin? Maxed out?

A debt philosophy is a filter you put all options through when it comes to significant spending and bringing on new debt. Think of it as your vision and mission when it comes to money. This could include growth initiatives like hiring, capital expenditures like equipment or buildings, or cash flow management tools like lines of credit.

As no two companies or two leaders are the same, there isn't a one-size-fits-all philosophy for debt. But not having a plan can be a killer. The philosophy is followed by the plan, which is usually managed by the owner or CFO.

I would suggest you spend an entire executive meeting discussing your current debt. How does it make you feel? What freedoms do you have and where are you limited? How stretched are you? Where are you comfortable in handling debt, and what is uncomfortable? Who owns the philosophy and keeps the team honest and adhering to it?

Here are some other questions you may consider:

- Do you use debt at all, or do you save and spend? The save philosophy implements slower growth. If you use debt, what thresholds do you want to put in place that are acceptable amounts of risk and rewards?
- Are you a renting or owning organization? There are many options to rent vs own now that are of strategic value. We rent software, technology, people, and more.

- Hire or outsource? Like renting physical space, specialists can create more value for your company than bringing on more people.
- What else should you talk about with your team?

Oh, and the other big lesson: don't cosign for anyone else's loan. Just don't do it.

Chapter 21

THE GENEROSITY TEST

We make a living by what we get, but we make a life by what we give.
—Winston Churchill

What we do with our income, wealth, assets, time, and expertise in terms of tithing and generosity is one of the ways we say thank you and show our gratitude to God. It's also something He has commanded us to do.

In fact, generosity is so important that it's the only thing that the Lord ever said we should use to test Him:

[10] *Bring the whole tithe into the storehouse, that there may be food in my house. Test me in this," says the Lord Almighty, "and see if I will not throw open the floodgates of heaven and pour out so much blessing that there will not be room enough to store it.* [11] *I will prevent pests from devouring your crops, and the vines in your fields will not drop their fruit before it is ripe," says the Lord Almighty.* [12] *"Then all the nations will call you blessed, for yours will be a delightful land," says the Lord Almighty.*
Malachi 3:10–12

Don't treat these verses like the yearly stewardship sermon you hear in church. Read and listen with new eyes and ears.

Proverbs 3:9-10

[9] Honor the LORD with your wealth, with the firstfruits of all your crops; [10] Then your barns will be filled to overflowing, and your vats will brim over with new wine.

Proverbs 11:24–26

[24] One person gives freely, yet gains even more; another withholds unduly, but comes to poverty. [25] A generous person will prosper; whoever refreshes others will be refreshed. [26] People curse the one who hoards grain, but they pray God's blessing on the one who is willing to sell.

Proverbs 14:31

Whoever oppresses the poor shows contempt for their Maker, but whoever is kind to the needy honors God.

Proverbs 22:9

The generous will themselves be blessed, for they share their food with the poor.

Proverbs 28:27

Those who give to the poor will lack nothing, but those who close their eyes to them receive many curses.

"Whoever refreshes others will be refreshed," it says in Proverbs 11:25. Are you refreshed in your generosity? I feel good when I write a check, but I'm not refreshed. I've found that the more often you take generosity and make it personal and relational that you truly find refreshment for both parties. One of the companies in our community offers to pay for a popular personal financial management course. If the employee finishes the course, the company will give them $500.00 as a bonus to their savings.

In one instance, after taking the course, an employee got totally out of debt and bought her first house. The impact on her, her family, and her company was high indeed and refreshing to both parties.

Application: Get It Started

As a leader, you have the opportunity to leverage your business and leadership platform to significantly impact the lives of people in your wake, including employees, their families, your community, and even the world with your time, money, talent, and assets. One could use the concept of a "ripple effect"—when we hit the water, the energy and influence of our rippling waves can impact countless thousands of lives and beyond.

The challenges are discerning what's right for you, being creative in the planning, and then actually doing it. The hardest part is getting started.

I've found for most business people, it's hard to come up with ideas beyond writing a check. So, to help you brainstorm, here's a list of some typical and creative ways a company can be generous and create an impact for their employees, their families, their community, and the world. These are idea starters. The specifics and execution details will need to be tailored based on you and your company. This is over and above employee benefits.

Ideas for you personally as a business leader:

- *Noncash giving: Carve out stock, real estate, or business interests to be placed in a donor advised fund.* (What's a donor advised fund? Two good resources are The Signatry: www.thesignatry.com, and The National Christian Foundation: www.ncfgiving.com).
- *Time and talent: What nonprofit boards do you have specific industry expertise or connections with that you could help grow? What other* skills or strengths do you have to give others? Examples include

finance, budget planning, resume writing, interview skills, networking, and connections.

- *Areas of passion: What issues or challenges grab your heart?* What organizations fit the list that you can you participate in as a volunteer?
- *Assets for others: For example, you may have a house perfect for hosting gatherings or a vacation home that you use for personal and rental.* I'm seeing a trend of using your homes to offer others time away, sabbaticals, and to host gatherings. Much gets done in the warmth of a home versus another large venue chicken dinner out or at company locations.

Ideas for inside your company:

- *Benevolence fund: This is cash set aside to help employees who are in a rough spot.* Privacy and dignity are key here. Another option is to allow employees to make a donation to the fund each pay period to facilitate team generosity. A company match of that giving is common. Then a committee of the employees decides on the grants.
- *Double the impact: Matching up to a certain amount any gift that an employee donates to a charity.*
- *Profit giving: Setting aside a percentage of profit to give to one particular charity each year voted on by the executive team or all employees.*
- Partner with a charity and set up volunteer days.

These are just a few ideas to get your wheels turning. If you are interested in a fascinating look at generosity at scale, read the book *Giving It All Away and Getting It Back Again* by David Green the CEO of Hobby Lobby. David spoke at an Acumen community event about Hobby Lobby's generosity plan, where they now give 50% of profits to charity. This book shares how they got there.

PART 5

VERSUS

Excellence is not a singular act but a habit. You are what you do repeatedly.
—Shaquille O'Neal

I (Dan) found out that "Versus" is now a verb with my kids. My eldest son said he was "versing" someone at school. It took me a couple of times before I got the context clues that they were playing each other.

In Proverbs, there are some big matchups where a lot of "versing" happens. The champions league of "versing" covers three matchups:

1. *The Fools Versus the Wise.* Two perennial powerhouses.
2. *Pride Versus Humility.* You wouldn't believe what Pride has been saying on social media.
3. *Hard Work Versus Laziness.* Also known as, what old people remember about themselves versus what they think about young people.

If Solomon were alive today, he would most likely be the color analyst. (Perhaps play by play would have been done by Isaiah.) In this section, we break down these three match-ups and pick up on Solomon's astute analysis and colorful language as he describes what happens when we choose to play for the wrong team.

Chapter 22

FOOL VERSUS WISE

*"It is remarkable how much long-term advantage
people like us have gotten by trying to be consistently not
stupid, instead of trying to be very intelligent."*
—Charlie Munger

In "The Case for Wisdom" in Part 1, we defined fools as people who want all the world can offer (money, power, sex, etc.) without thinking about the impact and consequences of blindly chasing those things. Fools don't learn, keep making mistakes over and over, tear down their own houses, are all about themselves, and are full of anger and rage.

We can all be foolish at times. The key is to limit your foolishness and your folly. Folly, as Solomon talks about, can be associated with youth. If you have teenagers or can remember your teenage years, they were full of folly and foolishness.

Solomon also uses some other great metaphors below.

First, fools are like:

- Tying a stone in a sling
- A thornbush in a drunkard's hand
- An archer who wounds at random
- A dog who returns to its vomit *(my personal favorite)*
- The useless legs of one who is lame

Doesn't that just sound like childhood? As parents, you discipline and guide your kids to be wiser.

Problems arise when those kids either don't learn their lessons or don't care, and then turn into adults.

Then fools:

- Devise wicked schemes
- Have no desire for wisdom or understanding
- Delight in airing their own opinions
- Trust only in themselves
- Give full vent to their rage

When compared to a fool, wisdom doesn't take a lot of knowledge, experience, or expertise. It's simply not being led by our emotions to do dumb things. Sometimes the smartest thing you can do is to not do the dumbest thing you can do.

It doesn't sell a lot of books, but "don't make stupid business decisions" is a pretty good strategy. I'm always amazed by the amount of people that don't do this and are amazingly foolish.

Proverbs 14:1
The wise woman builds her house, but with her own hands the foolish one tears hers down.

Proverbs 17:12
Better to meet a bear robbed of her cubs than a fool bent on folly.

Proverbs 17:16
Of what use is money in the hand of a fool, since he has no desire to get wisdom?

Proverbs 18:2
Fools find no pleasure in understanding but delight in airing their own opinions.

Proverbs 26:1

1 Like snow in summer or rain in harvest, honor is not fitting for a fool.

Proverbs 26:6–11

6 Sending a message by the hands of a fool is like cutting off one's feet or drinking poison. 7 Like the useless legs of one who is lame is a proverb in the mouth of a fool. 8 Like tying a stone in a sling is the giving of honor to a fool. 9 Like a thornbush in a drunkard's hand is a proverb in the mouth of a fool. 10 Like an archer who wounds at random is one who hires a fool or any passerby. 11 As a dog returns to its vomit, so fools repeat their folly.

Proverbs 27:3

Stone is heavy and sand a burden, but a fool's provocation is heavier than both.

Proverbs 28:26

Those who trust in themselves are fools, but those who walk in wisdom are kept safe.

Proverbs 29:8

Mockers stir up a city, but the wise turn away anger.

Proverbs 29:11

Fools give full vent to their rage, but the wise bring calm in the end.

Fools finance equipment they can't pay off with clients they don't have. Fools hire people they don't need hoping that person can magically make it rain. Fools hold on to jerkhole employees because "He's been with me from the start." Fools don't listen to their spouse, employees, friends, or partners because "They just don't understand my vision and what I see." Fools take their anger out on others because they can.

I (Dan) am an amazing fool.

As a young and new business owner, my driving force in leadership was financial only. I wanted to make millions of dollars by the age of 30. That financial goal caused me to run the company in a certain way. As we started to grow, we had the opportunity to bring a software developer in-house instead of outsourcing. He was awesome, but an army of one. You know what you do with an army of one when you have a financial-only dream? You use him like a rented mule.

As the work piled on, he finally blew up one day and stormed out of my office after I decreed what needed to be done with the usual overly aggressive timeline. (I mean most programmers want to go home and program all night, with the lights off, listening to death metal. It's what they do, right?) What was my response? Anger, of course. I stormed out of my office, chasing him into his office. How dare he walk out during our meeting? Who did he think he was? Well, he was a dude who was overworked, who wasn't happy or engaged, and was probably going to quit. He was sprinting a marathon. He laid into me pretty well. I deserved it.

That was beginning of my wake-up call. This is stupid to write now, but at the time, understanding that people are not just resources to deploy was a new concept. You mean you aren't just here to help me with my million-dollar dream?

Most of the time business and leadership is not about being awesome and visionary. It's about not being stupid. I was tearing down the house we were building one employee at a time to satisfy my need to hit an arbitrary monetary goal.

What about you? Are you tearing down your house anywhere? Where are you being foolish?

Mental Model: Multiply by Zero

Multiplying by Zero is a great concept because it's so easy to grasp. In basic multiplication, what is any number times zero? Yep ... zero. All places, all times, all people. Zero times anything is zero.

Not sure what I mean? Here's a simple business math example:

Client Need x Relationship x Face-to-Face Conversation = Possible Sale
Client Need x Relationship x Face-to-Face Conversation x Giant Blunder = ZERO

One time I (Dan) was on what had to be the worst sales call ever. By the worst, I mean the most excruciating, embarrassing, terrible, horrible, no good, bad sales call.

We flew into to Boston to see office supply giant Staples (before all the merging). We had an hour with ten people in their HR and Learning and Development departments. After a quick meet and greet, handshake, and chit chat, we all sat down to start the meeting and our usual needs assessment.

My partner and I took out our notebooks, and one of the Staples execs lightly mentioned, "Hey, ... so do you always bring competitors' products when talking with customers you are trying to sell?" We look down to see we have Office Depot branded notebooks.

Go ahead ... Insert the four-letter words here that you would silently be screaming in your head.

What followed was literally the most uncomfortable business meeting of my life. My partner's brain was faster than mine, and he calmly folded over his paper so you couldn't see the logo, apologized, and asked if it was okay to continue. For some reason, *they said yes.* Seriously, we talked like it was an actual sales call for an hour with ten people in the room. *They should have thrown us out!* I would have.

I mean, how much money did they waste by listening to two fools who they had no intention of working with?

What did anyone in that room hear that day? Nothing. Absolutely nothing. Zilch. Zero.

We almost laugh affectionately about it now (almost). On the way home, we devised a checklist and plan so that particular issue (and others) never happened again. It's hard enough to do business . . . there is no reason to multiply by zero and give yourself a zero percent chance to win before you even start.

Fools do this over and over and over again. Multiply by zero in their life, in their work, and then complain and get angry at the world for their mistakes.

Are you multiplying by zero anywhere in your company or your life?

Chapter 23

Pride Versus Humility

True humility isn't thinking less of yourself but thinking of yourself less.
—Rick Warren

You know what my favorite subject is? Me. You? Oh, that's nice about you, but let's talk more about me. Know someone like that? Comedian Brian Regan has a name for these people. He calls them Me Monsters.

Left to our own devices, we are all Me Monsters. Pride is the source of a lot of the problems we experience in life and in business. Egos, experts, gurus, ninjas, know it alls ... Solomon calls people with extreme pride mockers, those who can't be taught.

Are you teachable?

In leadership, this is a terrible issue because what got you here won't get you there. You got the opportunity to lead because you knew all the answers. You were the star of the show, and the spotlight was always on you. Once you manage and lead people, however, you need to learn to shine that spotlight on others, rely on your team and their expertise, and become the dumbest person in the room. That's hard when it's been all about you, when all your employees make it all about you, and all your vendors and partners help make it all about you.

What's a leader to do?

Proverbs 3:7–8

[7] Do not be wise in your own eyes; fear the LORD and shun evil. [8] This will bring health to your body and nourishment to your bones.

Proverbs 11:2

When pride comes, then comes disgrace, but with humility comes wisdom.

Proverbs 12:9

Better to be a nobody and yet have a servant than pretend to be somebody and have no food.

Proverbs 13:10

Pride only breeds quarrels, but wisdom is found in those who take advice.

Proverbs 16:18–19

[18] Pride goes before destruction, a haughty spirit before a fall. [19] Better to be lowly in spirit along with the oppressed than to share plunder with the proud.

Proverbs 18:12

Before a downfall a man's heart is proud, but humility comes before honor.

Proverbs 21:24

The proud and arrogant person—"Mocker" is his name—behaves with overweening pride.

Proverbs 24:17–18

[17] Do not gloat when your enemy falls; when they stumble, do not let your heart rejoice, [18] or the LORD will see and disapprove and turn his wrath away from them.

Proverbs 25:14

Like clouds and wind without rain is one who boasts of gifts never given.

Proverbs 25:27

It is not good to eat too much honey, nor is it honorable to seek one's own honor.

Proverbs 26:12

Do you see a person wise in their own eyes? There is more hope for a fool than for them.

Proverbs 27:1–2

[1] Do not boast about tomorrow, for you do not know what a day may bring. [2] Let someone else praise you, and not your own mouth; an outsider, and not your own lips.

Proverbs 27:21

The crucible for silver and the furnace for gold, but people are tested by their praise.

Proverbs 29:23

Pride brings a person low, but the lowly in spirit gain honor.

Are you a mocker? Are you prideful? I've found that most leaders (and humans) have varying degrees of blind spots when it comes to pride.

The biggest pillar of pride in leaders I have found is control, mainly that you are in it and can do it all. That your strength, ideas, leadership, and actions are the reason for your success. The fact that leaders believe they are in total control and the reliance on the things "I" do can change situations. "I" am the reason. "I" got us here. "I" can take us there.

You need to have understanding, visibility, management, and leadership over your company. But be straight with yourself. You aren't in control. You can look at any dip in the business and stock market or that large happy customer who leaves suddenly and creates a real financial crunch to understand that reality. You don't like to admit it. It makes your world too fragile.

What's the truth? The truth is that you are not in control. Remember that the fear of the Lord is the start to understanding wisdom. Being under God's authority and accepting it is the next big step. Whose authority are you under? The government? Your spouse? Yourself? Whose? How did you get where you are? You worked your butt off, but there were a lot of other people, paths, and some luck that helped. You had plans; God wove the web.

First and foremost, you are under God's authority. Isaiah 10:15 says, "Does the ax raise itself above the person who swings it, or the saw boast against the one who uses it? As if a rod were to wield the person who lifts it up, or a club brandish the one who is not wood!"

What Isaiah is saying is that the tool cannot be mightier than the one who uses it. We are the tools of God, therefore we are under Him. To that end, we are not in control but under His authority to carry out His will. It is His company, but yours to grow and profit from so that you can in turn build the Kingdom for Him.

Is your company under His authority? Are you grateful for what He has given you?

Application: The Pride Assessment

Pride creates blind spots. Here is a great assessment to see where your pride manifests itself. The assessment comes from Daniel Burke and Fr. John Bartunek's book, *Navigating the Interior Life: Spiritual Direction and the Journey to God*.

Take it now.

PRIDE ASSESSMENT

Pride: Excessive love of one's own excellence and desired excellence. Pride manifests itself when we seek our self-worth and security in our own abilities, traits, or strengths.

Never	Sometimes	Frequently	Focus	Manifestations of the Root Sin of pride 1st Review: Move quickly and assess by instinct. 2nd Review: Review items checked in Sometimes or Frequently categories. Determine manifestations that require attention and identify them in Focus column with a checkmark.
				Too high an opinion of myself or elevated concept of myself
				Annoyance with those who contradict me or question what I say
				Inability to submit to those whom I judge as less competent or less spiritual than I am
				Refusing or resisting assent to others without a satisfactory explanation
				Anger if I don't get my way or am not taken into account
				Easily judgmental, putting others down, gossiping about them
				Slow to recognize or acknowledge my own mistakes or weaknesses
				Slow to see when I hurt others and an inability to seek and give forgiveness
				Frustration or anger when others don't thank me for favors or work that I do
				Unwillingness to serve, rebellion against what I don't like or agree with
				Impatience, distance, brusqueness in my daily contact with others
				Thinking I am the only one who knows how to do things right
				Unwillingness to let others help me or advise me
				Inflated idea of my own intelligence and understanding
				Dismissing what I do not understand or what others see differently
				Not feeling a need for God, even though I do say prayers
				Nursing grudges, even in small matters
				Never taking orders or bristling when orders are given to me
				Inflexibility in preferences or perspective
				Always putting myself and my things first
				Indifference toward others and their needs, never putting myself out for them
				Centering everything (conversation, choices, recreation, etc.) on myself and my likes
				Calculating in my relations with God and with others

Chart used by permission. Daniel Burke, Fr. John Bartunek, *Navigating the Interior Life: Spiritual Direction and the Journey to God,* (Emmaus Road Publishing, 2012), 70–72.

What jumped out at you? Where does your pride manifest most often?

Humbling? You bet. But Burke says, "Be encouraged!" Then he outlines a great way to combat your pride. Wherever your pride is, find a corresponding virtue—the opposite. Whenever we focus on the negative, we do much worse than focusing on a positive. So, for example, I marked frequently that I get "frustrated or angry when others don't thank me for favors or work that I do." I mean c'mon, how about a little shout out for doing that extra load of laundry during the week, or connecting you two giants of business, which turned into a great deal for both of you?

Pride's corresponding virtue is humility. So, in order to work on my pride, I look for ways to change my mindset away from myself.

A friend suggested a prayer that I wound up saying every morning for a year to walk myself toward humility. It is bold, tough, and full of hard truth. If nothing else, it's a second assessment for you.

Litany of Humility
O Jesus! meek and humble of heart, Hear me.
- ~ From the desire of being esteemed, **Deliver me, Jesus.**
- ~ From the desire of being loved, Deliver me, Jesus.
- ~ From the desire of being extolled, Deliver me, Jesus.
- ~ From the desire of being honored, Deliver me, Jesus.
- ~ From the desire of being praised, Deliver me, Jesus.
- ~ From the desire of being preferred to others, Deliver me, Jesus.
- ~ From the desire of being consulted, Deliver me, Jesus.
- ~ From the desire of being approved, Deliver me, Jesus.
- ~ From the fear of being humiliated, Deliver me, Jesus.
- ~ From the fear of being despised, Deliver me, Jesus.
- ~ From the fear of suffering rebukes, Deliver me, Jesus.
- ~ From the fear of being calumniated, Deliver me, Jesus.
- ~ From the fear of being forgotten, Deliver me, Jesus.
- ~ From the fear of being ridiculed, Deliver me, Jesus.
- ~ From the fear of being wronged, Deliver me, Jesus.

- ~ From the fear of being suspected, Deliver me, Jesus.
- ~ That others may be loved more than I, **Jesus, grant me the grace to desire it.**
- ~ That others may be esteemed more than I, Jesus, grant me the grace to desire it.
- ~ That, in the opinion of the world, others may increase, and I may decrease, Jesus, grant me the grace to desire it.
- ~ That others may be chosen and I set aside, Jesus, grant me the grace to desire it.
- ~ That others may be praised and I unnoticed, Jesus, grant me the grace to desire it.
- ~ That others may be preferred to me in everything, Jesus, grant me the grace to desire it.
- ~ That others may become holier than I, provided that I may become as holy as I should, Jesus, grant me the grace to desire it.

Rafael Cardinal Merry del Val (1865–1930),
Secretary of State for Pope Saint Pius X

Which lines stood out during your reading as a desire or fear? What do you want to do about that?

Note: In your head you might be asking: *So does this mean I have to be weak and subservient?* No. Name a leader in the Bible that was weak and subservient. I can't think of one either. Leaders in the Bible were bold, creative, courageous, shrewd, fair, and honest. They also were about growth and people. Remember, being humble is not thinking less of yourself, but thinking of yourself less. What can you do this week that is positive and walks you toward humility?

Chapter 24

LAZINESS VERSUS HARD WORK

If a man is lazy, the rafters sag: if his hands are idle, the house leaks.
Ecclesiastes 10:18

I am not afraid of hard work. I (Dan) was washing dishes at an Italian restaurant at 14 to make a buck and save for a car, insurance, etc. (I still think my hands have burns from those hot pots.) If you are reading this, you probably aren't afraid of hard work either. It's what got you here. A lot of people fail for the lack of hard work. You are not one of them, at least not in the work category.

There is one place where I am fantastically simple and lazy, and that's my house. The grass just keeps growing and something is always broke. I just want to hang out with my kids and take naps on Sunday.

This laziness has cost me more time and money than just doing the hard work the first time. When we first moved into our house, the basement leaked. It drove me crazy because I couldn't figure out why it would because it was always somewhere new. The time it took to move the boxes, toys, furniture, squeegee the floor, and put fans was immense, and of course it happened late at night making it an even later night or early morning.

I finally got someone to come look at it, and he told me two simple things to do. One: Clean out our gutters. Two: Put dirt around the house so that there was a grading away from the foundation. That's it. No crazy basement construction or fancy systems to install. Just lay some dirt, check and clean the gutters.

Guess what? No more water. A little bit of work for a long-term gain.

The lazy are the simple, the sluggard: These people are just plain ignorant. They don't know and don't want to know. But it's not always tied to just work. It's everywhere in their life.

Proverbs 6:6–11

6 Go to the ant, you sluggard; consider its ways and be wise! 7 It has no commander, no overseer or ruler, 8 yet it stores its provisions in summer and gathers its food at harvest. 9 How long will you lie there, you sluggard? When will you get up from your sleep? 10 A little sleep, a little slumber, a little folding of the hands to rest—11 and poverty will come on you like a thief and scarcity like an armed man.

Proverbs 10:4

Lazy hands make for poverty, but diligent hands bring wealth.

Proverbs 12:11

Those who work their land will have abundant food, but those who chase fantasies have no sense.

Proverbs 13:4

A sluggard's appetite is never filled, but the desires of the diligent are fully satisfied.

Proverbs 14:23

All hard work brings a profit, but mere talk leads only to poverty.

Proverbs 15:19

The way of the sluggard is blocked with thorns, but the path of the upright is a highway.

Proverbs 19:24

A sluggard buries his hand in the dish; he will not even bring it back to his mouth!

Proverbs 24:30–34

[30] I went past the field of a sluggard, past the vineyard of someone who has no sense; [31] thorns had come up everywhere, the ground was covered with weeds, and the stone wall was in ruins. [32] I applied my heart to what I observed and learned a lesson from what I saw: [33] A little sleep, a little slumber, a little folding of the hands to rest—[34] and poverty will come on you like a thief and scarcity like an armed man.

Proverbs 26:16

A sluggard is wiser in his own eyes than seven people who answer discreetly.

My house was the vineyard described in Proverbs 24:30–34. It almost literally had thorns, weeds, and the proverbial stone walls could have been coming to ruin. I had to get to work.

Early in my career, my children were that vineyard. "Leave me alone, I have to work, sleep, relax ... we'll hang out later, later, later." My relationship vineyard with my children had grown dry and dead. At times, the same could be said about my relationship with my wife. How can you be lazy about something right in front of you? Actually, it's pretty easy. I saw it, I just didn't want to do anything about it or prioritize it. Lazy. Sometimes my body has been my ruined vineyard. I ignored it and the pounds came on as I ate terribly, drank too much, and didn't want to exercise. At one company, our employees were the vineyard. We focused so much on product and profit that we laid bare our employees instead of investing in them.

Laziness is not just about hard work when it comes to work. That's easy. Laziness affects us all somewhere and is tied to harmony—not just work/life balance but overall life balance and overall company harmony.

Where are your personal vineyards? Where are your company vineyards?

Application: Wheel of Reality

Below are two wheels. One is personal, and one is company focused. Color in each wheel with how you are doing on each topic. How round is your wheel? Are there any low spots that need work? What is one area you need to focus on personally? What is one area you need to focus on at your company? Where do you need to be like an ant?

Personal Wheel:

Personal Wheel of REALITY

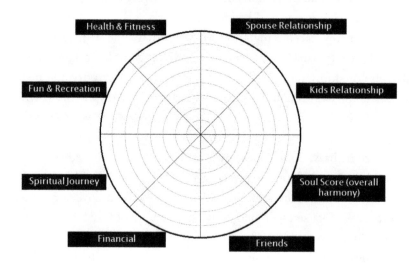

Company Wheel:

Organization Wheel of REALITY

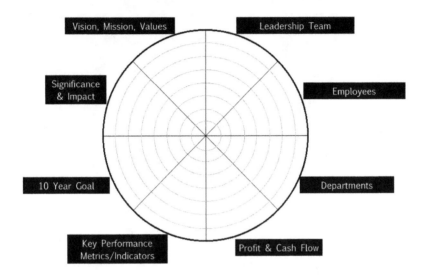

PART 6

YOUR TONGUE IS ON FIRE

⁴ Or take ships as an example. Although they are so large and are driven by strong winds, they are steered by a very small rudder wherever the pilot wants to go. ⁵ Likewise, the tongue is a small part of the body, but it makes great boasts. Consider what a great forest is set on fire by a small spark. ⁶ The tongue also is a fire, a world of evil among the parts of the body. It corrupts the whole body, sets the whole course of one's life on fire, and is itself set on fire by hell.

James 3:4–6

WHOA! James wasn't kidding around. The tongue is like a ship's rudder, tiny yet massive in impact and direction. Your tongue can corrupt the entire body and set forest fires! What comes out of us reveals who we are inside.

In a world with many communication options, platforms, and mediums, it's harder than ever to censor and react. If you have read any general outrage, angry social media posts, the yelling news, blitzkreig sports talk, blog comment sections, business review sites, and so on—it's easy to get a sense of what James is talking about.

When it comes to leadership, we have even more options to set things ablaze. Our very thoughts, mannerisms, suggestions, side comments, speeches, and meetings all communicate a lot about you, set the culture in your company, and describe what you think of your employees. Does your tongue set fires, or is it fresh water?

Chapter 25

Good Tongue
Bad Tongue

Better to be silent and thought a fool than to speak and remove all doubt.
—Mark Twain

As we've seen, James, the brother of Jesus, calls the tongue a rudder of a large ship (3:4). The tongue is a small part of your body, but it can steer your ship into dangerous waters very quickly. You must learn to control it.

A fiery tongue speaks perversity, corruption, maliciousness, hatred, slander, deceit, lies, crushing, gossip, and cursing.

A righteous tongue speaks truth, love, kindness, joy, and honesty.

How do you use your tongue? What direction is your rudder pointing your ship?

Proverbs 4:24
Keep your mouth free of perversity; keep corrupt talk far from your lips.

Proverbs 10:18–19
[18] Whoever conceals hatred with lying lips and spreads slander is a fool. [19] Sin is not ended by multiplying words, but the prudent hold their tongues.

Proverbs 11:13
A gossip betrays a confidence, but a trustworthy person keeps a secret.

Proverbs 12:18
The words of the reckless pierce like swords, but the tongue of the wise brings healing.

Proverbs 12:25
Anxiety weighs down the heart, but a kind word cheers it up.

Proverbs 14:3
A fool's mouth lashes out with pride, but the lips of the wise protect them.

Proverbs 15:1
A gentle answer turns away wrath, but a harsh word stirs up anger.

Proverbs 15:4
The soothing tongue is a tree of life, but a perverse tongue crushes the spirit.

Proverbs 16:13
Kings take pleasure in honest lips; they value the one who speaks what is right.

Proverbs 16:24
Gracious words are a honeycomb, sweet to the soul and healing to the bones.

Proverbs 16:28
A perverse person stirs up conflict, and a gossip separates close friends.

Proverbs 17:27–28

[27] The one who has knowledge uses words with restraint, and whoever has understanding is even-tempered. [28] Even fools are thought wise if they keep silent, and discerning if they hold their tongues.

Proverbs 18:4

The words of the mouth are deep waters, but the fountain of wisdom is a rushing stream.

Proverbs 18:8

The words of a gossip are like choice morsels; they go down to the inmost parts.

Proverbs 18:21

The tongue has the power of life and death, and those who love it will eat its fruit.

Proverbs 21:23

Those who guard their mouths and their tongues keep themselves from calamity.

Proverbs 25:25

Like cold water to a weary soul is good news from a distant land.

Proverbs 26:18–19

[18] Like a maniac shooting flaming arrows of death [19] is one who deceives their neighbor and says, "I was only joking!"

Proverbs 27:5

Better is open rebuke than hidden love.

Proverbs 30:32–33

[32] "If you play the fool and exalt yourself, or if you plan evil, clap your hand over your mouth! [33] For as churning cream produces butter, and as twisting the nose produces blood, so stirring up anger produces strife."

The sheer volume of Proverbs about talking is a key indicator of its importance. I suggest you read all of these Proverbs in the index, as there are nuances that require a deeper inquiry. When to speak, when to remain silent. The effects of lies, slander, rebukes, curses. How words can build others up or tear them to pieces.

I (Dan) once had three follow-up strategy meetings in three consecutive days with three companies. Two went well, the last one was fine, but it wasn't the same because of two words: "I" and "me."

Sitting in the team meeting with the "I/me" leader was different in how the team interacted. The conversation in that meeting was very hub and spoke. All the spokes (executive team) had to make sure the hub (CEO) was on board and get his "I/me" to own the idea before moving on. Conversation was stilted and inflexible because the spokes were trying to please the hub who needed to make sure everyone knew what "I" thought and how "me" would do it.

In the "we/us" leader meetings the team interaction was healthy, flowing across the table across team members much more like a multi-modal network. The differences in honesty and candor, and ultimately effectiveness was easy to see.

As a leader, your choice of words is important because everything you say carries weight with your employees, clients, partners, and vendors. One quick way to disengage your staff is to act like it's all coming from you. The words "I" and "me" show that. Not in normal conversation, but when talking in meetings, especially when the topics are about credit, ideas, and direction.

For example:

- "The reason why I decided to focus on manufacturing was because..."

- "The reason why we decided to focus on manufacturing was because..."

One word, but a totally different meaning to everyone listening. Yes, you made the decision to go in the new direction, but how many people researched, reported, recommended, and budgeted to get you to that decision?

Sometimes this is habit. Founders or companies that started in a garage have a leader where "I" was true for a long time. It's a habit, and it's tough to break. But it's necessary to break that habit as the business grows.

The other part is ego. "I want the credit. I want the kudos. I want everyone to think or know I'm smart." Stop it. This has the opposite effect.

Every rule has its exception. The exception to this rule is when it comes to taking heat. As a leader, "I" take the heat, "we" win.

Simple, right?

Bottom line: It's a choice between four words, but it makes a giant difference creating a healthy culture and being a true leader with your team.

Application: Good Tongue Principles

As a leader, how powerful are the words you use with your employees? Did you know that you can make their day, lift their spirits, knock them down, scare them to death, motivate, or demotivate—all in a single meeting?

I (Dan) remember one time when I announced we were going to focus on a new initiative for the year and had three people in my office afterwards asking if their job were at risk. What? Of course not...but that's what they heard.

Now, you can't go around worrying about everything you are going to say. But you can maximize the good and minimize the bad. Here are four ways to do that:

5. **Say less.** Like the quote at the beginning of the chapter, saying less is usually better. I know this well because I'm a "talk to think" person, so I scare and insult people and their positions frequently on accident by just thinking out loud. You'd be amazed that a simple yes or pointed question gets across the same message as explaining yourself and why you are saying no. Be quick to listen, slow to speak.

6. **Think about the other person's perspective.** More genius, right? I often find that leaders forget where their employees are coming from. I've seen quite a few eye rolls from employees who get life stage "ideas/advice" from the CEO who forgets that his wife stays at home and the employee and their spouse are both working. Want to sound all Ivory Tower? Innocently point out the big differences between your life and your employees.

7. **Ask more questions.** Asking questions, like listening, is a skill you can acquire. The business world is adopting coaching techniques like listening and questions quickly as they see benefits of the approach. This is a reminder to work this skill into your leadership kit bag.

8. **Find fresh water.** Intentional recognition and praise are fresh water to your team. When they deserve it, praise often and in large groups. It's so easy to talk improvement, fixing, and what's wrong. Be intentional in finding the good going on in your business.

There are so many tangents to this one topic it deserves a book of its own. But here and now, you can say less, and when talking, take five seconds to understand the other person's perspective, ask more questions, and when you need to talk, use a righteous tongue speaking truth, love, kindness, joy, and honesty.

Chapter 26

Know When to Shut Up

My dear brothers and sisters, take note of this: Everyone should
be quick to listen, slow to speak, and slow to become angry.
James 1:19

One of the most powerful gifts you can give someone is the gift of
being heard. When someone is really listened to, they feel more alive,
worthwhile, and free.

This is why people are always looking for a "seat at the table." They
have an opinion and want to know it counts. They want to be a part of
the solution.

When you listen first, and ask questions to make sure you fully
understand, you get the full picture. Too often we stop once we think
we hear the problem, challenge, or issue. And then we try to solve it—or
worse yet, we become angry.

Proverbs 18:13
He who answers before listening—that is his folly and shame.

Proverbs 18:15
The heart of the discerning acquires knowledge, for the ears of
the wise seek it out.

Proverbs 18:17
In a lawsuit, the first to speak seems right, until someone comes forward and questions him.

In verse 17 above, I like to have a little fun and replace the word "lawsuit" with "meeting." How many times have we taken the first person or only person who talks as correct, especially if the highest exec in the room jumps in and agrees or runs with the idea?

In my (Dan) first business, I was one of the founders, so I was the subject matter expert on everything we did. I was a problem solver for a good five years. The team grew and we hired functional staff that were more than capable. I'm ashamed to think back about how many times I stifled ideas, progress, and talking about hard issues by either being the answer man or knowing the answer before we had the meeting. How debilitating that must have been for my team. Later in my career, I led a change-management initiative as COO. Although I understood the business, I was anything but the subject matter expert, so I had to rely on others to inform me and help me make decisions. I asked a ton of questions, and the real experts had the lively discussions while my business knowledge guided the decisions.

The difference between those two scenarios was quite big in terms of engagement and trust.

Which scenario describes you? Your business? What benefit would your company receive if you listened more? What meetings are you having where you should be quick to listen and slow to speak? How will you be "the listener" in these meetings?

Application: Coaching Through Curiosity

So often we function as the "answer man." We wait for the other person to stop talking so that *we* can start talking, instead of listening and asking questions. Or people just bring us problems and dump them in our lap, and we take them on as our own instead of helping them work through to a solution.

As a certified executive coach, I'm (Dan) a big fan of the "coach" approach. Although I don't think you need to get certified, there are two concepts that you can use that go a long way toward learning to listen.

First, be curious. Come to conversations with listening in mind. Listening with humility, patience, and discernment. It's a sign of wisdom. Be curious. When you seek to understand and maintain your curiosity, it's easier to listen.

When you are curious about what the other person is saying, it's impossible not to ask questions. What happened? What do you think we should do? What impact would that have on us and the client? What do you want to do? What obstacles can I help remove?

And that's the second step: ask questions. In his book *The Coaching Habit*, Michael Bungay Stanier goes through the five questions every leader should have in his arsenal. The top three for me are:

1. What's on your mind?

    This question allows you to start any conversation with the other person in the lead.

2. And What Else? (AWE)

    Because the person is bringing you a situation, problem, or challenge, it's so very easy to jump into fix it mode. Maintain curiosity by staying in question mode. You'll also find that this brings out additional details that helps you understand where the real challenge may lie versus where the conversation started.

3. What do you want?

   One of my clients has a sign over his desk that reads "bring me solutions, not problems." In order to push your team towards this habit you need to ask them what they want to do in the situation. What options have they thought through? Which is the best one in their mind?

See how those questions are all open ended and allow the other person to create the solution? They lead the person through a thought process to arrive at next steps versus you delivering the answer. You can do the same to help your people. Sometimes it will be easier to just solve a problem yourself as it will save you time. But that's short-term gain for long-term pain. Don't do it.

Challenge: Your Next Meeting

Try to work through one of these challenges at your next meeting. (Or the next meeting that makes sense to try it.)

- Challenge # 1: Spend an entire meeting without saying anything. Of course, there are times you have to speak, but try to speak at just five percent of your normal percentage. You'll be amazed at what happens.
- Challenge # 2: Only ask questions at your next meeting or conversation. Often the real work of a meeting doesn't start until someone asks for your opinion or tries to get you to solve the problem. Don't let them. What can you ask them to help them create the solution or the next step? Here's a tip: If this is too hard to try at work, try it at home at the dinner table. It's especially hard with teenagers. If you can do it at home, work will seem easy.

Time Travel and Your Most Important Client

"I'm sorry, what?"

My (Dan) wife just stared at me. The five of us were out to lunch because my son had just returned from ten days at scout camp. He was regaling us with tales of raccoons and giant spiders in his tent. Meanwhile . . . I was time traveling.

Do you ever do that? Time travel either into the future (what is going to happen) or the past (relive what has already happened)? Funny thing is you can't control the first or change the second, so what's the point?

"I'm more prepared. I'm strategizing. I do this to be better." That is what I tell myself, but that's a lie. It's the worry, anxiety, and all the other junk from everyday life garbage-ing up my head.

So, back to my wife and her rude interruption of my time traveling. "I'm sorry, what?" I say.

"Want to join the conversation?" she asks politely.

Sigh. "Yes, just thinking about work."

"Well, then act like we're your client." BOOM! My head exploded.

How do I act with clients? I'm prepared for the meeting. I've got their challenges, opportunities, needs, and blind spots at the front of my mind. I show up and am present. I'm all theirs for the time we spend together. Nothing else is going on during that time except for the client interaction and engagement. During the meeting I listen—deep listening, trying to hear what is said but also what they are not saying. I wrap all that together and meet them where they are: empathizing, strategizing, ideating, connecting, holding accountable, or just listening.

Imagine if I gave my most important clients, my family, that kind of service all the time. The impact and influence would be off the charts, and the ROI would be exponential.

How do you need to come to your most important client meetings?

Chapter 27

Discipline for the Student

No discipline seems pleasant at the time, but painful.
Later on, however, it produces a harvest of righteousness
and peace for those who have been trained by it.
Hebrews 12:11

I (Dan) love to learn. I am a learning junkie. I love business models, decision models, mental models, and different perspectives. I love to implement new ideas and get feedback to see what works and what doesn't.

It's strange, I've always taken feedback and criticism well—until I was CEO. In order to live up to the title, I felt like I needed to be the smartest person in the room. It was all about my ideas, and anyone else's ideas or perspective didn't have all the information or didn't understand the vision. They didn't "get it." And who rebukes their boss when he's already made the decision? Nobody. That is unhealthy and egotistical and eventually will get you into a lot of trouble.

Are you teachable? Can you take yourself out of your own way and change your mind when the facts change, when the times change, when you change, when the business changes, or when the world changes?

How do you make sure you are open to learning or trying new things, and even admitting you are wrong?

Proverbs 3:11–12

[11] My son, do not despise the LORD's discipline, and do not resent his rebuke, [12] because the LORD disciplines those he loves, as a father the son he delights in.

Proverbs 5:11–14

[11] At the end of your life you will groan, when your flesh and body are spent. [12] You will say, "How I hated discipline! How my heart spurned correction! [13] I would not obey my teachers or turn my ear to my instructors. [14] And I was soon in serious trouble in the assembly of God's people."

Proverbs 10:17

Whoever heeds discipline shows the way to life, but whoever ignores correction leads others astray.

Proverbs 12:1

Whoever loves discipline loves knowledge, but whoever hates correction is stupid.

Proverbs 13:13

Whoever scorns instruction will pay for it, but whoever respects a command is rewarded.

Proverbs 15:10

Stern discipline awaits anyone who leaves the path; the one who hates correction will die.

Proverbs 15:12

Mockers resent correction, so they avoid the wise.

Proverbs 15:31–32

[31] Whoever heeds life-giving correction will be at home among the wise. [32] Those who disregard discipline despise themselves, but the one who heeds correction gains understanding.

Proverbs 19:27

Stop listening to instruction, my son, and you will stray from the words of knowledge.

Proverbs 23:12

Apply your heart to instruction and your ears to words of knowledge.

Proverbs 25:12

Like an earring of gold or an ornament of fine gold is the rebuke of a wise judge to a listening ear.

Do you "avoid the wise"? Do you hate correction, discipline, and instruction? In the above Scripture it says the people who love you will be the ones who help you. This is tough because it's so hard to say tough things to the people you love.

So, if someone gives you correction, instruction, or discipline—you should thank them. You may not agree with what they're saying, but you should be open to it and think about it and pray on it. If it's true, it can be an ornament of fine gold and help you gain understanding, be rewarded, and be among the wise.

This idea of being a good student goes back to having good advisors, but it's also about understanding yourself, your strengths/weaknesses, and giving yourself a checkup from the neck up from time to time to see where you are biased. Being the dumbest person in the room is a good thing. So is receiving candid, honest feedback in the form of instruction and discipline.

All of us are teachable if we can admit we don't know everything (or have to). Here's a quick check: If you are the CEO or Owner and are the "answer man" at your company; if there is a constant perpetual stream of people who need your approval, advice, permission; if people come to you with problems and no solutions—then you have some changing to do.

It's hard to hear real information about your company and yourself. You are proud of who you are and what you've accomplished. Proud can turn into pride and cause you to you rely on what got you to here. Pride turns into overconfidence and blind spots. A common blind spot in leaders is bias. You learned some things over the years, and based upon your life, you see the world in a certain way. So what happens when what you see isn't what is true in the world? You are biased. And we're all biased.

For example, I know soccer is better than football. A continuous game vs. eight seconds on and thirty seconds off? C'mon. There's no comparison. But hey, I've played soccer all my life, so I might be biased.

Drew loves football. He played. His three boys played. He can't stand "low scoring, ties, and fake injuries to bait calls." He also thinks there are more concussions in soccer than football. He might be biased.

How did you come up in business? What path did you take? Was it sales, operations, finance, or marketing? You are biased with your base of knowledge from that path, and so you start with a bias toward your experience in how you look at everything in the business.

One way we can become better leaders is to acknowledge our biases and make sure we don't fall into their traps. Here's the most common bias I've found within companies that create the biggest blind spots.

Application: Combat Confirmation Bias Through Debate

Confirmation bias is when we find facts, information, and stories that confirm what we already believe or want to believe.

In high school history class, I (Dan) had a project where we had to research and, in a debate format, argue for or against dropping the atomic bomb on Japan during WWII. Since we all knew the outcome, everyone wanted to be on the "for" side. I was of course placed on the "against" side. How were we going to argue against something that already happened? Funny thing is, the more research we did, the more questions, data, and valid viewpoints we found for why dropping the atomic bomb was not a good idea. The final debate was actually very even in terms of for and against arguments.

This format is a great way to unhook deep and long-held thoughts people hold on to as "truth" within a company's organization and uncover new ways of thinking.

What long-term biases are in your company? What status quo needs to be challenged? What sacred cows exist? What big decisions need to have many points of view before moving forward? Using a debate format can help.

There are private equity companies and venture capital firms that employ this format for every investment they make. Before an investment is made, two partners will argue in front of the decision committee for and against the investment so that all angles are looked at. Imagine arguing against an investment you want to make!

Of course, this process might not uncover every problem or challenge, but the entire team has the whole picture right up front and has the open forum to talk about it without fear of repercussion. The decision stands upon its own merit, not on the idea bringer's power, status, or ego.

Chapter 28

Discipline for the Teacher

If we don't shape our kids, they will be shaped by outside forces that don't care what shape our kids are in.
—Dr. Louise Hart

You know what this book is lacking? Science! Well, here you go.

In thermodynamics, there is a concept called entropy, also known as the law of disorder. It states that everything in our universe, when left to itself, moves toward disorder.

Without discipline, everything in order moves toward chaos. You know this to be true without thinking too hard about it. It's true with your kid's room (leave it alone for a month and see what happens), with the extension cords in the garage, your health, and the lawn. When left alone ... eventually chaos.

The same goes for your company. Your company is trying to become chaotic at all times. The world is throwing as much chaos at you and your employees as it can. It is your job to provide stability, direction, accountability, focus, instruction, and discipline.

Instruction (vision, mission, direction, focus, leadership, management) and discipline (accountability, cadence, consequences) are vital to your business surviving and thriving.

Proverbs 9:8–9

[8] Do not rebuke mockers or they will hate you; rebuke the wise and they will love you. [9] Instruct the wise and they will be wiser still; teach the righteous and they will add to their learning.

Proverbs 13:24

Whoever spares the rod hates their children, but the one who loves their children is careful to discipline them.

Proverbs 19:18

Discipline your children, for in that there is hope; do not be a willing party to their death.

Proverbs 19:25

Flog a mocker, and the simple will learn prudence; rebuke the discerning, and they will gain knowledge.

Proverbs 22:6

Start children off on the way they should go, and even when they are old, they will not turn from it.

Proverbs 22:15

Folly is bound up in the heart of a child, but the rod of discipline will drive it far away.

Proverbs 29:15

A rod and a reprimand impart wisdom, but a child left undisciplined disgraces its mother.

Proverbs 29:17

Discipline your children, and they will give you peace; they will bring you the delights you desire.

Proverbs 24:11

Rescue those being led away to death; hold back those staggering toward slaughter.

Proverbs 25:11

Like apples of gold in settings of silver is a ruling rightly given.

Proverbs 29:17

Discipline your children, and they will give you peace; they will bring you the delights you desire.

Proverbs 29:21

A servant pampered from youth will turn out to be insolent.

Tip: Read these verses a second time through and replace "children" with "employees." What do you think?

If you do not instruct, discipline, and hold your employees accountable, you hate them, are a party to their death, disgrace, and slaughter. Although we are talking about a metaphorical death and leaving your company isn't always a bad thing, if you had the opportunity to create a great employee and didn't do it—then their leaving is on you.

When you instruct, discipline, hold accountable, mentor, and coach your employees, then you improve your team, move toward excellence, and provide them and yourself with peace and delight.

I look at a company with no instruction or discipline like a high school party when the parents aren't home. There are a lot of bad decisions happening all night, and everything is just one stupid decision away from disaster.

Consequences ... Not Condemnation

I (Dan) had a client who had a good manager make a bad decision. The manager (he) was starting to become a little close to a particular female employee. The employee handbook strictly forbade relationships between managers and their direct reports to avoid conflicts of all kinds. It's not a crazy thing for people who work together to develop relationships and even date. But the policy of this company prohibited it—if a relationship was worth pursuing, one of the two would move departments or even find a job at another company.

This particular relationship was kept under wraps for some time, but soon the other employees noticed. By the time it got to my client, it was a full-blown dating relationship and causing problems within the department.

My client confronted the manager about the relationship, and the manager denied it several times and rather vehemently. He was lying. What a conundrum. By lying, the manager was harming the morale and culture of his team and going against the wishes of ownership. The third time the manager was confronted, he denied it again. My client let him go.

The manager was very upset. The manager was also married. Imagine how that conversation was going to go at home for the manager.

"Hi, honey. I got fired today ..."

"Oh, gosh, what happened ... ?"

My client was extremely upset as well, as this was a long-tenured employee.

The following week, my client reached out and met with the former manager and just listened to how his manager's marriage got to that point, the struggles, and where the relationship is now. The married couple decided to fight for their marriage. It wasn't going to be easy, but it was worth it. My client also brainstormed with and made several inquiries/referrals into other employment opportunities for the former manager.

When it's all said and done, this leadership thing is all about people. In this case, the manager had to live with the consequences of his decisions, but my client didn't condemn him forever. He helped pick him up.

We are all responsible for our actions, and therefore the consequences that come with those actions. But as leaders, once the consequences are given, what grace, mercy, hope, friendship, or help might your employees (and all your relationships) really need from you?

Application: FETCH

Frustration

Elimination

Through

Confrontation that's

Healthy

FETCH is time tested and quite literally *the most powerful tool* I've (Drew) seen used to deal with high-stakes challenges relating to people. Spouses. Children. Partners. Executives. Managers. Front-liners. Anyone who matters in your life and business. While relationships and performance shouldn't be always measured numerically, I've seen it foster multi-million-dollar outcomes. It works, and it's bathed in grace AND truth. Hard on the issue; soft on the person. What have been obstacles that prevented you from having effective conversations and confrontations?

FETCH is a tool that highlights the "8 Steps to Effective Confrontation" originally architected by Dr. John Townsend (www.TownsendNOW.com) and used with his permission to impact those we serve in our Acumen community.

I heard Dr. Townsend speak at a conference where he unpacked the eight steps of the "Effective Confrontation" process. I've used it ever since. I've coached others on how to use it. It's helped create amazing breakthrough and victory. It's given me a way to deal with people without belittling and hurting them.

Here's the Process:

- **Let them know I am "for" them.** It's important to let them know you are "for them" ... that you value them.
- **State the problem.** State this early. People are catastrophic thinkers so getting truth out there early is actually grace-giving versus our typical tendency to sugarcoat and delay reality.
- **Own my part.** In other words, what part of the problem do I own? How have I contributed to the problem at hand?
- **Hear their side.** "Please share your perspective of the situation." Then listen.
- **Deal with diversion (ex. "Let me get back to . . .").** Townsend explained that these five words will help you keep the conversation and dialogue from getting off on a rabbit trail. Often people will try to divert, blame, offer excuses . . . Anything to avoid the truth. It's very important to stay on track.
- **Request specifically what I want (be hard on the issue and soft on the person).** This should be specific and something you prepare in advance and articulate or outline with clarity and specificity.
- **Give consequences if needed.** Prepare this in advance. Be clear on what could happen or will happen if what you want in number five above is not achieved.
- **Reiterate that I am "for" them (grace leaves quickly).** It's important to extend grace ... In light of truth.

- **Check back with them within 24 hours.** It's important to circle back and check in. "How are you feeling about the issue? Now that you've slept on it, what is your reaction?

This process, when prepared for and followed, can be a catalyst for moving your business past hard conversations, eliminate frustrations and bottlenecks that are inhibiting progress and momentum.

- Who is someone you need to have a FETCH with?
- What about others in your life? Spouse, kids, organization? Who else might need FETCH tools?

We'd like to offer you the opportunity to download our FETCH ebook, which allows you to order FETCH cards for your entire team FREE of charge for you!

These business-card-sized reminders fit in your wallet or folder or purse just like your other cards. It's a perfect way to recall the process before you need to have a highstakes conversation.

Just visit: http://acumenimpact.com/fetch-ebook/

PART 7

DON'T BE EVIL (OR STUPID)

"It takes 20 years to build a reputation and five minutes to ruin it. If you think about that, you'll do things differently."
—Warren Buffett

A good name is more desirable than great riches; to be esteemed is better than silver or gold.
Proverbs 22:1

It's funny that Solomon and Warren Buffet are on the same page. They both value a good name and reputation. Again, Proverbs tells us that something is more precious than gold. What does a good name mean? Why is it more desirable than riches?

Without a good name, people will not trust you—and what is business without trust of how you are going to behave? That it is going to be good and valuable for others?

People can be taught what integrity and being ethical is, but that doesn't mean they are ethical or have integrity. Awareness does not translate into compliance.

According to an *Ethics and Compliance Initiative study*, 60 percent of ethical misconduct is by management, and the highest percentage of that is by senior management. That means the biggest opportunity and purveyors of misconduct are from the people you work with the closest and have the most impact on your organization.

Solomon dealt with his fair share of ethical dilemmas. His thoughts on integrity, injustice, and evil are revealed in the following chapters.

Chapter 29

INTEGRITY

*And this is my prayer: That your love may abound more and more in
knowledge and depth of insight, so that you may be able to discern
what is best and may be pure and blameless until the day of Christ.*
Philippians 1:9–10

That's a big word: Integrity. It is as simple as the middle portion of the
Ten Commandments: don't kill, commit adultery, steal/cheat, or lie.
We've also got the positive sides of those commandments with honesty,
trust, respect, justice, and sincerity.

These are good in and of themselves, and most people accept these
rules when it comes to our personal interactions. We all accept the
Golden Rule: Do unto others as you would have them do unto you. In
a servant leadership filter, you'd upgrade that to treat others how they
want to be treated.

In business, there is a culture of acceptability that these rules are
true except when there is something to gain or lose and the lines are
gray. And in business, there is a lot of gray. Specifically, I've found
that the more money, power, and glory are involved—the grayer the
lines become.

An action that was questionable at $10,000 can suddenly become
acceptable when $100,000 is on the line. And the numbers don't have
to be that high. (Remember the story that opened the book, where I
wanted to save $5,000 hiring an employee?) Our minds are great at

confirming our wants and needs and crowding out the reality of the situation.

Proverbs 3:27–28

[27] Do not withhold good from those to whom it is due, when it is in your power to act. [28] Do not say to your neighbor, "Come back tomorrow and I'll give it to you"—when you already have it with you.

Proverbs 3:30–32

[30] Do not accuse anyone for no reason—when they have done you no harm. [31] Do not envy the violent or choose any of their ways. [32] For the LORD detests the perverse but takes the upright into his confidence.

Proverbs 6:16–19

[16] There are six things the LORD hates, seven that are detestable to him: [17] haughty eyes, a lying tongue, hands that shed innocent blood, [18] a heart that devises wicked schemes, feet that are quick to rush into evil, [19] a false witness who pours out lies and a person who stirs up conflict in the community.

Proverbs 10:9

Whoever walks in integrity walks securely, but whoever takes crooked paths will be found out.

Proverbs 11:1

The LORD detests dishonest scales, but accurate weights find favor with him.

Proverbs 11:3

The integrity of the upright guides them, but the unfaithful are destroyed by their duplicity.

Proverbs 12:17
An honest witness tells the truth, but a false witness tells lies.

Proverbs 13:17
A wicked messenger falls into trouble, but a trustworthy envoy brings healing.

Proverbs 14:11
The house of the wicked will be destroyed, but the tent of the upright will flourish.

Proverbs 16:11
Honest scales and balances belong to the LORD; all the weights in the bag are of his making.

Proverbs 17:15
Acquitting the guilty and condemning the innocent—the LORD detests them both.

Proverbs 17:26
If imposing a fine on the innocent is not good, surely to flog honest officials is not right.

Proverbs 19:9
A false witness will not go unpunished, and whoever pours out lies will perish.

Proverbs 20:17
Food gained by fraud tastes sweet, but one ends up with a mouth full of gravel.

Proverbs 21:3
To do what is right and just is more acceptable to the LORD than sacrifice.

Proverbs 22:1

A good name is more desirable than great riches; to be esteemed is better than silver or gold.

Proverbs 24:26

An honest answer is like a kiss on the lips.

Proverbs 29:10

The bloodthirsty hate a person of integrity and seek to kill the upright.

I (Dan) had a client whom we'll call SaaSco who had a software as a service product coming up for renewal with one of his largest clients. The negotiation wasn't going well due to price and legal jargon disagreements. During this, his client sent over a one-page memorandum that basically called him a liar and a thief (in legalese so it sounded very nice), calling his ethics and morals into question while demanding a ridiculous contract. He called me, exasperated. "What do I do with this?" As we talked through this challenge, the Scripture that kept coming to the surface was Matthew 10:16, where Jesus was giving the 12 disciples instructions before he sends them out on their own: "I am sending you out like sheep among wolves. Therefore, be as shrewd as snakes and as innocent as doves."

Jesus knew that the world isn't all for and with you. In fact, some people are against you. You aren't supposed to be wimpy but innocent and prudent.

The first thing SaaSco did was see if he was as innocent as a dove. "Perhaps the client is right, and I just don't know the contract or have missed something." But after going through all the emails and the contract, he concluded that he was in fact innocent.

For this case, the second piece of the Scripture comes to light. If SaaSco was to be as shrewd as a snake, how might he work this negotiation? After sleeping on it, SaaSco decided to totally ignore the memorandum and to just put an offer on the table that was shrewd yet fair for both parties. SaaSco knew his client could walk. But after being called out falsely, perhaps that was best.

The client ended up signing a new five-year agreement with a predetermined separation clause at the end of the term. Obviously, there are a lot of details omitted from here, but the point of this example is that when you are pure and blameless, you can be bold and courageous standing tall against falsehood.

Could the client have not signed the contract and left? Yes. It would have hurt revenue, but the company would continue.

Is this the Scripture for how to handle all contract or ethical dilemmas? No. This was discerned for this specific challenge. (Read "Making Big Decisions" to learn more.)

Does doing the right and wise thing always turn out well by the world's definition? No. In the long run, ethical and wise choices allow you to be there when the next big opportunity comes calling. This is how trust and a good name are built—through time and repetition.

Application: What About You?

So, what about you? Is there any part of your life or your company that needs the integrity filter? When it comes to pricing, products, services, marketing, sales, operations, finance, safety, delivery, employees, partners, vendors, and clients—are any of your ways crooked, harmful, lies, false, stir up conflict, dishonest, or wicked?

Are you and your company pure and blameless? When you find out situations where you aren't, how do you react? Do you hide from it or do shine a light on it to make it right?

Chapter 30

EVIL (AND STUPID?)

*Everyone who does evil hates the light, and will not come
into the light for fear that their deeds will be exposed.*
John 3:20

There is evil and then there is stupid that looks like evil because of
the damage it does but is actually due to incompetence or ignorance.
Sometimes trying to tell the two apart is hard.

It is not often that we truly face evil. Sin, conflict, disagreement,
sure—but not true evil. Evil is genocide, slavery, sex trafficking, child
and spousal abuse, and harassment. True evil is detestable. It's often
done in secret and meant to be kept in the dark. Evil is premeditated
and intentional and full of pride, ego, and a disdain for accountability.

The line between evil and stupid is based on intent. Stupid is not
meant to harm, but it does anyway. Stupid is where incompetence and
ignorance meet adversity, decisions, actions, and challenges, all of
which can result in collateral damage and consequences.

- In business, evil exchanges profit and power at the expense
  of people, which could be employees, customers, and
  communities. Money, power, prestige, and even the game of
  acquiring those drive the intention. You, the public, don't find
  out about it until someone shines a light on it or does something
  stupid. For example:
- Uber: internal culture of sexual harassment, stealing of
  intellectual property from competitors (Google), and using

software (codenamed "hell"—I can't make this up) to target rival Lyft.
- Wells Fargo: 3.1 million fraudulent bank accounts and fraudulent charges to retail bank customers because "unrealistic sales goals were set."
- Volkswagen: Creating "defeat device" software to defeat EPA testing and make diesel engines pass emissions tests while actually spewing harmful compounds forty times over the EPA limit.
- Enron: False accounting leaving the company bankrupt and employees' retirements in shambles.
- Bernie Madoff: Ponzi Scheme that cost people over $18 Billion. With a B.

See what Proverbs says about evil below.

Proverbs 17:11
Evildoers foster rebellion against God; the messenger of death will be sent against them.

Proverbs 17:13
Evil will never leave the house of one who pays back evil for good.

Proverbs 19:28
A corrupt witness mocks at justice, and the mouth of the wicked gulps down evil.

Proverbs 21:10
The wicked crave evil; their neighbors get no mercy from them.

Proverbs 21:27
The sacrifice of the wicked is detestable—how much more so when brought with evil intent!

Proverbs 22:8

Whoever sows injustice reaps calamity, and the rod they wield in fury will be broken.

Proverbs 24:19–20

[19] Do not fret because of evildoers or be envious of the wicked, [20] for the evildoer has no future hope, and the lamp of the wicked will be snuffed out.

Proverbs 26:27

If a man digs a pit, he will fall into it; if a man rolls a stone, it will roll back on him.

Evil is detestable, a rebellion against God, shameful, corrupt, violent, merciless, and intentional. Proverbs states that evil and those that commit evil have no future, will be snuffed out, will fall into a pit, be crushed by his stone, and see the messenger of death.

Heavy.

If you are intentionally doing something in your business that hurts people—internally or externally, physically or monetarily, and if you are hiding in the dark, scared of the consequences if you got caught—then there is evil you must deal with. If there is anything that you are ignoring, a "don't ask, don't tell" scenario that you think might be hurting people and helping profit, then you are incompetent as a leader and stupid.

Application: The Zacchaeus Formula

Most of the time, our adversity and challenges are due to our sinful nature, not evil intent. How do we deal with evil if you find it? The same way we deal with sin. The story of Zacchaeus, the tax collector gives you the formula:

> [1] *Jesus entered Jericho and was passing through.* [2] *A man was there by the name of Zacchaeus; he was a chief tax collector and was wealthy.* [3] *He wanted to see who Jesus was, but because he was short, he could not see over the crowd.* [4] *So he ran ahead and climbed a sycamore-fig tree to see him, since Jesus was coming that way.*
>
> [5] *When Jesus reached the spot, he looked up and said to him, "Zacchaeus, come down immediately. I must stay at your house today."* [6] *So he came down at once and welcomed him gladly.* [7] *All the people saw this and began to mutter, "He has gone to be the guest of a sinner."* [8] *But Zacchaeus stood up and said to the Lord, "Look, Lord! Here and now I give half of my possessions to the poor, and if I have cheated anybody out of anything, I will pay back four times the amount."*
>
> [9] *Jesus said to him, "Today salvation has come to this house, because this man, too, is a son of Abraham.* [10] *For the Son of Man came to seek and to save the lost."*

Luke 19: 1-10

1. **Zacchaeus was seen as a sinner because he was a Jewish tax collector.** He worked for the Romans and had the power to overcharge his own people to make a bigger profit. Tax collectors did well financially and were hated. But Zacchaeus's interaction

with Jesus shows us a way to make restitution for evil and stupid actions.

2. **Shine the light on the darkness.** Figure out what is going on, who is involved, and how deep it goes. If it involves you, where do you go for counsel to bring this to light the right way? Zacchaeus went to Jesus. Where is Jesus for you in this situation?

3. **Accept responsibility.** Evil and sin comes with consequences. God forgives, and so do people, but not without you owning it.

4. **Ask for forgiveness.** True, authentic apologies are hard to come by in business. PR teams and lawyers have created a culture of releases and statements that desensitize us to authenticity. If you want to make up for a mistake, it has got to be real. Jesus wants to give you salvation, just like he did with Zacchaeus.

Make it right. What do you have to do to make it right? Who do you need to make it right with? How do you quantify right? For Zacchaeus, it was four times the amount he took. Wow.

You want to be wise. It would be great to make wise decisions *before* we are evil, stupid, or sinful. But that's impossible to do all the time. What we can do is shine the light, accept responsibility, ask for forgiveness, and make it right.

Chapter 31

INJUSTICE

[14] What good is it, my brothers and sisters, if someone claims to have faith but has no deeds? Can such faith save them? [15] Suppose a brother or a sister is without clothes and daily food. [16] If one of you says to them, "Go in peace; keep warm and well fed," but does nothing about their physical needs, what good is it? [17] In the same way, faith by itself, if it is not accompanied by action, is dead.

James 2:14–17

I'm (Dan) conservative by nature. I'm a believer in capitalism, profit, and small government. Justice, social justice, and injustice sound like war cries of the liberal agenda, yet they are anything but. It's the execution of these ideas that cause the most tension and separate us, not the ideal. The more I read about the life of Jesus and the growth of His church, the more aware I become of injustice in the world—and of my opportunity to combat it with the platform and resources at my disposal.

Do we build a wall? Do we change our immigration programs? Do we have too many social programs? Do we not have enough? This is not that book, and I'm not that author. What I do know is that inside cities, neighborhoods, communities, and companies, there are injustices that you need to be aware of and combat when you have the opportunity to do so.

If you are squinting or squirming at these words, please read the verses below with open eyes and an open heart, because injustice is as prevalent today as it was in Solomon's time.

Proverbs 10:15
The wealth of the rich is their fortified city, but poverty is the ruin of the poor.

Proverbs 13:23
A poor man's field may produce abundant food, but injustice sweeps it away.

Proverbs 14:20
The poor are shunned even by their neighbors, but the rich have many friends.

Proverbs 17:5
Whoever mocks the poor shows contempt for their Maker; whoever gloats over disaster will not go unpunished.

Proverbs 18:5
It is not good to be partial to the wicked and so deprive the innocent of justice.

Proverbs 18:23
The poor plead for mercy, but the rich answer harshly.

Proverbs 21:13
Whoever shuts their ears to the cry of the poor will also cry out and not be answered.

Proverbs 22:22–23

[22] Do not exploit the poor because they are poor and do not crush the needy in court, [23] for the LORD will take up their case and will exact life for life.

Proverbs 27:7

One who is full loathes honey from the comb, but to the hungry even what is bitter tastes sweet.

Proverbs 31:8–9

[8] Speak up for those who cannot speak for themselves, for the rights of all who are destitute. [9] Speak up and judge fairly; defend the rights of the poor and needy.

Who are the poor? They are the needy, the lowly, the impoverished, the oppressed, the orphan, the widow, the trembling, the debtor, the alien, the prisoner, and the beggar.

Another side of injustice is those who are poor in power. There are many stories of how larger companies squash smaller companies in lawsuits simply because the larger can last longer in a legal battle regardless of the validity or legality of the claim.

Application: Injustice Responsibility

Likewise, you have the same types of interactions going on inside your companies. If culture is bad or a manager is bad, there can be infighting, bullying, backstabbing, power struggles, or harassment—all of which demoralize, beat down, and oppress your employees. So what are you responsible to do about it? Two proverbs provide you the keys:

1. *Don't exploit the poor because they are poor and do not crush the needy in court, For the Lord will take up their case and extract life*

for life. **(Proverbs 22:22–23)** Don't exploit the poor just because you can. Cheap wages, extreme hours or working conditions, safety violations, and unethical business practices can exploit your employees because they are at your mercy. It's worth taking less margin to shepherd your employees under your care. You want to take the Big Guy on? Me neither.

2. *Speak up for those who cannot speak for themselves.* Defend the rights of the poor and needy. **(Proverbs 31:8–9)**

"That's just the way it is."
"It's always been that way."
"I don't have the power to change it."
"I'm just one person."

If everyone had that attitude, the very country we live in—the right to own land, vote, ride a bus, eat at restaurants, get medical care, work—would all be different. Yes, debate the execution of the ideal. But the ideal is mandated by our faith to take action.

Inside your company you have the poor. Inside your neighborhood you have the poor. Inside your church you have the poor. Inside your family you have the poor. You don't need to change the world or the country. But you can be a catalyst for change with who and what is close to you.

What are you being called to do? Who are you called to serve?

PART 8

BARRIERS
TO SUCCESS

Me, me, myself, and then I and me, me, I couldn't tell this one
about I, because I was talking about myself, and then mee,
meee, MEEE, MEEEEEEEEEEEE! Beware the Me Monster.
—**Brian Regan**

Everyone has a monster inside. It's all about you. Your wants and needs, pride and ego. You'd rather not have it, but you do anyway. It's okay to have this monster inside you. We all do. It's like Bruce Banner and the Hulk or Dr. Jekyll and Mr. Hyde. All is well until it isn't.

No one is perfect, and we are all broken at the foot of the cross. Managing your Hulk or Mr. Hyde is key if you are going to act wisely.

This concept of the Me Monster comes from one of my favorite comedians, Brian Regan. His Me Monster routine is based upon a super-egostical and self-absorbed character at a dinner party. The exact kind of person we hate to sit next to. A lot of head nodding and mm ... hmmm-ing. Yet, you have the opportunity to become this person and this kind leader if you let your emotions run wild. Anger, revenge, envy, and gluttony are all themes in Proverbs that can turn you into a Me Monster.

As a leader, it's hard not to become the Me Monster. Everyone "loves" you. You gave them a job, sign their paychecks, and have dominion over their time. Why wouldn't they cater to your wants, needs, and desires? It's not that they want you to be a monster, but it's easier to keep you happy than deal with hard issues.

If we allow ourselves to drink in the ego our employees and the world may fill us with, we are on a path to having Bruce Banner/ The Hulk-like tendencies and being a Me Monster.

Chapter 32

ANGER AND TEMPER

The size of a man can be measured by the size
of the things that make him angry.
—Dale Carnegie

When you own an outsourced payroll service company, the one call you don't want to get from the client is, "Where are my employees' paychecks?"

It was late Friday morning before a long three-day holiday weekend. The manager of our customer service team approached me and said, "We've had a handful of clients contact us indicating that their employees have not received their direct deposit funds. I think there must be a problem with the electronic file we sent to the bank."

Translated, this means that every client who had direct deposit funds that were due that Friday was going to face the same issue. In short, their employees were not going to get their payroll funds until the following business day (ie. the following Tuesday). Not good! If there's one thing you *don't* do in the outsourced payroll service business, it's screw with the timing and accuracy of employee paychecks and funds availability.

My (Drew) heart fell. My stomach collapsed. I had actually planned to leave early that day to make the weekend even longer. I could feel the rage pulsing through my veins and body. I was pissed beyond words. A careless and very avoidable oversight by an individual on our team was going to result in absolute chaos and anarchy for everyone, and it was going to cost our firm a substantial amount of money—not to mention a good chance that we might lose many clients as a result.

Not only did this cast a very ugly shadow over each of our client relationships, but it also cast a seed of doubt with each of their respective employees about the accuracy/timeliness of their future paychecks.

This was not your typical toss-the-pitching-wedge-in-the-trees moment. I was ready to throw the entire golf bag, clubs and all, into the pond and push the golf cart in to join them. We're talking *rage*! I actually had a golf club in my office at the time, and I so badly wanted to grab it and just start hitting things.

But there I was standing front and center. Funny how everybody turns toward you when you're the top dog and there's a massive crisis. Their eyes are fully fixed on how you are going to react and how this adverse situation is going to impact you as the leader.

I wish I could say that I suddenly recited a great Scripture like Proverbs 15:18, which says "a hot-tempered person stirs up conflict, but one slow to anger calms strife." But my veins were pumping blood so fast that my brain had lost any ability to put something so eloquent together. Though I was in no mental or emotional condition to recite Scripture, I did sense the Holy Spirit nudging that this was an opportunity to make lemonade out of lemons. To demonstrate leadership strength to our team during crisis and create a battle plan to serve our clients and their respective employees—and to make any shortfall whole, no matter what the cost or remedy.

It was awful, draining, taxing, and difficult to attempt to explain to employers and employees that money would not be arriving until the following Tuesday. The collateral damage was expensive in lost confidence and trust eroded. Plus, we made a promise to cover any bounced checks or other penalties that employees incurred because of our gaffe.

Frankly, I think everyone on our team thought the individual who messed up would get the ax. If I would've allowed my anger to prevail, that likely would've been the case. But this was a strong individual who simply made an honest mistake. No one felt worse than she, and terminating her employment would've been an action born out of anger and bitterness, not truth and grace.

Several weeks later, after the storm had passed, I actually had an employee thank me for demonstrating what they said was the best example of leadership they had ever witnessed. I'm not sharing this to shine a light on me, but rather to illustrate how our leadership influences and impacts the lives of other people, whether it be during times of adversity or times of victory.

What are your hot buttons? Are there things that just set you off on the inside and then make their way to the outside? How do you handle your anger? What "makes you angry?"

Proverbs 14:17
A quick-tempered person does foolish things, and the one who devises evil schemes is hated.

Proverbs 15:18
A hot-tempered person stirs up conflict, but the one who is patient calms a quarrel.

Proverbs 16:29
A violent person entices their neighbor and leads them down a path that is not good.

Proverbs 16:32
Better a patient person than a warrior, one with self-control than one who takes a city.

Proverbs 17:14
Starting a quarrel is like breaching a dam; so drop the matter before a dispute breaks out.

Proverbs 17:19

Whoever loves a quarrel loves sin; whoever builds a high gate invites destruction.

Proverbs 18:19

A brother wronged is more unyielding than a fortified city; disputes are like the barred gates of a citadel.

Proverbs 19:19

A hot-tempered person must pay the penalty; rescue them, and you will have to do it again.

Proverbs 20:3

It is to one's honor to avoid strife, but every fool is quick to quarrel.

Proverbs 22:10

Drive out the mocker, and out goes strife; quarrels and insults are ended.

Proverbs 22:24–25

24 Do not make friends with a hot-tempered person, do not associate with one easily angered, 25 or you may learn their ways and get yourself ensnared.

When anger is a default emotion for you, as seen by the Scripture above, you will do foolish things, create conflict, and invite destruction. You and your company don't need any extra of any of those things. Anger is a distraction. It's a waste of time and energy, and it will cloud your judgment.

Can someone make you angry? My dad asked me (Dan) this often when I was young. I believe the anger output during my teenage years may have increased severely at one point. My initial response was,

"Yes, of course someone can make me angry. In fact, I'm angry right now at..."

He'd calmly ask it again. *Oh great, here we go, a lesson from my father. Awesome.* "Okay, I give. Can someone make me angry?"

"Who is in charge of your emotions?"

Me.

"Who is in charge of your outlook, response, and actions tied to those emotions?"

Me.

"So can someone make you angry?"

No. I can choose to get angry, to feel anger, to be angry, but no one can make me angry. *Well crap, I have to take responsibility for my emotions. Sweet.*

The easiest place that this plays out is in junior high. Most junior high boys like to haze each other by tearing down, ridiculing, and making fun. It's all in the name of good fun...but not really.

- "Dan likes Ali!"
- "You suck at basketball!"
- "Wow man, *nice* shirt!"

All of these are hoping to invoke a response. They immediately make you feel like you must protect yourself.

"I do not!"

"You suck!" And the game is afoot. They "got" you, and now it's a fight where you have a stake in the outcome, and they don't other than to see how hot you get.

We're not in junior high anymore, but the world acts the same way. Every employee, client, and vendor has things they care about that don't align with what you care about. So, there are opportunities to turn on your red angry light based on situations and people you can't control.

Mental Model: Could Be Good, Could Be Bad, I Don't Know

There once was a poor farmer with a field and a prized stallion. One day, the stallion broke through the fence and ran off. The neighbor heard of what happened and came to console the farmer. "I'm so sorry to hear that you lost your stallion. That is terrible. What are you going to do?"

The farmer shrugged and simply said, "Could be good. Could be bad. I don't know."

Three days later the stallion returned and brought with him seventeen wild mares. The farmer quickly fixed the fence. Hearing about this, the neighbor rushed over to congratulate the farmer. "That is so lucky for you that your stallion came back and with seventeen mares as well. Congratulations!"

The farmer shrugs and simply said, "Could be good. Could be bad. I don't know."

The farmer's only son went out the next day to break the wild mares, and he got bucked off and broke his leg. Hearing this, the neighbor rushed over to console the farmer. "What are you going to do? Harvest is soon and your only son is hurt?"

The farmer shrugged and simply said, "Could be good. Could be bad. I don't know."

Later that week, soldiers came into the town and announced a decree from the king that all able-bodied young men must report to the capital to join the war effort. Due to his broken leg, the son did not have to go. Hearing this, the neighbor rushed over to celebrate with the farmer. "You must be so happy, your son doesn't have to go to war."

The farmer shrugged and simply said, "Could be good. Could be bad. I don't know."

And this could go on and on. What's the point?

You are too attached to the goings on of every move in your company, especially in the short term. Your business can give you all kinds of stress, tension, angst, problems, and anger. If you look back on your life and the history of your business, you can see times where "bad" things turned out to be good, and "great" things didn't turn out to be so great at all.

We don't know the purposes of God. If we believe the Scripture that all things are there for us to grow and strengthen, then we should consider it all joy:

> *"Consider it pure joy, my brothers and sisters, whenever you face trials of many kinds, because you know that the testing of your faith produces perseverance."*
> **James 1:2–3**

All you have is how you look at life's events, your attitudes, and your perspective, but you get to add Jesus and the knowledge that it's all for His glory and that He has already won. Pretty cool.

Does it make it any better or easier when tough times show up? No.

Your star salesperson resigned without notice. Your biggest client called to cancel their contract. You tore your ankle coaching sixth grade basketball. Your bank has just called your loan. Your partners have come to you and want to buy you out.

All of these things can make you angry. In the long term, could be good, could be bad. You don't know. So do what James says and persevere through your faith with joy.

Your Emotions are Contagious

You might be thinking, *So I'm just supposed to be Zen and happy all the time? Really?*

Not at all. Be human and have real emotions. Celebrate and mourn. Just know that on the whole, as you go, so goes your company. Whoever you are on the outside will be emulated by your team.

Former Navy Seal Rorke Denver has a wonderful take on leadership where his focus is on emotion. "Calm is contagious," he says. He gives an example from a particular exercise during Seal training where the leaders were running around like chickens with their heads cut off, trying to finish the training mission in the time allotted.

Seeing the chaos, his master chief rounded up the leaders and gave them a simple message: "If you lose your head, you'll lose your head." For them, quite literally. Out on the battlefield, if a soldier loses their cool, they are more likely to be injured or killed, and they are much more dangerous to their own team.

Calm is contagious.

When you as the leader project calm and confidence in the face of whatever you are seeing, your team will emulate you. In fact, in a group of achievers, they will turn it up a notch or three. Then it rolls downhill to all of your employees.

When you are calm, they are calm.

It actually works with all emotions. You are contagious when you project fear, anxiousness, anger, envy, resentment, and freaking out. You can also project joy, trust, and calm. It's okay to acknowledge the situation you are in. It's not okay to put others at risk with emotions that make a situation worse. What emotions are you choosing to infect your team with?

Chapter 33

REVENGE

Hello, my name is Inigo Montoya. You killed my father. Prepare to die.
—**Inigo Montoya:** *The Princess Bride*

When you are filled with anger, resentment, disappointment, and fear, you can make bad decisions. One of those bad decisions is revenge, where you inflict harm on others for something harmful done to you.

Revenge is not justice. Justice is righting a wrong. It's okay to protect, fight for, and stand for justice.

Revenge is eye for an eye, tooth for a tooth. It's two wrongs. Solomon says that yours is not to get revenge—that is for the Lord.

Proverbs 20:22
Do not say, "I'll pay you back for this wrong!" Wait for the LORD, and he will deliver you.

Proverbs 24:28–29
28 Do not testify against your neighbor without cause—would you use your lips to mislead? 29 Do not say, "I'll do to them as they have done to me; I'll pay them back for what they did."

Proverbs 25:21–22
21 If your enemy is hungry, give him food to eat; if he is thirsty, give him water to drink. 22 In doing this, you will heap burning coals on his head, and the LORD will reward you.

Proverbs 29:6
Many seek an audience with a ruler, but it is from the LORD that
one gets justice.

The NFL is a great place to see the results of revenge. How many
times have you seen a defender hit someone after the play is over and no
flag gets thrown? Then, an offensive teammate comes over and levels
the defender. Since there is no other action going on, he's easily seen
by the referee and a penalty flag is thrown immediately, penalizing the
team in an almost always critical time in the game and spot on the field.

For whatever reason, in the heat of the moment, the initial action
is not caught. Afterward, the premeditation of revenge, the anger that
is behind it and the execution, put a giant spotlight on the illegal hit.

It happens in normal guy life too. I (Dan) play in an over-30 indoor
soccer league. Yeah, that's right. Over 30. This is over-30 soccer where
we win a T-shirt if we win the league. This shirt is highly coveted.

For some reason, a lot of guys still like to talk trash during games.
I'm not sure if this is just a leftover from earlier days of playing or if
guys really think it gets into the other players' head.

One night, a particular player on the other team took a disliking to
me. Let's call him Frank. He was a big fan of trash talking, to which I
always have one response: "Good Job." It's a congratulatory phrase that
says "Great trash talk!" and "You're a dumb dumb!" without actually
saying it.

On a play early in the game, I defended well against Frank, and he
fell. No foul was called. The game went on. Frank came up and chest
bumped me and told me if I did that again, he was going to punch
me. Punch me? What were we playing for? That's right, a T-shirt. My
response? "Good job," and I ran down the field to join the play.

Apparently, that was the wrong thing to say to Frank. He ran down
behind me, and when the ball was on the opposite side of the field,
elbowed me. I think he was aiming for my chest as a way to warn
me. His aim was poor, and he elbowed me right over the eye, which

exploded in blood. I literally saw red and thought that if I was bleeding, he should be too.

Frank was surprised that he spilled blood, but he didn't back down. I yelled several choice words and with no response started in for the kill. Or what probably looked like wild flailing from a maniac. I couldn't see, so there was a lot of guessing going on in my fighting tactics.

Real fights are quick, and old guy fights are even quicker. The two teams pulled us away from each other. There was a doctor on our team who told me I needed stiches.

Frank left the field and the facility immediately. I have never seen Frank again.

In the aftermath, I was livid. Who did that guy think he was? It's over-30 soccer! We all have to go to work the next day. That is not how you continue playing into your 30s and 40s. On top of the humbling of being in a fight, looking like an idiot trying to fight when I couldn't see, getting stiches, and a black eye, I had to call my wife and tell her why I wasn't going to be home. "Hey! Your winner of a husband got in a fight at soccer." Sweet.

That's when I got the email from the soccer complex that I was suspended for three months. Any violence is an automatic suspension. I got suspended for getting elbowed and stiches? Oh, that's right, I tried to hit him back.

I wanted revenge. I wanted justice. Old men don't punch each other without consequences. What he did was a felony. So, I went to the police department the next day while my eye looked nice and shiny and filled out a report.

A detective interviewed me, and Frank, and the soccer complex manager. Frank said I ran into his elbow, and the soccer complex played dumb. The detective told me that If I really wanted to, I could get my team to testify to what they saw, and his team, too.

I was also going to a doctor to see if there was anything wrong with my eye. I wanted to sue. I wanted to take his house, his life. Fricking meathead, punch me, will you?!? I almost pursued both the charge and a lawyer.

And then this from Paul:

[17] *Do not repay anyone evil for evil. Be careful to do what is right in the eyes of everyone.* [18] *If it is possible, as far as it depends on you, live at peace with everyone.* [19] *Do not take revenge, my dear friends, but leave room for God's wrath, for it is written: "It is mine to avenge; I will repay," says the Lord.* [20] *On the contrary: If your enemy is hungry, feed him; if he is thirsty, give him something to drink. In doing this, you will heap burning coals on his head.* [21] *Do not be overcome by evil, but overcome evil with good.*

Romans 12:17-21

Well, poop. I could make a case that I was pursuing justice based upon actions Frank had taken, and those come with consequences. I also knew in my heart that it was becoming a burning fire in me to get an eye for an eye from Frank.

I let it all go.

I didn't pursue any legal action, criminal or civil. I let all the anger and pride go. I waited out my suspension and jumped back into soccer three months later. And I now have this story that comes up every session or two about when "Dan went crazy" on that guy. I'll probably never kick that "badge of honor" I bestowed upon myself. I get to be humbled over and over.

It's just like that in the business world too.

Partners sue each other into oblivion wasting precious time and resources for revenge. Companies make sure the other party is on the losing end of a venture to make up for a deal they got screwed on five years ago to "make it even." People hire or promote the wrong person because the right person did something to them that they have never forgotten. Employees sue employers unjustly because they are mad about . . . everything.

Revenge is a desire to harm and can gnaw on your soul if you don't do something about it. That something needs to be healthy.

Application: Look Up, Let It Go, Move Forward

I wish I had a great process for dealing with the desire to take revenge. From my own experience, I can say it's two things that worked for me.

1. Look up:

    It's not on you to take revenge. If any is to be taken, it's from the Lord. I don't know how you get past whatever hurt, pain, circumstance, tragedy, or evil that has been done to you. It took Jesus to let me let it go, and my eye healed. How much more do you need him if it's something that won't heal?

2. Let it Go:

    Red, Morgan Freeman's character in "Shawshank Redemption," said something that has stuck with me. "Get busy living, or get busy dying." Living for revenge is to live in death. To be consumed with someone else's life subtracts from your own. Let it go. I had to "let it go" 30 times a day for a month. Then 10 times a week. Then one day, I finally and truly let it go. I don't know how deep your scar is or how hurt you are. Letting it go takes time. Some of us can't let it go. It can only fade. Let it fade, but don't let it gnaw at your soul any longer.

3. Move Forward:

    What is the first step you need to take to move forward? Momentum is a powerful thing. Get heading downhill, and get busy living.

Chapter 34

ENVY

"Envy is the art of counting the other fellow's blessings instead of your own."
—Harold Coffin

In this social-media-moment-sharing world, there is more anxiety about keeping up, hanging out, and living the good life than ever before. There's more room for envy than ever before. Someone will always have more stuff, money, relationships, intelligence, connections, looks, strengths (physical, charisma, speaking, math), and opportunity.

In the business world, you see companies that have better profits, margins, employees, clients, leaders, products, services, brand, vision, growth, visibility, and sales—and this is especially true when it comes to direct competition. It always seems easier for the other guy. What you usually don't know is that whatever company you envy is having similar problems to yours—just on a different cycle than yours. Sales might be up, but their culture is starting to crumble due to maxing out capacity. The brand is hot but it's all air; there's no meat on that bone.

Envy is in your own head, and it robs you of joy. It can even impact your decision making negatively.

Proverbs 23:17–18
[17] Do not let your heart envy sinners, but always be zealous for the fear of the LORD. [18] There is surely a future hope for you, and your hope will not be cut off.

Proverbs 24:1–2

[1] Do not envy the wicked, do not desire their company; [2] for their hearts plot violence, and their lips talk about making trouble.

"Uh...I don't envy sinners or the wicked. So, what's up with that?"

We're all sinners, so when you envy others, your heart is envying sinners.

"And the wicked?"

How many companies have we seen rise to power and look fantastic on the outside, only to find that the inside is dark and black and corrupt and dysfunctional? Remember too much too fast?

In 2012, the Kansas City business community witnessed a large payday loan scandal. A network of companies were defrauding the lowest economic class and doing it with a lot of churchgoing people's money.

Some financial advisor friends of mine commented on the weird conversations they were having with potential clients on their investment in these enterprises. The potential clients would say something like, "I'm currently getting a thirty percent return on my money in thirty to sixty days. Can you do that?"

"Um, no, not legally. Where are you getting those types of returns?"

"Well, that is what my guy is getting me now. We're really investing and growing this enterprise."

"What's the enterprise?"

"We're just leaning into our entrepreneurial spirit and growing this thing."

(This thing?) "Okay. Then you should probably stay with him."

Conversations like that could cause envy. Wow. Thirty percent in thirty days—sign me up. Imagine that conversation at the backyard BBQ. Except that it's not normal. It was dark and mysterious. This group of investors gave more money, invested in more new companies, and did a lot of good during this time of growth. It looked great on the outside. Unfortunately, it was wrong and illegal, and it all came crashing down.

Names were taken off stadiums, building projects were stopped in their tracks, some executives went to jail, and one even committed suicide.

Wicked.

Envious thinking is a slippery slope, and it only goes down. It also makes you concentrate on the wrong things. Just like keeping up with the Joneses personally will make you unhappier, so will keeping up with the Acmes. Instead of concentrating on what you have and your company strengths, you focus on what needs to be more like "them." This has nothing to do with improving profit, margin, employees, clients, leaders, products, services, vision, growth, visibility, and sales. It has everything to do with why you are doing what you are doing.

Emulation is not envy. If you need to start another service or carry another product to compete in the marketplace, by all means do it. Respecting another company's excellence and growth and wanting to learn from others is key. Another leader can be your mentor or advisor. Striving for excellence based upon what you know to be true somewhere else isn't envy . . . it's a value to strive for.

So, what's the difference?

Envy creates feelings of doubt, unworthiness, less than, scarcity, and pain. Envy stagnates you and your company. Envy can ruin you and your company's self-esteem.

How do you combat envy?

Mental Model: You Vs. You

Jordan Peterson, author of *12 Rules for Life: An Antidote to Chaos*, says the following as rule number 4: "Compare yourself to who you were yesterday, not to who someone else is today." He makes this point about you the person. I think it extends to your company as well.

What was your company like three years ago? How was the culture, your executive team, revenues, your leadership capability, and product and service mix? Is it better, worse, different, evolved? Talking personally again, Peterson explains that if you really want what the other person has, then you would have to get all of that person, not just the part you like. Part of envy is singling out one characteristic for comparison. Would you want to trade for someone's entire life or the entire company, or just the good part?

"Man, what we could do with that revenue . . . but could you imagine working under those conditions?"

"They are killing it now, but I heard they had 10 years of living on the edge of bankruptcy to get where they are today."

Based on your company history, opportunities, challenges, good things, bad things, time in the world, and so on, how does your company of yesterday compare to your company today?

What do you want it to look like three years from now?

Jordan states, "What you aim at determines what you see." This is why knowing where you are going, why you are going, and how you are going to get there is so important. Without direction, there is no path—wherever you go, there you are. Wherever makes it easy to start looking at others and want what they have. What you really want is their perceived direction and accomplishments.

Know who you are, where you are, and where you want to go. Then compare you against you, and watch how you will grow.

Chapter 35

HEDONISM OVERBOARD

One martini is alright, two are too many, and three is not enough.
—James Thurber

Hedonism is the advanced search for pleasure.

I (Dan) can remember (quite contritely) instances in college where I was studying for a minor in hedonism. Too many parties, too much sleep, too much partying, too much food, too much TV, too much gaming. Too much.

That extreme search for pleasure was exhausting, expensive, and took a toll on my body, my relationships, and my soul. It was toward the end of college that I really understood the effects of the all-encompassing intentional pleasure hunt. It was easy to see when extreme behavior was detrimental. My body hurt, my head hurt, and relationships needed mending. I had made my pleasure an ultimate thing, which turned into a bad thing.

Proverbs 21:17
Whoever loves pleasure will become poor; whoever loves wine and olive oil will never be rich.

Proverbs 23:19–21
19 Listen, my son, and be wise, and set your heart on the right path: 20 Do not join those who drink too much wine or gorge

themselves on meat, [21] for drunkards and gluttons become poor, and drowsiness clothes them in rags.

Proverbs 25:16–17
[16] If you find honey, eat just enough—too much of it, and you will vomit. [17] Seldom set foot in your neighbor's house—too much of you, and they will hate you.

Proverbs 27:20
Death and Destruction are never satisfied, and neither are the eyes of man.

Proverbs focuses on food and booze. But, it's Proverbs 27:20 that lays out the real deal. Like Death, the eyes of man are never satisfied. There are parts of your life where the hole is bottomless.

By nature, we're just not satisfied. When we take dissatisfaction and the advanced search of anything to another level, it can become an unhealthy focus. When that unhealthy focuses on our pleasure and satisfaction, and I would add achievement, it becomes hedonism overboard.

The "-aholic" and addiction list comes to mind. Workaholic, alcoholic, opioid addiction, porn addiction. Working, sports, watching TV, food, friends, wine, beer, exercise, sex, video games, social media, email, hobbies, and phone checking can all be hedonistic if we don't watch out.

How do you know if you are hedonistic anywhere? Ask someone who loves you. "Hey, _____. Do I have anything that I take to the extreme?"

So, do you have any extremes?

If there are any identified, what impact are they having on you, your life, and your family?

Finally, is your company hedonistic?

Work Overboard

The most common hedonistic trait I see in high achievers and companies is being a workaholic. There is satisfaction and pleasure in work completed, recognition, feeling of importance, moving up the ladder, getting emails and invitation to meetings, and excelling at something you are good at. The results also give you pleasure.

There is a lot of lip service to a balance of work and life, but the undercurrent at many companies is exactly the opposite. I'm not talking about sprinting. We all need to sprint from time to time because there is more work to do than time to do it. But we're made to sprint short distances. I'm talking about when everyone is sprinting a marathon. When everything is always on fire, everything is a priority, and it all has to be done ASAP—for years.

It makes me think of all the large enterprises that hire and lay off in eighteen-month cycles as a strategy. We have one of these in our town. Get in, work your tail off, hopefully make it to Director or VP. If your number gets called, you are either let go or perhaps you are lucky enough take a package. Some people actually go back for three or four tours of this cycle as they play the game.

I've heard former employees mention executives saying things like, "I don't have a life, so that's too bad for you," and, "If I'm here, you're here."

Companies like this begin to consume their employees. Some thrive in this culture, some tolerate it, and others just burn out. The thrivers tend to be those with broken relationships at home. (Ever work in order to avoid a hard conversation with your spouse?) Or those chasing the title or monetary incentive. (If we can just hit $10 million in revenue this year, *that* would be the difference maker.) Or those who work out of sheer boredom. (What else would I do?)

"That may be them, but I have to work this hard. This place would crumble without me here."

Yeah? Then you are a poor leader. Charles De Gaulle said that "Graveyards are filled with indispensable men." He's right. Life will go on after you die. Your company will too. If companies like Apple, Ford, and General Electric can grow and innovate after the death of their legendary founders, then your company can too.

When the leader of the company is a workaholic, he is stating to everyone with his actions that he values those that work like him. It's a steep slope into building a culture of total workaholism. Everything moves downhill and very fast.

Application: The Sabbatical

I've found that the hardest thing for an owner or CEO to do when this is a concern is leave and unplug for any extended period of time.

What's the longest period of time you have unplugged? A long weekend, one week, two weeks? More? How about a month? Why a sabbatical and not a vacation? A sabbatical is about rest and unplugging. A vacation oftentimes is about action, activity, and doing. A sabbatical is about being.

Why do we need to "be?" Our brain needs it.

In Cal Newport's book *Deep Work,* he discusses how we have become a society that is entertained and distracted. Because of that you have a hard time focusing long enough to do deep work, or "work efforts that create new value, improve your skill, and are hard to replicate."

You need breaks to get out of the distracted and entertained zone. When you do, you'll be a better leader and more creative.

You cannot build muscle unless you rest between workouts. Imagine working out the same muscle group every day without rest in between. Eventually, those muscles will atrophy. The same is true with our brains. Unless you truly rest your brain, you cannot build your concentration muscles, your thinking muscles, or your deep work muscles. Sprinting all the time will hurt your body and brain in the long term. Your company will also atrophy. When it's all go all the time, turnover increases, work product is mediocre, stress increases, conflict increases, and overall performance declines.

Resting your brain aids insight and creativity, helps recharge your mental batteries, and increases your capacity to concentrate and do deep work. You need it, and so does your team.

Back to the sabbatical. What's the most amount of time you've ever taken off and unplugged? Whatever it is, double it in the next twelve months. If you've only taken a week, take two. Taken two? Take a month.

Sound crazy? It isn't. The feedback from leaders who have pushed the limit on unplugging are positive and confirming. What happens at the office? They figure it out. What happens to you? You come back invigorated, with a clear mind, perhaps some new clarity, and a brain muscle that is ripped and ready to lead your company.

Chapter 36

TEMPTATION

*For true peace of heart is to be found in resisting
passion, not in yielding to it.*
—Thomas a Kempis, *Imitation of Christ*

We are a society of immediate gratification. This country is so blessed with infrastructure, resources, opportunity, government, and freedom that you can satisfy any need at any place any time—so much so that it's become a challenge for society to manage. Because you have the opportunity to eat anything, buy anything, go anywhere whenever you want, you are left to your own devices to control those desires. How wonderfully horrible for us all.

From the simple candy bowl in the break room and shiny-object projects or people to the more complicated opportunity to win the big contract if you're willing to look the other way on a couple of safety issues, you are tempted by your desires frequently.

In Proverbs, Solomon preaches caution and a taming of our desires.

Proverbs 1:10–19

[10] My son, if sinful men entice you, do not give in to them. [11] If they say, "Come along with us; let's lie in wait for innocent blood, let's ambush some harmless soul; [12] let's swallow them alive, like the grave, and whole, like those who go down to the pit; [13] we will get all sorts of valuable things and fill our houses with plunder; [14] cast lots with us; we will all share the loot"—[15] my son, do not

go along with them, do not set foot on their paths; [16] for their feet rush into evil, they are swift to shed blood. [17] How useless to spread a net where every bird can see it! [18] These men lie in wait for their own blood; they ambush only themselves! [19] Such are the paths of all who go after ill-gotten gain; it takes away the life of those who get it.

Proverbs 25:28
Like a city whose walls are broken through is a person who lacks self-control.

Proverbs 31:1–7
[1] The sayings of King Lemuel—an inspired utterance his mother taught him. [2] Listen, my son! Listen, son of my womb! Listen, my son, the answer to my prayers! [3] Do not spend your strength on women, your vigor on those who ruin kings. [4] It is not for kings, Lemuel—it is not for kings to drink wine, not for rulers to crave beer, [5] lest they drink and forget what has been decreed, and deprive all the oppressed of their rights. [6] Let beer be for those who are perishing, wine for those who are in anguish! [7] Let them drink and forget their poverty and remember their misery no more.

Where are your walls broken through? Are you ambushing innocent souls anywhere? Are you benefiting from ill-gotten gains?

I know. Who am I to question you? You are "the king" of your business, of your household, and you have it all under control. Right. Me too. Except when I don't.

The hardest person to lead is yourself.

We're all broken at the foot of the cross. It's these internal carnal desires that will drag you and your company down. Giving into the desires isn't a one-time fall down and die. It's a slow builder, and eventually you're so deep in it, you don't know how to get out.

Enter the Ninja

Ever been a ninja? Hiding sleek and very discreet. It becomes a game. All of us are ninjas somewhere. We were trained back when we were kids.

At the age of 30, I (Dan) did the hardest thing I have ever done. Not the biggest, most monumental, or even the greatest—but physically and mentally the hardest. Seriously I'd rather go through junior high again than to have to go through it.

What was it? I quit dipping. (This entails smokeless tobacco in the round can that you put inside the front or side of your lip. There is lots of spitting involved.)

In college, I smoked and dipped. Smoked first, dipped as an alternative. Once I graduated, I didn't want to smoke anymore, so dip became how I quit smoking. Since dipping was socially unacceptable, it would be easy to give up once I couldn't do it in public. Or so I thought.

Funny thing is that I just became good at hiding it. Like a ninja, I would dip where no one would know or see and be able to put one in or take it out of my mouth without anyone noticing. It became my best friend; I did everything with dip.

It became apparent about five years in that this was the new normal. Why so long? Because I kept saying I was going to stop. So stopping was always right around the corner. Except it wasn't.

That's when the quitting started, and started, and restarted, and started again. I probably tried to stop dipping fifty times, each time failing. This is a little addict stuff here, but most of the time I would start again because it was for someone else. I would quit for my wife. Then when she would make me angry, I'd get her back by dipping. Sweet, huh?

Or it would be that I had created such a habit that I couldn't imagine life without it. Dip on the way to work. Dip after coffee. Dip after every meal. Dip while on the phone. Dip with a drink.

See, most of the areas where we lack self-control are about our appetites vs. ourselves. It's not about other people in these instances; it's only really about us and what we think and feel about ourselves.

I finally got to that rock-bottom moment. I was feeding my firstborn son a bottle while spitting in another. I sat there thinking how ridiculous that is, and yet how many times I had tried and failed to stop. I didn't want to have to become an even better ninja to hide it from my kids. I had tried everything in the world . . . so, what was next?

This was the first thing that I ever gave up to God. That's one of those phrases you hear from "Jesus people" that they say in passing, and it sounds weird, and you just nod your head. I get it now. I literally said a small haphazard prayer that went something like, "Lord, you are going to have to do this, because I know I can't."

About a week later I'm surfing the internet and find my way to www.killthecan.org. It's a site dedicated to helping guys stop dipping. There is a virtual team you get on, and then you are held accountable by checking in every day and counting the days without dip.

Before you start, they also ask that you print out a contract to put in your wallet. This was what you would sign before you gave up again and went into the convenience store to buy another can. It's brilliant:

I give up my quit. Quitting is impossible, and I cannot do it. I love dipping more than I love myself. I care about dipping more than I care about my personal health. I love dipping more than I love my family. I know this addiction will kill me, and I ACCEPT that fact. I enjoy spending time alone with my can more than I enjoy spending time with anyone else on the planet. I look forward to losing my jaw, my tongue, my throat, my life—it's worth it. When I am lying in my hospital bed fighting a losing battle against cancer, I will feel a sense of satisfaction knowing that this is the path I CHOSE. My only regret will be that I didn't start dipping earlier in life. I will feel sorrow for my family's heartbreak and suffer untold pain, but I know you must sacrifice for the things you truly love. I know ALL the consequences of my actions and I accept them fully and without regret. I hereby choose to give my life to this addiction—I do so with a smile on my face.

Signature: _____

Date: _____

That contract saved me many a time. I'd be sitting in the car at a gas station ready to go in, and then read it. And then drive away. The more I read it, the more biblical I think it is. "You must sacrifice for the things you truly love." What did I love? Truly, what did I love? I think you can substitute lots of words in the above contract in exchange for dipping. What word came to mind when you were reading it?

They asked me to do this for one hundred days. You have to build new habits during that on hundred days. The nicotine is actually out of your body in two weeks. But your brain—oh, your brain wants it forever. Your brain is basically the devil and tells you lies for quite some time until you rewire it.

It's funny, I didn't meet one "real" person on the site. I checked in every day and read my contract as a prayer. I did meet God. I met the person who cared so much that He found me the one thing to get me through the hardest thing I ever did. Notice I didn't pray and wait. You have to work with God. This is not something that happens from the bleachers. It's a full-contact sport.

Every once in a while, I'll get whiff of someone else's dip can, and a flood of memories and triggers fills my brain and body. It's nuts that over a decade later, I can still think and feel strongly about something I never wanted to be a part of me to begin with.

As I read the contract again, I feel like I've quit lots of addictions in my life. I quit dipping, porn, love of money, love of work, and more. Addiction is anything that you do in such a volume that it becomes harmful to yourself and others. Smoking, drugs, work, running, working out—it's a giant list.

In moments of weakness, just remember this can be done. Anything is possible. One day you will not need it to feel normal, you will not need it to function, and you will get over those feelings of sadness and loss. Keep your eye on the Lord, and never forget—the ultimate price in this battle is your life, both here on earth and for eternity. And that's always worth fighting for.

Mental Model: The Marshmallow Test

In his book *The Marshmallow Test: Why Self Control is the Engine of Success*, psychologist Walter Michel discusses his experiment where he placed preschool children into a room with one marshmallow. The experimenter would explain to the child that they could either eat the initial marshmallow or wait until she comes back and get a second marshmallow—the reward of waiting being the chance to eat two versus one. The videos on YouTube of this experiment are great as you see kids coming up with fun ways to not eat the marshmallow; you can literally "see" the wheels turning as the kids lose their resolve and eat it.

The original hypothesis on the study was that delaying gratification allows people to be more successful. In many instances, this is true. In business, that is especially true. Jeff Bezos, CEO of Amazon, takes the long outlook of, "If we are successful now, it's because of the things we've done three to four years ago." For most large companies, this flies in the face of Wall Street, which is more aligned to short-term, 90-day results. Those short cycle times create decisions that maximize for today but are not always beneficial for tomorrow.

As business executives and leaders, there is pressure to make decisions quickly and decisively. Shiny objects, which we've discussed, often are a perfect example of how eating this marshmallow now can keep you from having two later.

Upon further study, it's not just about delayed gratification but also trust. Did the preschooler trust that the experimenter would actually come back and give them another marshmallow? New research is pointing out how much that depends on personal factors like environment, socioeconomic status, and family background.

I don't have a science experiment to prove this, but I find that the more often you can make patient decisions that have longer time horizons, the better off you and your company will be. In business, when you start eating your marshmallow is when you deviate from your initial plan or budget so much that it's not the original plan anymore.

A common marshmallow that leaders eat involves hiring. I've had too many conversations with executives where someone looked good on paper, had a great first interview with the CEO, was fast tracked in the hiring process, and ninety days later, the company is looking for a way out of the situation. The first ninety days turned into a nightmare because the executive took command and filled a need instead of following what is usually a set process that involves assessments, other team interviewing, and background checks. That all takes time . . . and yields a second marshmallow.

Of course, there are exceptions where you need to strike while the iron is hot. Discerning when it is hot and when to leave the marshmallow is why you have a team. For those of you in the shorter-term game (venture/startup, private equity, public), you can either sell a longer-term vision to your investors or look more personally rather than organizationally.

When have you pulled the trigger on a marshmallow? When have you waited and gotten two?

How will you recognize marshmallow situations when they appear?

PART 9

ME
MANAGEMENT

The toughest person to lead is always yourself.
—**John C. Maxwell**

I (Dan) recently went on a vision trip with the Global Orphan Project (www.goproject.com) to Haiti. They specialize in orphan care across the world, partnering with local resources to help provide sustainable family-style care. One of the executives is in our accelerator community and offered to lead a trip. A group of eight went down, not to work but to see, experience, and understand the challenges in a country decimated by natural disaster and of people who are at the bottom of Maslow's Hierarchy searching for safety, food, and water consuming a majority of the daily grind.

In the United States, we have money and resources to "fix" many things. I learned in Haiti that our American attitude and mindset can't solve every problem, and at times can make problems worse due our cultural ignorance.

After we had visited several local businesses and an orphan-care residence, we met to discuss what we learned and felt from the meetings of the day. Sitting on a balcony in the 90-degree weather in February when it was 15 degrees at home, it's impossible not to compare/contrast the two cultures.

Haiti is poor in possessions, privacy, choice, convenience, riches, opportunity, government, future vision, and natural resources. Haiti is rich in hope, spirit, family, patience, and joy. The community is very strong. People are firmly in the present and are independent and self-sufficient.

I found that to be in stark contrast to what we have. The United States is rich in possessions, choice, convenience, privacy, natural resources, efficiency, vision, future, government, and the list can go on and on. I believe that we lack the same richness and depth in our inner lives. We have poverty of hope, spirit, family, joy, and contentment. We chase mortgages and stuff and are ruled by time and commitments that crowd out the ability to engage at deeper and richer levels.

In our busyness, it's hard to see Jesus working in our lives and the lives of others. In Haiti, you can see and hear Jesus clearly.

This section isn't here to bash the United States or our culture or people. It's here to be a wake-up call or a poke in the chest to see where you are when it comes to the most important things in life. What seeds are you planting? What fruit are you harvesting? What is your legacy? Can you see Jesus working in your life, your family, and your company?

Chapter 37

JOY

When anxiety was great within me, your consolation brought me joy.
Psalm 94:19

I (Dan) misunderstood joy for a long time. I thought it was being happy, or close to the same thing anyway. They are not the same. Happy is external. Happy is momentary. It's tied to outcomes and stimuli. Getting a new contract makes me happy. That first sip of coffee in the morning make me uber happy.

Happy is not joy.

Joy is internal. Joy is tied to impact and belief. Impact as it relates to helping others. Doing something for someone else brings joy. Employing people brings me joy. Belief in knowing my values and beliefs and being rooted in those brings me joy. Knowing Jesus brings me joy. Putting my family ahead of my work life brings me joy.

Joy is eternal.

The only eternal part of this world is people. When you invest in, listen to, serve, develop, value, recognize, help, and celebrate people, you create joy and build up others for eternity.

Proverbs 13:19

A longing fulfilled is sweet to the soul, but fools detest turning from evil.

Proverbs 14:30

A heart at peace gives life to the body, but envy rots the bones.

Proverbs 15:15

All the days of the oppressed are wretched, but the cheerful heart has a continual feast.

Proverbs 17:22

A cheerful heart is good medicine, but a crushed spirit dries up the bones.

Proverbs 15:15 above says we're wretched when we're oppressed! Yuck. But I've felt wretched before.

You sabotage your own joy. Anxiety, worry, fears, boredom, numbness, envy, and extreme self-interest all suck the joy from us and "rots the bones."

The world does it too. Life isn't fair, but it's alarmingly not fair when it happens to you.

When you let yourself and the world take hold of your joy, it can put you in a funk. When the funk gets big enough, you can sink further into yourself and shut others out. Not a good way to keep our bones fed.

Application: How to Maintain a Cheerful Heart

Once you identified your funkiness, then you need a path to a cheerful heart. Proverbs says that a cheerful heart is good medicine, so we'll treat it as such.

There are two parts to this prescription: spiritual vitamins and physical therapy.

Vitamins are great. They make you better by increasing nutrients inside that you may not have or don't have enough. Spiritual vitamins are better.

The first spiritual vitamin is thanksgiving. Each day, get up and list all of the things you are thankful for. Start with the fact that you woke up. Seriously, 151,600 people die every day. Congrats, you ain't one of them. Then go to your health, talents, abilities, family, friends, pets, work, interests, coffee, weekends, laughter, mistakes, trees—it's a pretty long list once you get going.

You need to take that vitamin with the water of prayer to help it go down. When you lift your thanks to God, he hears you. It fills Him with joy. He loves that you are so thankful for all that he has given you. After your thanksgiving, if you want to ask forgiveness for anything, talk about your heart and what's heavy on it, and pray for others . . . *go for it.* Then listen. Listen for that still small whisper back. What is his will for you today?

Vitamins need to be taken daily, as your body will use up the nutrients quickly. Spiritual vitamins too. Therefore, I'm prescribing that you take thanksgiving with prayer every day for the rest of your life.

Now for the physical therapy. While thanksgiving is working on the inside, we need to strengthen your joy muscles on the outside.

In his letter to the Philippians, Paul said that joy is "true, noble, right, pure, lovely, admirable, excellent, and praiseworthy" (Philippians 4:8). What can you do that is all of those things? Serving others can check all the boxes. When you give yourself out by serving others, you actually get more in return. Yes, you've heard this a bunch of times. That's because it's true. What happens is that the world is too busy, and people just don't do it.

The gym won't come to you. You have to go to the gym! The frequency and length of your physical therapy is up to you.

You could be someone who daily prays for the opportunity to serve someone that day. This could be as simple as a smile, having a meaningful conversation with the office "sandpaper person" in the break room, or offering to pick up the kids from school.

And/Or you could decrease the volume but increase the time and serve or volunteer at church, school, a nonprofit, your sister's house, your niece or nephew, etc. on a weekly or monthly basis.

It doesn't matter what you choose to do; the point is that you serve someone else and strengthen your joy muscle.

Application: Philippians

Take this week and read Philippians in the Bible all the way through. Paul has a wonderful point of view on joy, given that he wrote that letter from prison. It's only four chapters and has big truth on how we should look at the world and joy. Ask Jesus to light your cheerful heart.

After you read a section each day, complete these:

What I learned about joy today is:

Today, I am going to: (action item on what to do moving forward)

Chapter 38

FAITH

When God says run through a brick wall, you start
sprinting and have faith that He'll create a hole.
—Andy Stanley (via his grandfather)

Have you ever had a brick wall experience? It's knowing—just purely knowing something in the pit of your gut, without any logical explanation to go with it. One of my (Dan) Acumen teams calls this being the "weird uncle." It's when you feel like you are being *called* to do or say something—and you *know* it comes from up above—but you are afraid that you'll come across as the weird uncle or a wacky religious person.

I had my first weird uncle experience in a sports bar and restaurant called the Blue Moose. It was lunchtime and busy. I was meeting with someone who at the time was a business friend but not a close friend. His father had recently passed away, and he was talking very openly how hard it was and what he was feeling. I got this tiny knock in the back of my head that I should ask him if I could pray with him.

I shook the feeling off.

My internal dialogue was saying, "Uh ... it's the middle of lunch. This place is packed. I know this guy, but not *that* well. I've never done anything like that before. How about, No."

The guy kept talking and pouring his heart out. After another couple of minutes, I got the tiny knock again. "Hey, ask if you can pray with him."

Internal Dialogue: "Hey back at you. I thought we talked about this. Weird uncle stuff. No thank you."

Still more conversation. I thought I was in the clear. The guy stopped talking and what was a tiny knock became a loud gong, "Ask him now!"

I said aloud, "Uh ... wow, I'm so sorry. Would you mind if I said a prayer right now?"

That's it. It's official. I'm the weird uncle. Let's get ready for the most awkward lunch we've both ever had. The pause got really long. He looked at me and said ... "That'd be great."

Stunned, I realized I then had to pray. I have no idea what I said. He thanked me. The rest of lunch was normal.

I had never done that before.

The guy and I have become close friends, and being the weird uncle was the jumping off point for me to have faith in listening to that still small voice and saying "yes."

Solomon doesn't write a lot of verses specifically on faith, but what he does write packs a punch.

Proverbs 3:3–4
3 Let love and faithfulness never leave you; bind them around your neck, write them on the tablet of your heart. 4 Then you will win favor and a good name in the sight of God and man.

Proverbs 3:5–6
5 Trust in the LORD with all your heart and lean not on your own understanding; 6 in all your ways submit to him, and he will make your paths straight.

Proverbs 3:5–6 is a butt kicker. Trust Him with everything; don't lean on your understanding. Submit to Him.

Every one of those things is hard.

Faith is the belief in things you cannot see. Trust is confidence and the reliability of someone or something. Our faith needs both.

Mental Model: Could You Bet the Farm?

The farm, as in your business, your lifestyle, house, promises to your spouse and children. The farm.

When you create a vision for your company, it's usually in the far future, say ten years. Now you must motivate your team to believe they can get there. Oftentimes it's a big goal, daring, almost outrageous. Your team must trust that you aren't loony.

Many times in business, we want the answer right away—to see the end, to know the outcome, to be guaranteed the result, avoid all the risk, get all the reward. But what would you do if you had to make a value and belief-based decision that could put your business in jeopardy of closing if you chose the wrong path? Could you do it?

The Green family from Hobby Lobby did just that. In 2012, the Affordable Care Act was rolling out, and the government was making changes to what would be required for many business healthcare plans. For Hobby Lobby, a four-billion-dollar company at the time with 25,000 employees, that meant including four particular drugs in their insurance policy when it renewed. These drugs were considered life-taking contraceptives by the Greens. To be clear, Hobby Lobby was providing sixteen different contraceptives, but it was with these four drugs where they decided to take a stand.

Is there any issue or situation where you would take a stand and risk everything you have and have built?

The fine for noncompliance would have been 1.3 million dollars ... a day. How long could your business handle a fine like that? Would that keep you up at night?

Provide the drugs, or pay the fine. Both bad options. So, Hobby Lobby sued the government. It was quite a battle with some interesting twists. One of the big ones was that the 10th circuit court provided relief the Friday before the new plan needed to be in place and the fine would have started. This was rare and gave them time to take the case to the Supreme Court, which decided in Hobby Lobby's favor.

That was a happy ending. But it could have gone the other way. The fine could have been upheld and then there would have been the slow death of a company and loss of jobs for all its employees . . . or give in, which they weren't going to do.

Could you live with making the right decision and "losing"?

In our faith, we know the end—Christ has won. Yet we toil in fear and worry and doubt. How much harder is it to trust God with the blessing of the business that he gave you?

Yet that's what he asks us to do: make the right decisions that align with our faith. To trust and have faith that our decisions, when aligned with him, will be honored. Not every story ends like the Hobby Lobby saga. The decision could have gone against the Green family. Hobby Lobby could have ceased to exist. They would have moved on.

The Greens had a brick wall put in front of them, and God said run. So they did.

Most likely, you won't have a wall this big to run through, and it's the little daily walls that are the most challenging. Trust the Lord, and He will make your paths straight.

Chapter 39

PATIENCE

Patience is not simply the ability to wait. It's how we behave while waiting.
—Joyce Meyer

I have gotten more patient as I've gotten older. Which means I've added five seconds onto my "patient time" since I was twenty. I'm not a patient person. Especially with my children. I'm more so in business but not much—I can't bend employees and staff to my will, so I have to fake my patience longer. Matter of fact, I can't do it to my children, either, but my overreactions at least make me feel better.

We are not a patient society, and yet it's a characteristic that can serve us all well. Why do you get impatient? Because you're an emotional being. Impatience is spurred on by emotion. Desire, hastiness, arrogance, and anger all kill patience and the wisdom it brings. These emotions are usually followed by rash and speedy decisions—the opposite of patience. Even a high dose of good emotions can help you make bad decisions.

According to Proverbs, the decisions you make with roller coaster emotions guiding you will have the propensity to be hasty and bad.

Proverbs 14:29
Whoever is patient has great understanding, but one who is quick-tempered displays folly.

Proverbs 16:32
Better a patient person than a warrior, one with self-control than one who takes a city.

Proverbs 19:2
Desire without knowledge is not good—how much more will hasty feet miss the way!

Proverbs 19:11
A person's wisdom yields patience; it is to one's glory to overlook an offense.

Proverbs 20:25
It is a trap to dedicate something rashly and only later to consider one's vows.

Proverbs 21:5
The plans of the diligent lead to profit as surely as haste leads to poverty.

The verse that really strikes me about patience in business is Proverbs 16:32, "Better a patient person than a warrior, one with self-control than one who take a city." We use so many war analogies in business that sometimes that's the only option we see. You have to make hard fast decisions when you are in battle. The stakes are just too high. Except it's not life and death; it's business. You don't have split-second decisions you need to make or everyone dies. But you feel like you do.

Early in my (Dan's) leadership career, we had an HR nightmare. Two employees were having an online affair through our internal chat system. When we learned of the relationship and started investigating the situation. Warnings along with a cease and desist offered a way out for all parties. Unfortunately, one party was not happy with the end result and became vindictive, retaliatory, and downright mean. It was a culture killer for the company.

Emotions riding high, I was the queen of hearts. "Off with their heads!" Our lawyer had to keep asking me to "put away the sword" and be patient with the process. It seemed like months went by as we interviewed, set processes and further meetings, communicated, and walked through the necessary steps to unravel the full situation. The costs were killing me on the inside as they felt wasteful, and the air in the office was thick. I really just wanted the whole thing to go away. Thankfully, cooler heads prevailed. Finally, we came to an agreement and parted ways with one party.

By waiting and going through the process, we had a better outcome that honored both parties and was legal versus making a rash decision creating a bigger battle and more liability, and crushing people. I didn't feel better. But that's the point. Patience is about giving up your emotional attachment to winning and justice—right now or ever—or avoiding any trouble or delay. When I look back on most instances where I wanted to take out my sword, six months later, it wasn't big enough of a deal to freak out and use my emotions to drive my decisions. How many times I've wished I was more patient. Hiring a rock star only to find that there was a culture clash or they were just a good interviewer. Shiny object syndrome excitement only to find that it would derail the rest of our plans for the year and kill productivity to do my bidding of the day. Patience is one of those things we can only gain with clear commitment to the process and usually it's by experience.

Where do you need to be more patient?

The Patience Continuum

Patience is a funny thing. It's having the power to something and not do anything until you are supposed to do something. Knowing when to do that something is key.

Daily patience is the thing of annoyance. Waiting in line at the DMV or behind the person who still writes checks at the grocery store counter. Waiting for Bob to stop talking about his arthritis so you can start the meeting.

There is short-term patience like the example above. There is also mid-term patience where you stretch a scenario out into months.

A client of mine had purchased a company and said he was going to take the first ninety days and just sit and listen to the executive team, watch all interactions, learn the business better, and get to know clients. He announced this to the entire company. So two weeks later, when he knew what changes he wanted to make, he had a decision. Would he go back on what he told his team and start implementing, or hold to the ninety days?

Could you wait the ninety days? What benefit would there be with waiting? What harm would there be to not wait?

Then there's longer-term patience. Take the above example and push it out even further. Brent Beshore, founder of Adventur.es, a unique private (and permanent) equity firm, expects to own portfolio companies forever and makes decisions on a thirty-year time horizon. *Thirty years!* It's a good thing he is young.

What kind of decisions would you make if that was your outlook? How would you invest, recruit, hire, fire, market, set values, strategize, invest in growth, and distribute profits?

One example Brent discussed at a presentation in Columbia, Missouri, was their company onboarding strategy. Upon the purchase of a company, they just sit and listen ... for a year. In year two, they promote from within and look at close peer relationships for other talent. If ninety days was tough not to take action, how would you do for a year?

Lastly, there is purposeful patience. This is the one that define people's lives—the one they make movies about. This is Jacob waiting seven years so he could take Rachel for his wife, and agreeing to work another seven years ... and doing it (Genesis 29:14–30). This is going to night school a little at a time to get your degree while you work a full-time day job.

Patience is tied to emotion. You can always ask yourself, "Where is my emotion?" Not that you remove your emotion and replace it with logic. That's impossible and not very healthy. But once you understand your emotion, you can acknowledge it and then move forward.

A client bought into a new company that sold safety equipment to large corporations. Historically, they had been reactive to opportunity. His arrival to the company shifted that focus to proactive. His background included M and A and private equity. The "obvious" strategy was to acquire or start new locations in key cities where current clients were to offer same-day, walk-in service. The pro-forma numbers all said yes. One thing kept nagging at him, though—they weren't ready. The systems weren't there, the processes weren't there, the people's knowledge wouldn't scale. But the money was there, and the opportunity was there.

The world said go go go, and he said no no no. He didn't pass on the opportunity or refuse to chase it. He patiently got the systems, team, and business ready by building a firm foundation before looking at the big scaling opportunity.

What about when the business is running well, you have the right players in the right seats, the strategy is unfolding as planned, and the future looks bright? Well, you change and add to it, of course! Let's get into a new market, acquire someone, develop a new product, etc. I'm all for innovation, experimentation, and progress. But there are times when holding the ship steady is prudent.

That takes active patience.

Mental Model: Active Patience

Another client had taken over his family business in fire system service and installation. He'd made it through the 2008 downturn in the economy and built it back up to be stronger and more diversified. The business was running well, with revenues and profits at a level that surpassed his original goals, and he was content with the maturity and size of the company. Growth was an option but only if he wanted to take on significant risk through a new location or acquisition. Being acquired was also an option, but there was no triggering event that made it a priority.

So, what do you do? You lead the company with active patience, checking the story frequently to see if anything changes, and if not ... do nothing. When I pushed him to explain his mindset, he laid out his thinking:

> The slower you go, the faster you get there. When things are going well, you don't need to push or drag on issues. When it's happening right, it will continue to happen right. Why change when 80–90 percent is going well? People don't like change. The less you change, the better people get. What's the point of shaking things up for the sake of change and ticking people off?

What about growth?

> It's growing albeit slowly. Could it grow more? Sure, but is it worth the pain to get it to grow more? Is it worth the twisting and struggle to pump out an extra three to five percent? For what? More work, higher risk, and a lot of pain for the team. When a mistake is made, it's not the end of the world.

What is important to know that makes this Active Patience work for you?

The key for me is that I don't get my identity from my job or the business. I don't need to prove to myself or my team that it's about me every day. There are a lot more important things that I'd like to focus on like family and relationships with people. Is it laziness, contentment, or God's grace to not want to go do the next thing? I'm definitely content, which has come through maturity and time. I've accomplished plenty and am proud of that. I don't need to be two to three times our current size. I'm focusing on the being, not the doing. As a be-er, I can focus on people and relationships.

Whether you are starting up, ramping up, scaling up, or keeping up, there are opportunities and times when doing nothing is the right strategy. Where do you need to be actively patient in your business?

Chapter 40

RIGHTEOUSNESS: THE OUTPUT OF WISDOM

This is how the birth of Jesus Christ came about: His mother Mary
was pledged to be married to Joseph, but before they came together,
she was found to be with child through the Holy Spirit. Because
Joseph her husband was a righteous man and did not want to expose
her to public disgrace, he had in mind to divorce her quietly.

But after he had considered this, an angel of the Lord appeared to
him in a dream and said, "Joseph son of David, do not be afraid to
take Mary home as your wife, because what is conceived in her is from
the Holy Spirit. She will give birth to a son, and you are to give him
the name Jesus, because he will save his people from their sins."
Matthew 1:18–21

According to Old Testament law, Joseph had the right to divorce
his fiancée and have Mary stoned for being pregnant without being
married. Yet he didn't. Why? The above Scripture in Matthew states,
"because Joseph her husband was a righteous man." What about him
was righteous, and how did that inform his decision about Mary?

Righteousness is one of those words that feels very big, mysterious,
holy, and unattainable. Most of us understand the negative connotation
better than the positive. Someone who is self-righteous is morally
superior and holier-than-thou. The negative comes from adding self.
The "I" compared to "you." Righteousness is about others.

But the wisdom that comes from heaven is first of all pure, then peace-loving, considerate, submissive, full of mercy, and good fruit, impartial and sincere. Peacemakers who sow in peace raise a harvest of righteousness.

James 3:17–18

According to James, how was Joseph righteous in his dealing with Mary? He was loving, considerate, and merciful in his initial reaction because he didn't want to shame her. Then, because of his dream, he was submissive and obedient to God's plan and said "Yes" to taking Mary as his wife. Today, we call that a shotgun wedding. The town gossips must have been in full effect. What did Joseph have to endure in terms of dirty looks, gossip, and direct conversations about what he was getting into? The world probably didn't agree with his decision.

When you act with wisdom according to the principles of Proverbs, you are "raising a harvest of righteousness," and you are therefore afforded the fruits of righteousness revealed in the verses below.

Righteousness is doing the right things, the right way.

When discussing righteousness, Proverbs' compare/contrast style helps you understand where a path of righteousness leads to versus the wicked. Surprisingly, this section has the most verses of all the sections in this book—78 verses in all specifically about righteousness. If there was any section that I would suggest that you read all of the verses in the index, this would be the one. Why? Because the culmination of everything you've read to this point creates righteousness.

Righteousness is the output of Wisdom.

Proverbs 3:33
The LORD's curse is on the house of the wicked, but he blesses the home of the righteous.

Proverbs 10:11
The mouth of the righteous is a fountain of life, but the mouth of the wicked conceals violence.

Proverbs 10:28
The prospect of the righteous is joy, but the hopes of the wicked come to nothing.

Proverbs 11:5
The righteousness of the blameless makes their paths straight, but the wicked are brought down by their own wickedness.

Proverbs 11:18
A wicked person earns deceptive wages, but the one who sows righteousness reaps a sure reward.

Proverbs 11:28
Those who trust in their riches will fall, but the righteous will thrive like a green leaf.

Proverbs 11:30
The fruit of the righteous is a tree of life, and the one who is wise saves lives.

Proverbs 12:26
The righteous choose their friends carefully, but the way of the wicked leads them astray.

Proverbs 13:5
The righteous hate what is false, but the wicked make themselves a stench and bring shame on themselves.

Proverbs 14:32
When calamity comes, the wicked are brought down, but even in death the righteous seek refuge in God.

Proverbs 14:34
Righteousness exalts a nation, but sin condemns any people.

Proverbs 15:28
The heart of the righteous weighs its answers, but the mouth of the wicked gushes evil.

Proverbs 16:12
Kings detest wrongdoing, for a throne is established through righteousness.

Proverbs 16:31
Gray hair is a crown of splendor; it is attained in the way of righteousness.

Proverbs 18:10
The name of the LORD is a fortified tower; the righteous run to it and are safe.

Proverbs 21:21
Whoever pursues righteousness and love finds life, prosperity, and honor.

Proverbs 28:1
The wicked flee though no one pursues, but the righteous are as bold as a lion.

Proverbs 29:7
The righteous care about justice for the poor, but the wicked have no such concern . . .

If righteousness is the output of wisdom, then action is the key to righteousness. God works through us. We need wisdom to know what to do (or not to do) and the courage to act on it and follow through.

Knowing what is right is not doing what is right. Knowledge without application is useless. As James wrote:

> [23] *Anyone who listens to the word but does not do what it says is like someone who looks at his face in a mirror* [24] *and, after looking at himself, goes away and immediately forgets what he looks like.*
> **James 1:23–24**

Solomon asked for wisdom to do his job (1 Kings ch 3). He didn't ask for God to do his job for him:

> *So give your servant a discerning heart to govern your people and to distinguish between right and wrong. For who is able to govern this great people of yours?"*
> **1 Kings 3:9**

It's the same with you. You have asked for wisdom, which comes from the fear of the Lord. Now it is time for you to discern and distinguish between right and wrong, action and inaction with these scriptures on your heart, in your head, and through your company.

Application: Have You Seen a Yellow Jeep?

"Have you seen a yellow jeep lately?"

What a weird question. This came from a friend, mentor, and sometimes coach of mine Ace Wagner.

With a quizzical look, and not quite sure where he was going I (Dan) said, "No."

"OK, text me when you see one."

And then he was silent. I'm thinking, really? That's it? You're not going to explain it? Uh … OK. But knowing him, there is a pony in there somewhere so I let it lie.

I leave our morning coffee and go on about my day. I'm heading to lunch with a client and low and behold, what do I see going into the restaurant but this yellow jeep parked out front. You've got to be kidding me. Not two hours after his creepy "text me when you see it" I see one. So I text him.

"Seen it. Now what?"

"Call me."

After lunch I do. Here's his explanation.

"Have you ever been looking for a car to buy and all of the sudden you see it everywhere?"

"Funny, I hadn't thought about it in that way, but yes."

This is the power of your subconscious. You've seen yellow jeeps everywhere all the time before now. It wasn't until I asked you to be aware that your subconscious started working on noticing the yellow jeep.

Makes sense. So … what?

What is your yellow jeep for the week?

Ah, now I got it, and here's what I learned.

Be Intentionally Aware to Take Action

The world is throwing as much at you as it possibly can in terms of information and messages. In order for your brain to cope, it has to filter most of it out. You have process, habit, and patterns that allow you to function without much thought (think driving or taking a shower).

With focus and attention, you can raise your awareness for all kinds of things. The "yellow jeep" exercise shows that YOU can intentionally decide what is important and therefore notice people, events, and things that were previously "hidden."

This happens all the time with goals. You set a goal, you focus on it, you achieve it. You want to find a new project manager for this open spot in your organization. You start looking and listening for opportunities to find that person. That person has become a yellow jeep.

I have found that yellow jeep-ing is powerful when you use it as a tool for awareness to help you identify opportunities to take action.

If you are going to use anything you've learned in this book, you need to be aware of the opportunities. How will you notice, stop, think, discern, communicate, and then act? You can't keep everything a priority, so you need to decide what is most important right now and then a way to trigger that awareness.

What should your yellow jeep be this month? What is one thing you can look for that will be positive for your employees, your company, and at home? Write it down, choose it with your team, and be ready to see it everywhere, and take action.

See a yellow jeep? Text us the pic to 913-735-0194.

Chapter 41

GOTCHAS AND WARNINGS

There is a foolish corner in the brain of the wisest man.
—Aristotle

My line of work is interesting. When I (Dan) consistently talk to business owners and CEOs month after month, getting deep into issues and working through situations, challenges, and opportunities, I see trends and themes. One of those themes involves common mistakes that are made over and over.

As I was doing the research and reading for this book, I also found that Solomon made many of those same mistakes. So if the wisest, richest man ever made them, then this list should be an assessment you make with annual frequency. These warnings and gotchas are broad and overarching and will help you finish well.

The One

We are all broken at the foot of the cross. That brokenness gives the enemy opportunity to turn you from your mission and make you stray from your vision. Many leaders have "the one." This is the one big weakness that can seal your downfall. David and Solomon both had women as their weakness. David with his adultery with Bathsheba. Solomon with his many wives.

If you are not familiar with Solomon's story, check out 1 Kings 11. He married wives from tribes that the Lord forbade, and over time, he allowed his wives to "turn his heart after other gods." We all make mistakes, errors, and just do things that are wrong. David was a man after God's heart. He had similar issues to Solomon, so what gives?

The difference between the two was repentance. David was repentant of his sin. His heart was for the Lord. Solomon's fear of the Lord waned, and so the Lord took his kingdom away from Solomon's son, leaving him just one tribe out of the entire kingdom.

The comparison of those two stories is a warning and an example of what can happen to you when you turn your heart away from God. We sin; we're all sinners. But sinners repent, that is rethink, and turn back to the Lord. Solomon got comfortable and lazy, and it was easier to please his wives than to honor the Lord.

With the wealth and freedom that owning and running a company gives you, there is an opportunity for the same thing to happen to you. Guard your heart against this and be alert. The hardest person to manage is yourself. You need to do it well.

What is your one? What could be the one thing that takes down your defenses and lulls you into sleep toward the Lord? How can you guard your heart against it?

The over problem

> [16] *Do not be overrighteous, neither be overwise—why destroy yourself?* [17] *Do not be overwicked, and do not be a fool—why die before your time?* [18] *It is good to grasp the one and not let go of the other. Whoever fears God will avoid all extremes.*
> ### Ecclesiastes 7:16–18

You are already the expert in your company. You have built a wealth of experience and are in the position you are in for a reason. It becomes easy to think you know it all, have seen it all, and therefore are the wisest. The two worst offenders in the over problem are the overwise and the overrighteous. The overwise know it all and have nothing left to learn. They rely on no one else and lead with a command mentality.

The overrighteous are legalistic, especially when it comes to religious practices. They know more, interpret it more correctly, worship harder, and love the Lord more than you—and they let you know it too. Their way is right, yours is wrong (or less right than theirs). These are the Pharisees of today. Rules over relationship and lots of judging. So heavenly minded that they are no earthly good.

Don't be either of these. Seriously, just stop it.

Peace is Important

Peace is important in God's work. Many times, the answer lies in knowing that peace is preferred to war. That isn't to say there isn't a time for war, anger, etc. But usually there is a path to peace for you to listen to and discern.

Wisdom ≠ Success

Finally, and this is the one that is hardest to take. Just because you make wise choices doesn't mean the world will bend to your will and you will enjoy the fruits of it. You can do the wise thing and lose. You can do the wise thing and not get justice. The world isn't perfect—even in wisdom.

But it's all about your perspective. When you have an eternal perspective and make wise choices that honor God, you know that your reward may not be today or even in this life. But you will receive your reward.

The Conclusion of the Matter:
The Narrow Gate

[13] Enter through the narrow gate. For wide is the gate and broad is the road that leads to destruction, and many enter through it. [14] But small is the gate and narrow the road that leads to life, and only a few find it.

Matthew 7:13–14

Jesus is the narrow gate. Many of us try to find salvation other ways, but he is the only way. I used to think that choosing the narrow gate was a one-time thing. In one way, it is. Accepting Christ is the narrow gate we choose at the point of salvation. Looked at another way, however, you are presented with the narrow gate all day every day through the decisions, situations, opportunities, and challenges presented to you.

How often is it easier to take the broad path? How many times do you choose the narrow gate? Christ's way, the wise way, is the narrow gate. You need to strive to take it. Doing so requires work, intentionality, effort, consistency, community, and faith. It is a journey not a destination.

Wisdom helps you know where to find the narrow gate and then act to walk through it.

I (Dan) started on the broad path. It was easy and helped me get what I wanted. I chose to cheat to save $5,000. Now, I try to choose the narrow gate at all times. It's not easy. I don't succeed all the time, but I try to do it anyway.

Mother Theresa has a great poem that sums up the narrow gate mentality perfectly.

Do it anyway

People are often unreasonable, illogical and self-centered;
Forgive them anyway.

If you are kind, people may accuse you of selfish, ulterior motives;
Be kind anyway.

If you are successful, you will win some false friends
and some true enemies;
Succeed anyway.

If you are honest and frank, people may cheat you;
Be honest and frank anyway.

What you spend years building, some could destroy overnight;
Build anyway.

If you find serenity and happiness, they may be jealous;
Be happy anyway.

The good you do today, people will often forget tomorrow;
Do good anyway.

Give the world the best you have, and it may never be enough;
Give the world the best you've got anyway.

You see, in the final analysis, it is between you and God;
It was never between you and them anyway.

Amen!

One More Thing

I (Dan) love books. Books have been a driving force of ideas, change, and reflection in my leadership, my business, my family, and my life.

It was a book that was the jumping off point for my renewed relationship with Jesus. It wasn't the Bible but a book about rediscovery. I had to rediscover my faith and find a new relationship with God, Jesus, and the Holy Spirit.

It's easier to be the weird uncle in print. I don't have to stare back at you in the restaurant and wonder what you are thinking or if we'll ever talk again. Here's a weird uncle moment.

If you are reading this page, and something in this book spoke to you and you don't know what to really think about Jesus, faith, God, the Holy Spirit, can I ask you a question? Do you want to know Jesus personally?

Paul wrote in Romans:

[9] *If you declare with your mouth, "Jesus is Lord," and believe in your heart that God raised him from the dead, you will be saved.* [10] *For it is with your heart that you believe and are justified, and it is with your mouth that you profess your faith and are saved.*
Romans 10:9

You don't have to know it all, be a Bible scholar, believe everything or all of "it." You just have to start somewhere. So start at the beginning. Say "Yes" to a relationship or a renewed relationship with Jesus. How? A simple prayer.

Literally just say this prayer out loud as you read it.

"Jesus, I declare with my mouth right now that you are my Lord and Savior. I don't fully understand or comprehend what that means, but I want you to be Lord of my life. I believe in my heart that God raised you from the dead and because of your victory over death, I too can have victory over sin in my life. Thank you for this gift of eternal life that is not something I can earn but simply receive. Thank you, Jesus. Amen."

Pretty cool, huh? Now the fun part. Go share what just happened with someone! Your spouse, a friend, mentor, priest, pastor. You knocked, the door is open, now you need community and guidance. Find a circle. Plug in.

Don't know where to start? Here are some resources for you to kick things off.

www.alpha.org/try: A training curriculum run in cities across the globe answering the most basic questions of faith.

www.church.org: Find a church near you.

NOTES

Introduction: The Why
1. Shane Parrish, *Mental Models: The Best Way to Make Intelligent Decisions (109 Models Explained)*, https://fs.blog/mental-models/
2. Dale Carnegie, *How to Win Friends and Influence People*, reissued edition (New York: Gallery Books, 1998), 14

Chapter 3: The Beginning of Wisdom: Do I (Really) Believe?
1. Donald S. Whitney, *Praying the Bible*, (Illinois: Crossway, 2015).
2. Chapter 4: The Value of Wisdom
3. Benjamin Franklinn, Poor Richards Almanac, (New York: H.M. Caldwell Co, 1900).

Chapter 7: The King, the Shepherd, and the Ruler
4. Mark Sanborn, *The Potential Principle: A Proven System for Closing the Gap Between How Good You Are and How Good You Could Be*, (Tennessee: Thomas Nelson, 2017)

Chapter 8: Who Are Your Prophets?
1. Ken Blanchard and Phil Hodges, *The Servant Leader: Transforming Your Heart, Head, Hands, and Habits*, (Tennessee: Thomas Nelson, 2003)

Chapter 9: Planning: Useless and Indispensable
1. Jeff Spadafora, *The Joy Model: A Step-by-Step Guide to Peace, Purpose, and Balance*, (Tennessee: Thomas Nelson, 2016)
2. Eric Ries, *The Lean Startup: How Today's Entrepreneurs Use Continuous Innovation to Create Radically Successful Businesses*, (New York: Crown Business, 2011)

Chapter 11: Prudence is Sexy
1. "Prudence." Merriam-Webster.com 2018. https://www.merriam-webster.com (15 June 2018)
2. *The Matrix*, directed by Andy Wachowski, Larry Wachowski (1999; Hollywood: Warner Home Video, Warner Bros.)
3. Suzy Welch, *10-10-10: 10 Minutes, 10 Month, 10 Years: A Life Transforming Idea,* (New York: Scribner, 2009)

Chapter 12: Recognition and Celebration
1. Bob Chapman, Raj Sisodia, *Everybody Matter: The Extraordinary Power of Caring for Your People Like Family,* (New York: Portfolio, 2015)

Chapter 13: Your Business Marriage
1. Adam Bryant, "What If You Had to Write a "User Manual" About Your Leadership Style? *Linkedin.com*, January 6th, 2014, accessed August 1st 2018, https://www.linkedin.com/pulse/20140106124338-35894743-what-if-you-had-to-write-a-user-manual-about-your-leadership-style/
2. Abby Falik, "Leaders need "User Manuals" – and what I learned by writing mine, *Linkedin.com, July 27th, 2017, accessed August 1st 2018,* https://www.linkedin.com/pulse/leaders-need-user-manuals-what-i-learned-writing-mine-abby-falik/

Chapter 14: Adultery
1. *The Big Sick*, directed by Michael Showalter, (2017: Los Angeles, Amazon Studios)

Chapter 18: Better a Little—The Deceitfulness of Wealth
1. *Davos 2017 Global Wage Calculator: Find out how your wage compares to the average in your country, then see where you sit Globally*, CNN.com, accessed August 5th 2018, https://money.cnn.com/interactive/news/economy/davos/global-wage-calculator/index.html
2. C.S. Lewis, *The Screwtape Letters*, reprint edition. (New York: HarperOne, 2015)

3. Greg McKeown, *Essentialism: The Disciplined Pursuit of Less,* (New York: Crown Business, 2014)
4. Stanford Graduate School of Business. February 10, 2014. Greg McKeown: Essentialism—The Disciplined Pursuit of Less [Video file] Retrieved from https://www.youtube.com/watch?v=T9x6D09AKBU GuzerVideo. March 14, 2008. Marriage Proposal Rejected at Basketball game [Video file] https://youtu.be/UtPkxzHKLpk

Chapter 19: Just Right

1. Murray T.D., (2016, January 15), *Why do 70 percent of lottery winners end up bankrupt?,* http://www.cleveland.com/business/index.ssf/2016/01/why_do_70_percent_of_lottery_w.html
2. Wikipedia contributors. (2018, October 25). Goldilocks principle. In *Wikipedia, The Free Encyclopedia.* Retrieved 21:31, December 8, 2018, from https://en.wikipedia.org/w/index.php?title=Goldilocks_principle&oldid=865670408

Chapter 20: Debt Philosophy

1. 1969 October 5, The Seattle Times (Seattle Daily Times), Odd Parcels by Alf Collins, Quote Page A-4, Column 1, Seattle, Washington. (GenealogyBank)

Chapter 21: The Generosity Test

1. David Green, Bill High, *Giving it All Away, And Getting it All Back Again: The Way of Living Generously,* (Grand Rapids: Zondervan, 2017)

Chapter 23: Pride vs. Humility

1. Daniel Burke, Fr. John Bartunek, *Navigating the Interior Life: Spiritual Direction and the Journey to God,* (Stubenville, OH, Emmaus Road Publishing, 2012), 70–72
2. Val, D.M., Litany of Humilty, retrieved from https://www.ewtn.com/devotionals/prayers/humility.htm

Chapter 26: Know When to Shut Up
1. Michael Bungay Stanier, *The Coaching Habit: Say Less, Ask More & Change the Way You Lead Forever,* Toronto: Box of Crayons Press, 2016)

Part 7: Don't be Evil (or Stupid)
1. Jena McGregor, (February 4, 2014) *Ethical Misconduct, by the numbers,* https://www.washingtonpost.com/news/on-leadership/wp/2014/02/04/ethical-misconduct-by-the-numbers/?utm_term=.e7e69b681001

Part 8: Barriers to Success
1. John Doe. July 5, 2012 10. Brian Regan—Me Monster [Video file] Retrieved from https://www.youtube.com/watch?v=vymaDgJ7KLg

Chapter 32: Anger and Temper
1. CAASpeakers. August 28, 2014. CAA Speakers—Rorke Denver [Video file] Retrieved from https://www.youtube.com/watch?v=xaxroF9yEH0

Chapter 33: Revenge
1. *The Princess Bride*, directed by Rob Reiner, (1987: Hollywood, MGM)

Chapter 34: Envy
1. Jordan B. Peterson, *12 Rules for Life: An Antidote to Chaos,* (Ontario: Random House Canada, 2018), 85, 96

Chapter 35: Hedonism Overboard
1. Cal Newport, *Deep Work: Rules for Focused Success in a Distracted World,* (New York: Grand Central Publishing, 2016), 3

Chapter 36: Temptation
1. *Contract to Give up,* retrieved at: https://www.killthecan.org/facts-figures/contract-to-give-up/

2. Walter Mischel, *The Marshmallow Test: Why Self Control is the Engine of Success,* (New York: Little, Brown and Company, 2014)

Chapter 40: Righteousness: The Output of Wisdom
1. Ace Wagner: http://acewagnerco.com

ACKNOWLEDGMENTS

A book starts as an idea and becomes a labor of love which then turns into a hard grind to the end. Here's to all the people who helped us grind.

I want to thank my (Dan) wife, Ali, and kids Owen, Josie, and Ben for putting up with the early mornings, late nights and helping me persevere through countless listening sessions while I verbally vomited everywhere. I love you first, team.

I (Drew) also want to thank my wife, Sarah, for her sacrificial love, service, support and devotion as a wife and mother to our four young adult children and their growing families (Jesse + wife Ty; Caleb + wife Paige; Jared and Rachel).

To the Premier team who were catalysts to get this project off the ground and test many of the ideas real time that are now in this book. With a special thanks to Dusty Clevenger, Travis Carpenter, Ricky Paradise, Trace Thurlby, Kevin Tews, Chris Ballard, Scott Clark, Jacqueline Doherty, Jason Doll, Lauren Vohland, Brent Blacklock, and Tim James.

Thank you to all the Acumen Partners and Teams who helped us flesh out the ideas and added stories and flavor to this book especially Velocity, Triumph, Pioneer, Accel, Ignite, and Ascend.

To those early readers and feedback givers that helped shape the entire book especially Andrew Stafford, Core Group, Jon Bachura, and the entire Cooper clan.

To those who offered their insights, wisdom, expertise, and advice on how to go about writing, editing, and publishing especially Ken Cooper, Bill High, Jeff Spadafora, Joe Calhoon, and Brian Phipps.

To the editing, design teams, and people behind the curtain: Mike Loomis, and that guy that we cannot name.

DAN COOPER

Dan Cooper co-founded ej4, a video-based online training company, in 2003, and was its CEO until selling in 2012. During his time with ej4, he grew the company from a startup to a nationally-recognized firm, serving Fortune 500 clients. As of the 2012, ej4 was serving 1,000+ customers, delivering millions of program views, was highly profitable and debt-free.

Dan took his leadership and technology experience to work on and in the Sparklab startup business accelerator as well as lead change management and profit building initiatives for mid-market companies.

Today, he is the President and partner of Acumen, an accelerator community experience built for CEOs and Owners of strong and growing companies. Dan is also a certified Executive Coach credentialed through the International Coaching Federation.

He and his wife, Ali, have been married for 19 years, have three children and attend Cure of Ars church in Leawood, KS. Dan enjoys all things soccer, snowboarding, and burning meat on the backyard barbecue grill.

DREW HISS

Drew Hiss launched his outsourced payroll and HR technology solutions company, Checkdate Solutions, in 1994. The entrepreneurial venture was a classic bootstrap start-up whose launch plan underestimated capital needs and ramp up time by significant multiples. The adventure predictably included scrapping for cash, overhauling the business model, rebranding, refocusing, redirecting resources, shifting tech platforms, praying, seeking counsel and wisdom, etc.. Not surprisingly, deep entrepreneurial scar tissue was forged. Ultimately Checkdate Solutions became one of Kansas City's fastest growing companies and was named one of the Greater KC Chamber of Commerce Best Businesses not once, but twice. Additionally, Checkdate Solutions ranked as one of KC's top 100 fastest growing companies for nine consecutive years and was in the top 25 nationally in its industry.

Today's workplace culture tends to compartmentalize personal virtues from commerce, creating silos and compartmentalization between business, family, community, values and faith. But as a CEO, Drew and his company grew when he "decompartmentalized:" on his journey, he learned to integrate his life of commerce and his life of family, faith and values.

Drew merged Checkdate Solutions with payroll industry leader Paycor, stepping away from the company in 2008 and serving on its board for eight years. Drew remains an owner in the firm. Today, Drew's heart to help business owners leverage the influence of their business platform for eternal impact is at the core of Acumen which he founded late in 2015. Acumen is a catalytic iron-sharpening-iron environment forged from the fiery furnace of entrepreneurial battle, marketplace survival and integration of the timeless wisdom of the ages.

Drew and his wife, Sarah have been married for 30 years and have four children (plus two beautiful daughters in law) ranging in age from 25 to 20. He is a raving distance congregant of Flatirons Community Church in Lafayette, CO. Drew enjoys snowboarding, hunting, cycling, hiking and a variety of outdoor activities and adventures including running with his three dogs.

Business is an adventure

Join us for council, coaching, and community to sharpen your edge.
www.AcumenImpact.com

Sharpen Verse Index

Table of Contents

SHARPEN VERSE INDEX

PART 1: GETTING WISDOM

James 1:5

If any of you lacks wisdom, he should ask God, who gives generously to all without finding fault, and it will be given to him.

Chapter 1: Wisdom's Origin and Birth

James 3:17

But the wisdom that comes from heaven is first of all pure; then peace-loving, considerate, submissive, full of mercy and good fruit, impartial, and sincere.

Proverbs 8:22–31

22 The LORD brought me forth as the first of his works, before his deeds of old; 23 I was formed long ages ago, at the very beginning, when the world came to be. 24 When there were no watery depths, I was given birth, when there were no springs overflowing with water; 25 before the mountains were settled in place, before the hills, I was given birth, 26 before he made the world or its fields or any of the dust of the earth. 27 I was there when he set the heavens in place, when he marked out the horizon on the face of the deep, 28 when he established the clouds above and fixed securely the fountains of the deep, 29 when he gave the sea its boundary so the waters would not overstep his command, and when he marked out the foundations of the earth. 30 Then I was constantly at his side. I was filled with delight day after day, rejoicing always in his presence, 31 rejoicing in his whole world and delighting in mankind.

Chapter 2: The Case for Wisdom

Proverbs 1:20–33

20 Out in the open wisdom calls aloud, she raises her voice in the public square; 21 on top of the wall she cries out, at the city gate she

makes her speech: 22 "How long will you who are simple love your simple ways? How long will mockers delight in mockery and fools hate knowledge? 23 Repent at my rebuke! Then I will pour out my thoughts to you, I will make known to you my teachings. 24 But since you refuse to listen when I call and no one pays attention when I stretch out my hand, 25 since you disregard all my advice and do not accept my rebuke, 26 I in turn will laugh when disaster strikes you; I will mock when calamity overtakes you—27 when calamity overtakes you like a storm, when disaster sweeps over you like a whirlwind, when distress and trouble overwhelm you. 28 "Then they will call to me but I will not answer; they will look for me but will not find me, 29 since they hated knowledge and did not choose to fear the LORD. 30 Since they would not accept my advice and spurned my rebuke, 31 they will eat the fruit of their ways and be filled with the fruit of their schemes. 32 For the waywardness of the simple will kill them, and the complacency of fools will destroy them; 33 but whoever listens to me will live in safety and be at ease, without fear of harm."

Chapter 3: The Beginning of Wisdom: Do I (really) Believe
Proverbs 1:1–7

1 The proverbs of Solomon son of David, king of Israel: 2 for gaining wisdom and instruction; for understanding words of insight; 3 for receiving instruction in prudent behavior, doing what is right and just and fair; 4 for giving prudence to those who are simple, knowledge and discretion to the young—5 let the wise listen and add to their learning, and let the discerning get guidance—6 for understanding proverbs and parables, the sayings and riddles of the wise. 7 The fear of the LORD is the beginning of knowledge, but fools despise wisdom and instruction.
Proverbs 8:13

13 To fear the LORD is to hate evil; I hate pride and arrogance, evil behavior, and perverse speech.

Proverbs 10:27
27 The fear of the LORD adds length to life, but the years of the wicked are cut short.

Proverbs 14:13, 26–27
13 Even in laughter the heart may ache, and rejoicing may end in grief. 26 Whoever fears the LORD has a secure fortress, and for their children it will be a refuge. 27 The fear of the LORD is a fountain of life, turning a person from the snares of death.

Proverbs 15:11
11 Death and Destruction lie open before the LORD— how much more do human hearts!

Proverbs 16:6–7
6 Through love and faithfulness sin is atoned for; through the fear of the LORD evil is avoided. 7 When the LORD takes pleasure in anyone's way, he causes their enemies to make peace with them.

Proverbs 19:23
23 The fear of the LORD leads to life; then one rests content, untouched by trouble.

Proverbs 24:21–22
21 Fear the LORD and the king, my son, and do not join with rebellious officials, 22 for those two will send sudden destruction on them, and who knows what calamities they can bring?

Proverbs 25:1–2

1 These are more proverbs of Solomon, compiled by the men of Hezekiah king of Judah: 2 It is the glory of God to conceal a matter; to search out a matter is the glory of kings.

Proverbs 28:14

14 Blessed is the one who always trembles before God, but whoever hardens their heart falls into trouble.

Proverbs 29:13

13 The poor and the oppressor have this in common: The LORD gives sight to the eyes of both.

Proverbs 30:1–5, 18–19

1 The sayings of Agur son of Jakeh—an inspired utterance. This man's utterance to Ithiel: "I am weary, God, but I can prevail. 2 Surely I am only a brute, not a man; I do not have human understanding. 3 I have not learned wisdom, nor have I attained to the knowledge of the Holy One. 4 Who has gone up to heaven and come down? Whose hands have gathered up the wind? Who has wrapped up the waters in a cloak? Who has established all the ends of the earth? What is his name, and what is the name of his son? Surely you know! 5 "Every word of God is flawless; he is a shield to those who take refuge in him. 6 Do not add to his words, or he will rebuke you and prove you a liar.

18 There are three things that are too amazing for me, four that I do not understand: 19 the way of an eagle in the sky, the way of a snake on a rock, the way of a ship on the high seas, and the way of a man with a young woman.

Chapter 4: The Value of Wisdom

Proverbs 3:1–2

1 My son, do not forget my teaching, but keep my commands in your heart, 2 for they will prolong your life many years and bring you peace and prosperity.

Proverbs 3:13–24

13 Blessed are those who find wisdom, those who gain under-standing, 14 for she is more profitable than silver and yields better returns than gold. 15 She is more precious than rubies; nothing you desire can compare with her. 16 Long life is in her right hand; in her left hand are riches and honor. 17 Her ways are pleasant ways, and all her paths are peace. 18 She is a tree of life to those who take hold of her; those who hold her fast will be blessed. 19 By wisdom the LORD laid the earth's foundations, by understanding he set the heavens in place; 20 by his knowledge the watery depths were divided, and the clouds let drop the dew. 21 My son, do not let wisdom and understanding out of your sight, preserve sound judgment and discretion; 22 they will be life for you, an ornament to grace your neck. 23 Then you will go on your way in safety, and your foot will not stumble. 24 When you lie down, you will not be afraid; when you lie down, your sleep will be sweet.

Proverbs 9:10–12

10 The fear of the LORD is the beginning of wisdom, and knowledge of the Holy One is understanding. 11 For through wisdom your days will be many, and years will be added to your life. 12 If you are wise, your wisdom will reward you; if you are a mocker, you alone will suffer.

Proverbs 12:8

8 A person is praised according to their wisdom, and one with a warped mind is despised.

Proverbs 24:3–4, 13–14

3 By wisdom a house is built, and through understanding it is estab-lished; 4 through knowledge its rooms are filled with rare and beautiful treasures.

13 Eat honey, my son, for it is good; honey from the comb is sweet to your taste. 14 Know also that wisdom is like honey for you: If you find it, there is a future hope for you, and your hope will not be cut off.

Ecclesiastes 5:8–20

10 Whoever loves money never has enough; whoever loves wealth is never satisfied with their income. This too is meaningless. 11 As goods increase, so do those who consume them. And what benefit are they to the owners except to feast their eyes on them? 12 The sleep of a laborer is sweet, whether they eat little or much, but as for the rich, their abundance permits them no sleep.

Chapter 5: Walking with Wisdom
Proverbs 2:1–22

1 My son, if you accept my words and store up my commands within you, 2 turning your ear to wisdom and applying your heart to understanding—3 indeed, if you call out for insight and cry aloud for understanding, 4 and if you look for it as for silver and search for it as for hidden treasure, 5 then you will understand the fear of the LORD and find the knowledge of God. 6 For the LORD gives wisdom; from his mouth come knowledge and understanding. 7 He holds success in store for the upright, he is a shield to those whose walk is blameless, 8 for he guards the course of the just and protects the way of his faithful ones. 9 Then you will understand what is right and just and fair—every good path. 10 For wisdom will enter your heart, and knowledge will be pleasant to your soul. 11 Discretion will protect you, and understanding will guard you. 12 Wisdom will save you from the ways of wicked men, from men whose words are perverse, 13 who have left the straight paths to walk in dark ways, 14 who delight in doing wrong and rejoice in the perverseness of evil, 15 whose paths are crooked and who are devious in their ways. 16 Wisdom will save you also from the adulterous woman, from the wayward woman with her seductive words, 17 who has left the partner of her youth and ignored the covenant she made before God. 18 Surely her house leads down to death and her paths to the spirits of the dead. 19 None who go to her return or attain the paths of life. 20 Thus you will walk in the ways of the good and keep to the paths of the righteous. 21 For the upright will live in the land, and the blameless will remain in it; 22 but the wicked will be cut off from the land, and the unfaithful will be torn from it.

Matthew 7:7–8
Ask and it will be given to you; seek and you will find; knock and the door will be opened to you. For everyone who asks receives; he who seeks finds; and to him who knocks, the door will be opened.

Chapter 6: Keeping Wisdom
Joshua 1:8
Do not let this Book of the Law depart from your mouth; meditate on it day and night, so that you may be careful to do everything written in it. Then you will be prosperous and successful.

Proverbs 4:5–13
5 Get wisdom, get understanding; do not forget my words or turn away from them. 6 Do not forsake wisdom, and she will protect you; love her, and she will watch over you. 7 The beginning of wisdom is this: Get wisdom. Though it cost all you have, get understanding. 8 Cherish her, and she will exalt you; embrace her, and she will honor you. 9 She will give you a garland to grace your head and present you with a glorious crown. 10 Listen, my son, accept what I say, and the years of your life will be many. 11 I instruct you in the way of wisdom and lead you along straight paths. 12 When you walk, your steps will not be hampered; when you run, you will not stumble. 13 Hold on to instruction, do not let it go; guard it well, for it is your life.

Proverbs 4:20–23
20 My son, pay attention to what I say; turn your ear to my words. 21 Do not let them out of your sight, keep them within your heart; 22 for they are life to those who find them and health to one's whole body. 23 Above all else, guard your heart, for everything you do flows from it.

Proverbs 8:1–21, 32–36
1 Does not wisdom call out? Does not understanding raise her voice? 2 At the highest point along the way, where the paths meet, she takes her stand; 3 beside the gate leading into the city, at the entrance,

she cries aloud: 4 "To you, O people, I call out; I raise my voice to all mankind. 5 You who are simple, gain prudence; you who are foolish, set your hearts on it. 6 Listen, for I have trustworthy things to say; I open my lips to speak what is right. 7 My mouth speaks what is true, for my lips detest wickedness. 8 All the words of my mouth are just; none of them is crooked or perverse. 9 To the discerning all of them are right; they are upright to those who have found knowledge. 10 Choose my instruction instead of silver, knowledge rather than choice gold, 11 for wisdom is more precious than rubies, and nothing you desire can compare with her. 12 "I, wisdom, dwell together with prudence; I possess knowledge and discretion. 13 To fear the LORD is to hate evil; I hate pride and arrogance, evil behavior and perverse speech. 14 Counsel and sound judgment are mine; I have insight, I have power. 15 By me kings reign and rulers issue decrees that are just; 16 by me princes govern, and nobles—all who rule on earth. 17 I love those who love me, and those who seek me find me. 18 With me are riches and honor, enduring wealth and prosperity. 19 My fruit is better than fine gold; what I yield surpasses choice silver. 20 I walk in the way of righteousness, along the paths of justice, 21 bestowing a rich inheritance on those who love me and making their treasuries full."

32 Now then, my children, listen to me; blessed are those who keep my ways. 33 Listen to my instruction and be wise; do not disregard it. 34 Blessed are those who listen to me, watching daily at my doors, waiting at my doorway. 35 For those who find me find life and receive favor from the LORD. 36 But those who fail to find me harm themselves; all who hate me love death.

Proverbs 9:1–6, 13–18

1 Wisdom has built her house; she has set up its seven pillars. 2 She has prepared her meat and mixed her wine; she has also set her table. 3 She has sent out her servants, and she calls from the highest point of the city, 4 "Let all who are simple come to my house!" To those who have no sense she says, 5 "Come, eat my food and drink the wine I have

mixed. 6 Leave your simple ways and you will live; walk in the way of insight."

13 Folly is an unruly woman; she is simple and knows nothing. 14 She sits at the door of her house, on a seat at the highest point of the city, 15 calling out to those who pass by, who go straight on their way, 16 "Let all who are simple come to my house!" To those who have no sense she says,17 "Stolen water is sweet; food eaten in secret is delicious!" 18 But little do they know that the dead are there, that her guests are deep in the realm of the dead.

Proverbs 16:16
16 How much better to get wisdom than gold, to get insight rather than silver!

Proverbs 19:8
8 The one who gets wisdom loves his own soul; the one who cherishes understanding prospers.

PART 2: LEADERS LEAD. GET ON WITH IT.
Chapter 7: The King, The Shepherd, and The Ruler
Luke 12:48
Everyone who has been given much, much will be demanded; and from the one who has been entrusted with much, much more will be asked.

Proverbs 14:35
35 A king delights in a wise servant, but a shameful servant arouses his fury.

Proverbs 16:10, 14–15
10 The lips of a king speak as an oracle, and his mouth does not betray justice.
14 A king's wrath is a messenger of death, but the wise will appease it. 15 When a king's face brightens, it means life; his favor is like a rain cloud in spring.

Proverbs 19: 6, 12

6 Many curry favor with a ruler, and everyone is the friend of one who gives gifts.

12 A king's rage is like the roar of a lion, but his favor is like dew on the grass.

Proverbs 20:2, 8, 26, 28

2 A king's wrath strikes terror like the roar of a lion; those who anger him forfeit their lives.

8 When a king sits on his throne to judge, he winnows out all evil with his eyes.

26 A wise king winnows out the wicked; he drives the threshing wheel over them.

28 Love and faithfulness keep a king safe; through love his throne is made secure.

Proverbs 25:3

3 As the heavens are high and the earth is deep, so the hearts of kings are unsearchable.

Proverbs: 28:2–3, 10, 12, 15, 16, 28

2 When a country is rebellious, it has many rulers, but a ruler with discernment and knowledge maintains order. 3 A ruler who oppresses the poor is like a driving rain that leaves no crops.

10 Whoever leads the upright along an evil path will fall into their own trap, but the blameless will receive a good inheritance.

12 When the righteous triumph, there is great elation; but when the wicked rise to power, people go into hiding.

15 Like a roaring lion or a charging bear is a wicked ruler over a helpless people.

16 A tyrannical ruler practices extortion, but one who hates ill-gotten gain will enjoy a long reign.

28 When the wicked rise to power, people go into hiding; but when the wicked perish, the righteous thrive.

Proverbs 29:2, 12, 14

2 When the righteous thrive, the people rejoice; when the wicked rule, the people groan.

12 If a ruler listens to lies, all his officials become wicked.

14 If a king judges the poor with fairness, his throne will be established forever.

Proverbs 30:29–31

29 There are three things that are stately in their stride, four that move with stately bearing: 30 a lion, mighty among beasts, who retreats before nothing; 31 a strutting rooster, a he-goat, and a king secure against revolt.

Chapter 8: Who are your prophets?

Proverbs 11:14

14 For lack of guidance a nation falls, but victory is won through many advisers.

Proverbs 12:15

15 The way of fools seems right to them, but the wise listen to advice.

Proverbs 14:28

28 A large population is a king's glory, but without subjects a prince is ruined.

Proverbs 15:22

22 Plans fail for lack of counsel, but with many advisers they succeed

Proverbs 19:20

20 Listen to advice and accept instruction, and at the end you will be counted among the wise.

Proverbs 20:5, 18

5 The purposes of a person's heart are deep waters, but a man of understanding draws them out.

18 Make plans by seeking advice; if you wage war, obtain guidance.

Proverbs 22:17–21

17 Pay attention and turn your ear to the sayings of the wise; apply your heart to what I teach, 18 for it is pleasing when you keep them in your heart and have all of them ready on your lips. 19 So that your trust may be in the LORD, I teach you today, even you. 20 Have I not written thirty sayings for you, sayings of counsel and knowledge, 21 teaching you to be honest and to speak the truth, so that you bring back truthful reports to those you serve?

Proverbs 23:9

9 Do not speak to fools, for they will scorn your prudent words.

Proverbs 24:5–6

5 The wise prevail through great power, and those who have knowledge muster their strength. 6 Surely you need guidance to wage war, and victory is won through many advisers.

Proverbs 27:17

17 As iron sharpens iron, so one person sharpens another.

Chapter 9: Planning: Useless and Indispensable

James 4:13–16

13 Now listen, you who say, "Today or tomorrow we will go to this or that city, spend a year there, carry on business and make money." 14 Why, you do not even know what will happen tomorrow. What is your life? You are a mist that appears for a little while and then vanishes. 15 Instead, you ought to say, "If it is the Lord's will, we will live and do this or that." 16 As it is, you boast in your arrogant schemes. All such boasting is evil.

Proverbs 14:12
2 There is a way that appears to be right, but in the end it leads to death.

Proverbs 16:1–4, 9, 25, 33
1 To humans belong the plans of the heart, but from the LORD comes the proper answer of the tongue. 2 All a person's ways seem pure to them, but motives are weighed by the LORD. 3 Commit to the LORD whatever you do, and he will establish your plans. 4 The LORD works out everything to its proper end—even the wicked for a day of disaster.
9 In their hearts humans plan their course, but the LORD establishes their steps.
25 There is a way that appears to be right, but in the end it leads to death.
33 The lot is cast into the lap, but its every decision is from the LORD.

Proverbs 16:3
3 The crucible for silver and the furnace for gold, but the LORD tests the heart.

Proverbs 19:21
21 Many are the plans in a person's heart, but it is the LORD's purpose that prevails.

Proverbs 20:24, 27
24 A person's steps are directed by the LORD. How then can anyone understand their own way?
27 The lamp of the LORD searches the spirit of a man; It searches out his inmost being.

Proverbs 21: 1–2, 22, 30–31
1 In the LORD's hand the king's heart is a stream of water that he channels toward all who please him. 2 A person may think their own ways are right, but the LORD weighs the heart.
22 One who is wise can go up against the city of the mighty and pull down the stronghold in which they trust.

30 There is no wisdom, no insight, no plan that can succeed against the LORD. 31 The horse is made ready for the day of battle, but victory rests with the LORD.

Proverbs 24: 27
27 Put your outdoor work in order and get your fields ready; after that, build your house.

Proverbs 27:23-27
23 Be sure you know the condition of your flocks, give careful attention to your herds; 24 for riches do not endure forever, and a crown is not secure for all generations. 25 When the hay is removed and new growth appears and the grass from the hills is gathered in, 26 the lambs will provide you with clothing, and the goats with the price of a field. 27 You will have plenty of goats' milk to feed your family and to nourish your female servants.

Proverbs 29:25
25 Fear of man will prove to be a snare, but whoever trusts in the LORD is kept safe.

Chapter 10: Making Big Decisions
Ecclesiastes 3:1–8
1 There is a time for everything, and a season for every activity under the heavens: 2 a time to be born and a time to die, a time to plant and a time to uproot, 3 a time to kill and a time to heal, a time to tear down and a time to build, 4 a time to weep and a time to laugh, a time to mourn and a time to dance, 5 a time to scatter stones and a time to gather them, a time to embrace and a time to refrain from embracing, 6 a time to search and a time to give up, a time to keep and a time to throw away, 7 a time to tear and a time to mend, a time to be silent and a time to speak, 8 a time to love and a time to hate, a time for war and a time for peace.

Proverbs 10:13, 23

13 Wisdom is found on the lips of the discerning, but a rod is for the back of one who has no sense.

23 A fool finds pleasure in wicked schemes, but a person of understanding delights in wisdom.

Proverbs 14:6–7, 33

6 The mocker seeks wisdom and finds none, but knowledge comes easily to the discerning. 7 Stay away from a fool, for you will not find knowledge on their lips.

33 Wisdom reposes in the heart of the discerning and even among fools she lets herself be known.

Proverbs 15:14, 21

14 The discerning heart seeks knowledge, but the mouth of a fool feeds on folly.

21 Folly brings joy to one who has no sense, but whoever has understanding keeps a straight course.

Proverbs 16:21

21 The wise in heart are called discerning, and gracious words promote instruction.

Proverbs 17:10, 24

10 A rebuke impresses a discerning person more than a hundred lashes a fool.

24 A discerning person keeps wisdom in view, but a fool's eyes wander to the ends of the earth.

Proverbs 20:12

12 Ears that hear and eyes that see—the LORD has made them both.

Proverbs 28:5, 9, 11

5 Evildoers do not understand what is right, but those who seek the LORD understand it fully.

9 If anyone turns a deaf ear to my instruction, even their prayers are detestable. 11 The rich are wise in their own eyes; one who is poor and discerning sees how deluded they are.

Chapter 11: Prudence Is Sexy

Proverbs 12:16, 23

16 Fools show their annoyance at once, but the prudent overlook an insult. 23 The prudent keep their knowledge to themselves, but a fool's heart blurts out folly.

Proverbs 13:16

16 All who are prudent act with knowledge, but fools expose their folly.

Proverbs 14:8, 15, 18

8 The wisdom of the prudent is to give thought to their ways, but the folly of fools is deception.

15 The simple believe anything, but the prudent give thought to their steps. 18 The simple inherit folly, but the prudent are crowned with knowledge.

Proverbs 16:22

22 Prudence is a fountain of life to those who have it, but folly brings punishment to fools.

Proverbs 21:16

16 Whoever strays from the path of prudence comes to rest in the company of the dead.

Proverbs 22:3

3 The prudent see danger and take refuge, but the simple keep going and pay the penalty.

Proverbs 27:12

12 The prudent see danger and take refuge, but the simple keep going and pay the penalty.

Chapter 12: Recognition and Celebration

Proverbs 22:29

29 Do you see someone skilled in their work? They will serve before kings; they will not serve before officials of low rank.

Proverbs: 25:13

13 Like a snow-cooled drink at harvest time is a trustworthy messenger to the one who sends him; he refreshes the spirit of his master.

Proverbs: 27:18

18 The one who guards a fig tree will eat its fruit, and whoever protects their master will be honored.

PART 3: BUILDING KEY RELATIONSHIPS
Chapter 13: Your Business Marriage

Hebrews 11:25

Let us not give up meeting together, as some are in the habit of doing, but let us encourage one another—and all the more as you see the Day approaching.

Proverbs 11:22

22 Like a gold ring in a pig's snout is a beautiful woman who shows no discretion.

Proverbs 12:4

4 A wife of noble character is her husband's crown, but a disgraceful wife is like decay in his bones.

Proverbs 19:14

14 Houses and wealth are inherited from parents, but a prudent wife is from the LORD.

Proverbs 18:22

22 He who finds a wife finds what is good and receives favor from the LORD.

Proverbs 21:9, 19

9 Better to live on a corner of the roof than share a house with a quarrelsome wife.

19 Better to live in a desert than with a quarrelsome and nagging wife.

Proverbs 25:24

24 Better to live on a corner of the roof than share a house with a quarrelsome wife.

Proverbs 27:15–16

15 A quarrelsome wife is like the dripping of a leaky roof in a rainstorm; 16 restraining her is like restraining the wind or grasping oil with the hand.

Proverbs 31:10–31

10 A wife of noble character who can find? She is worth far more than rubies. 11 Her husband has full confidence in her and lacks nothing of value. 12 She brings him good, not harm, all the days of her life. 13 She selects wool and flax and works with eager hands. 14 She is like the merchant ships, bringing her food from afar. 15 She gets up while it is still night; she provides food for her family and portions for her female servants. 16 She considers a field and buys it; out of her earnings she plants a vineyard. 17 She sets about her work vigorously; her arms are strong for her tasks. 18 She sees that her trading is profitable, and her lamp does not go out at night. 19 In her hand she holds the distaff and grasps the spindle with her fingers. 20 She opens her arms to the poor

and extends her hands to the needy. 21 When it snows, she has no fear for her household; for all of them are clothed in scarlet. 22 She makes coverings for her bed; she is clothed in fine linen and purple. 23 Her husband is respected at the city gate, where he takes his seat among the elders of the land. 24 She makes linen garments and sells them, and supplies the merchants with sashes. 25 She is clothed with strength and dignity; she can laugh at the days to come. 26 She speaks with wisdom, and faithful instruction is on her tongue. 27 She watches over the affairs of her household and does not eat the bread of idleness. 28 Her children arise and call her blessed; her husband also, and he praises her: 29 "Many women do noble things, but you surpass them all." 30 Charm is deceptive, and beauty is fleeting; but a woman who fears the LORD is to be praised. 31 Honor her for all that her hands have done, and let her works bring her praise at the city gate.

Ecclesiastes 4:9–10

9 Two are better than one, because they have a good return for their work: 10 If one falls down, his friend can help him up, but pity a man who falls and has no one to help him up!

Chapter 14: Adultery

Proverbs 5:1–10, 15–20

1 My son, pay attention to my wisdom, turn your ear to my words of insight, 2 that you may maintain discretion and your lips may preserve knowledge. 3 For the lips of the adulterous woman drip honey, and her speech is smoother than oil; 4 but in the end she is bitter as gall, sharp as a double-edged sword. 5 Her feet go down to death; her steps lead straight to the grave. 6 She gives no thought to the way of life; her paths wander aimlessly, but she does not know it. 7 Now then, my sons, listen to me; do not turn aside from what I say. 8 Keep to a path far from her, do not go near the door of her house, 9 lest you lose your honor to others and your dignity to one who is cruel, 10 lest strangers feast on your wealth and your toil enrich the house of another.

15 Drink water from your own cistern, running water from your own well. 16 Should your springs overflow in the streets, your streams of

water in the public squares? 17 Let them be yours alone, never to be shared with strangers. 18 May your fountain be blessed, and may you rejoice in the wife of your youth. 19 A loving doe, a graceful deer— may her breasts satisfy you always, may you ever be intoxicated with her love. 20 Why, my son, be intoxicated with another man's wife? Why embrace the bosom of a wayward woman?

Proverbs 6:23–28
23 For this command is a lamp, this teaching is a light, and correction and instruction are the way to life, 24 keeping you from your neighbor's wife, from the smooth talk of a wayward woman. 25 Do not lust in your heart after her beauty or let her captivate you with her eyes. 26 For a prostitute can be had for a loaf of bread, but another man's wife preys on your very life. 27 Can a man scoop fire into his lap without his clothes being burned? 28 Can a man walk on hot coals without his feet being scorched? 29 So is he who sleeps with another man's wife; no one who touches her will go unpunished. 30 People do not despise a thief if he steals to satisfy his hunger when he is starving. 31 Yet if he is caught, he must pay sevenfold, though it costs him all the wealth of his house. 32 But a man who commits adultery has no sense; whoever does so destroys himself. 33 Blows and disgrace are his lot, and his shame will never be wiped away. 34 For jealousy arouses a husband's fury, and he will show no mercy when he takes revenge. 35 He will not accept any compensation; he will refuse a bribe, however great it is.

Proverbs 7:1–27
1 My son, keep my words and store up my commands within you. 2 Keep my commands and you will live; guard my teachings as the apple of your eye. 3 Bind them on your fingers; write them on the tablet of your heart. 4 Say to wisdom, "You are my sister," and to insight, "You are my relative." 5 They will keep you from the adulterous woman, from the wayward woman with her seductive words. 6 At the window of my house I looked down through the lattice. 7 I saw among the simple, I noticed among the young men, a youth who had no sense. 8 He was

going down the street near her corner, walking along in the direction of her house 9 at twilight, as the day was fading, as the dark of night set in. 10 Then out came a woman to meet him, dressed like a prostitute and with crafty intent. 11 (She is unruly and defiant, her feet never stay at home; 12 now in the street, now in the squares, at every corner she lurks.) 13 She took hold of him and kissed him and with a brazen face she said: 14 "Today I fulfilled my vows, and I have food from my fellowship offering at home. 15 So I came out to meet you; I looked for you and have found you! 16 I have covered my bed with colored linens from Egypt. 17 I have perfumed my bed with myrrh, aloes and cinnamon. 18 Come, let's drink deeply of love till morning; let's enjoy ourselves with love! 19 My husband is not at home; he has gone on a long journey. 20 He took his purse filled with money and will not be home till full moon." 21 With persuasive words she led him astray; she seduced him with her smooth talk. 22 All at once he followed her like an ox going to the slaughter, like a deer stepping into a noose 23 till an arrow pierces his liver, like a bird darting into a snare, little knowing it will cost him his life. 24 Now then, my sons, listen to me; pay attention to what I say. 25 Do not let your heart turn to her ways or stray into her paths. 26 Many are the victims she has brought down; her slain are a mighty throng. 27 Her house is a highway to the grave, leading down to the chambers of death.

Proverbs 22:14
14 The mouth of an adulterous woman is a deep pit; a man who is under the LORD's wrath falls into it.

Proverbs 23:26–28
26 My son, give me your heart and let your eyes delight in my ways, 27 for an adulterous woman is a deep pit, and a wayward wife is a narrow well. 28 Like a bandit she lies in wait and multiplies the unfaithful among men.

Proverbs 27:8
8 Like a bird that strays from its nest is a man who flees from his home.

Proverbs 30:20
20 This is the way of an adulterous woman: She eats and wipes her mouth and says, "I've done nothing wrong."
1 Corinthians 6:18–20
18 Flee from sexual immorality. All other sins a person commits are outside the body, but whoever sins sexually, sins against their own body. 19 Do you not know that your bodies are temples of the Holy Spirit, who is in you, whom you have received from God? You are not your own; 20 you were bought at a price. Therefore honor God with your bodies.

Chapter 15: Do What You Say
Proverbs 4:1–4
1 Listen, my sons, to a father's instruction; pay attention and gain understanding. 2 I give you sound learning, so do not forsake my teaching. 3 For I too was a son to my father, still tender, and cherished by my mother. 4 Then he taught me, and he said to me, "Take hold of my words with all your heart; keep my commands, and you will live.

Proverbs 6:20–22
20 My son, keep your father's command and do not forsake your mother's teaching. 21 Bind them always on your heart; fasten them around your neck. 22 When you walk, they will guide you; when you sleep, they will watch over you; when you awake, they will speak to you.

Proverbs 10:1
1 The proverbs of Solomon: A wise son brings joy to his father, but a foolish son brings grief to his mother.
Proverbs 11:29
29 Whoever brings ruin on their family will inherit only wind, and the fool will be servant to the wise.

Proverbs 13:1, 14–15, 20

1 A wise son heeds his father's instruction, but a mocker does not respond to rebukes.

14 The teaching of the wise is a fountain of life, turning a person from the snares of death. 15 Good judgment wins favor, but the way of the unfaithful leads to their destruction.

20 Walk with the wise and become wise, for a companion of fools suffers harm.

Proverbs 20: 29

29 The glory of young men is their strength, gray hair the splendor of the old.

Chapter 16: The Family Business

Proverbs 17:2, 6, 21, 25

2 A wise servant will rule over a disgraceful son and will share the inheritance as one of the family.

6 Children's children are a crown to the aged, and parents are the pride of their children.

21 To have a fool for a child brings grief; there is no joy for the parent of a godless fool.

25 A foolish son brings grief to his father and bitterness to the mother who bore him.

Proverbs 19:13, 26

13 A foolish child is a father's ruin, and a quarrelsome wife is like the constant dripping of a leaky roof.

26 Whoever robs their father and drives out their mother is a child who brings shame and disgrace.

Proverbs 20:11, 20

11 Even a child is known by his actions, by whether his conduct is pure and upright.

20 If a man curses his father or mother, his lamp will be snuffed out in pitch darkness.

Proverbs 23:22–25

22 Listen to your father, who gave you life, and do not despise your mother when she is old. 23 Buy the truth and do not sell it— wisdom, instruction and insight as well. 24 The father of a righteous child has great joy; a man who fathers a wise son rejoices in him. 25 May your father and mother rejoice; may she who gave you birth be joyful!

Proverbs 27:11

11 Be wise, my son, and bring joy to my heart; then I can answer anyone who treats me with contempt.

Proverbs 28:7, 24

7 A discerning son heeds instruction, but a companion of gluttons disgraces his father.
24 Whoever robs their father or mother and says, "It's not wrong," is partner to one who destroys.

Proverbs 29:3

3 A man who loves wisdom brings joy to his father, but a companion of prostitutes squanders his wealth.

Proverbs 30:17

17 The eye that mocks a father, that scorns an aged mother, will be pecked out by the ravens of the valley, will be eaten by the vultures.

Chapter 17: The Value of Your Network (and real friends)
Proverbs 17:17

17 A friend loves at all times, and a brother is born for a time of adversity.

Proverbs 18:24
24 One who has unreliable friends soon comes to ruin, but there is a friend who sticks closer than a brother.

Proverbs 27:6, 9–10, 14, 19
6 Wounds from a friend can be trusted, but an enemy multiplies kisses. 9 Perfume and incense bring joy to the heart, and the pleasantness of a friend springs from their heartfelt advice. 10 Do not forsake your friend or a friend of your family, and do not go to your relative's house when disaster strikes you— better a neighbor nearby than a relative far away.
14 If anyone loudly blesses their neighbor early in the morning, it will be taken as a curse.
19 As water reflects the face, so a man's heart reflects the man.

PART 4: LOVE PEOPLE, USE MONEY
Proverbs 30:8–9
8 Keep falsehood and lies far from me; give me neither poverty nor riches, but give me only my daily bread. 9 Otherwise, I may have too much and disown you and say, 'Who is the LORD?' Or I may become poor and steal, and so dishonor the name of my God.

Matthew 6:24
No one can serve two masters. Either you will hate the one and love the other, or you will be devoted to the one and despise the other. You cannot serve both God and money.

Chapter 18: Better a Little—The Deceitfulness of Wealth
Mark 10:25
It is easier for a camel to go through the eye of a needle than for someone who is rich to enter the kingdom of God.
Proverb 13:22
22 A good person leaves an inheritance for their children's children, but a sinner's wealth is stored up for the righteous.

Proverbs 15:16–17

16 Better a little with the fear of the LORD than great wealth with turmoil. 17 Better a small serving of vegetables with love than a fattened calf with hatred.

Proverbs 16:8

8 Better a little with righteousness than much gain with injustice.

Proverbs 17:1

1 Better a dry crust with peace and quiet than a house full of feasting, with strife.

Proverbs 18:11

11 The wealth of the rich is their fortified city; they imagine it a wall too high to scale.

Proverbs 19:1, 22

1 Better the poor whose walk is blameless than a fool whose lips are perverse.
22 What a person desires is unfailing love; better to be poor than a liar.

Proverbs 22:16

16 One who oppresses the poor to increase his wealth and one who gives gifts to the rich—both come to poverty.

Proverbs 23:4–5

4 Do not wear yourself out to get rich; do not trust your own cleverness. 5 Cast but a glance at riches, and they are gone, for they will surely sprout wings and fly off to the sky like an eagle.

Proverbs 28:6, 8, 20, 22, 25

6 Better the poor whose walk is blameless than the rich whose ways are perverse.

8 He who increases his wealth by exorbitant interest amasses it for another, who will be kind to the poor.

20 A faithful person will be richly blessed, but one eager to get rich will not go unpunished.

22 The stingy are eager to get rich and are unaware that poverty awaits them.

25 The greedy stir up conflict, but those who trust in the LORD will prosper.

Proverbs 29:4

4 By justice a king gives a country stability, but those who are greedy for bribes tear it down.

Proverbs 30:7–9

7 Two things I ask of you, LORD; do not refuse me before I die: 8 Keep falsehood and lies far from me; give me neither poverty nor riches, but give me only my daily bread. 9 Otherwise, I may have too much and disown you and say, 'Who is the LORD?' Or I may become poor and steal, and so dishonor the name of my God.

Chapter 19: Just Right

Proverb 13:11

11 Dishonest money dwindles away, but whoever gathers money little by little makes it grow.

Proverbs 20:21

21 An inheritance quickly gained at the beginning, will not be blessed at the end.

Proverbs 21:20

20 The wise store up choice food and olive oil, but fools gulp theirs down.

Chapter 20: Debt Philosophy

Proverbs 6:1–5

1 My son, if you have put up security for your neighbor, if you have shaken hands in pledge for a stranger, 2 you have been trapped by what you said, ensnared by the words of your mouth. 3 So do this, my son, to free yourself, since you have fallen into your neighbor's hands: Go— to the point of exhaustion—and give your neighbor no rest! 4 Allow no sleep to your eyes, no slumber to your eyelids. 5 Free yourself, like a gazelle from the hand of the hunter, like a bird from the snare of the fowler.

Proverbs 11:15

15 Whoever puts up security for a stranger will surely suffer, but whoever refuses to shake hands in pledge is safe.

Proverbs 17:18

18 One who has no sense shakes hands in pledge and puts up security for a neighbor.

Proverbs 20:16

16 Take the garment of one who puts up security for a stranger; hold it in pledge if it is done for an outsider.

Proverbs 22:7, 26–27

7 The rich rule over the poor, and the borrower is slave to the lender. 26 Do not be one who shakes hands in pledge or puts up security for debts; 27 if you lack the means to pay, your very bed will be snatched from under you.

Proverbs 27:13

13 Take the garment of one who puts up security for a stranger; hold it in pledge if it is done for an outsider.

Chapter 21: The Generosity Test

Malachi 3:10–12

10 Bring the whole tithe into the storehouse, that there may be food in my house. Test me in this," says the Lord Almighty, "and see if I will not throw open the floodgates of heaven and pour out so much blessing that there will not be room enough to store it. 11 I will prevent pests from devouring your crops, and the vines in your fields will not drop their fruit before it is ripe," says the Lord Almighty. 12 "Then all the nations will call you blessed, for yours will be a delightful land," says the Lord Almighty.

Proverbs 3:9–10

9 Honor the LORD with your wealth, with the firstfruits of all your crops; 10 then your barns will be filled to overflowing, and your vats will brim over with new wine.

Proverbs 11:24–26

24 One person gives freely, yet gains even more; another withholds unduly, but comes to poverty. 25 A generous person will prosper; whoever refreshes others will be refreshed. 26 People curse the one who hoards grain, but they pray God's blessing on the one who is willing to sell.

Proverbs 14:21

21 It is a sin to despise one's neighbor, but blessed is the one who is kind to the needy.

Proverbs 14:31

31 Whoever oppresses the poor shows contempt for their Maker, but whoever is kind to the needy honors God.

Proverbs 19:17

17 Whoever is kind to the poor lends to the LORD, and he will reward them for what they have done.

Proverbs 22:9

9 The generous will themselves be blessed, for they share their food with the poor.

Proverbs 23:6–8

6 Do not eat the food of a begrudging host, do not crave his delicacies; 7 for he is the kind of person who is always thinking about the cost. "Eat and drink," he says to you, but his heart is not with you. 8 You will vomit up the little you have eaten and will have wasted your compliments.

Proverbs 28:27

27 Those who give to the poor will lack nothing, but those who close their eyes to them receive many curses.

Proverbs 18:16

16 A gift opens the way and ushers the giver into the presence of the great.

PART 5: VERSUS

Chapter 22: Fool versus Wise

Proverbs 12:2

2 Good people obtain favor from the LORD, but he condemns those who devise wicked schemes.

Proverbs 14:1, 9, 24

1 The wise woman builds her house, but with her own hands the foolish one tears hers down.

9 Fools mock at making amends for sin, but goodwill is found among the upright.

24 The wealth of the wise is their crown, but the folly of fools yields folly.

Proverbs 17:12, 16

12 Better to meet a bear robbed of her cubs than a fool bent on folly.

16 Of what use is money in the hand of a fool, since he has no desire to get wisdom.

Proverbs 18:2
2 Fools find no pleasure in understanding but delight in airing their own opinions.

Proverbs 19:10
10 It is not fitting for a fool to live in luxury—how much worse for a slave to rule over princes!

Proverbs 24:7
7 Wisdom is too high for fools; in the assembly at the gate they must not open their mouths.

Proverbs 26:1, 4–11
1 Like snow in summer or rain in harvest, honor is not fitting for a fool. 4 Do not answer a fool according to his folly, or you yourself will be just like him. 5 Answer a fool according to his folly, or he will be wise in his own eyes. 6Sending a message by the hands of a fool is like cutting off one's feet or drinking poison. 7 Like the useless legs of one who is lame is a proverb in the mouth of a fool. 8 Like tying a stone in a sling is the giving of honor to a fool. 9 Like a thornbush in a drunkard's hand is a proverb in the mouth of a fool. 10 Like an archer who wounds at random is one who hires a fool or any passer-by. 11 As a dog returns to its vomit, so fools repeat their folly.

Proverbs 27:3, 22
3 Stone is heavy and sand a burden, but a fool's provocation is heavier than both.
22 Though you grind a fool in a mortar, grinding them like grain with a pestle, you will not remove their folly from them.

Proverbs 28:26

26 Those who trust in themselves are fools, but those who walk in wisdom are kept safe.

Proverbs 29:8–9, 11

8 Mockers stir up a city, but the wise turn away anger. 9 If a wise person goes to court with a fool, the fool rages and scoffs, and there is no peace. 11 Fools give full vent to their rage, but the wise bring calm in the end.

Chapter 23: Pride versus Humility

Proverbs 3:7–8

7 Do not be wise in your own eyes; fear the LORD and shun evil. 8 This will bring health to your body and nourishment to your bones.

Proverbs 11:2

2 When pride comes, then comes disgrace, but with humility comes wisdom.

Proverbs 12:9

9 Better to be a nobody and yet have a servant than pretend to be somebody and have no food.

Proverbs 13:7–8, 10

7 One person pretends to be rich, yet has nothing; another pretends to be poor, yet has great wealth. 8 A person's riches may ransom their life, but the poor cannot respond to threatening rebukes.
10 Pride only breeds quarrels, but wisdom is found in those who take advice.

Proverbs 15:25, 33

25 The LORD tears down the house of the proud, but he sets the widow's boundary stones in place.
33 Wisdom's instruction is to fear the LORD, and humility comes before honor.

Proverbs 16: 5, 18–19

5 The LORD detests all the proud of heart. Be sure of this: They will not go unpunished.

18 Pride goes before destruction, a haughty spirit before a fall. 19 Better to be lowly in spirit along with the oppressed than to share plunder with the proud.

Proverbs 18:12

12 Before a downfall a man's heart is proud, but humility comes before honor.

Proverbs 20:6, 9

6 Many claim to have unfailing love, but a faithful person who can find? 9 Who can say, "I have kept my heart pure; I am clean and without sin?"

Proverbs 21:2, 4, 24

2 Rich and poor have this in common: The LORD is the Maker of them all.

4 Haughty eyes and a proud heart—the lamp of the wicked—produce sin.

24 The proud and arrogant person—"Mocker" is his name—behaves with overweening pride.

Proverbs 22:4

4 Humility is the fear of the LORD; its wages are riches and honor and life.

Proverbs 24:17–18

17 Do not gloat when your enemy falls; when they stumble, do not let your heart rejoice, 18 or the LORD will see and disapprove and turn his wrath away from them.

Proverbs 25:6–8, 14, 27

6 Do not exalt yourself in the king's presence, and do not claim a place among his great men; 7 it is better for him to say to you, "Come up

here," than for him to humiliate you before his nobles. What you have seen with your eyes 8 do not bring hastily to court, for what will you do in the end if your neighbor puts you to shame?

14 Like clouds and wind without rain is one who boasts of gifts never given.

27 It is not good to eat too much honey, nor is it honorable to seek one's own honor.

Proverbs 26:12

12 Do you see a person wise in their own eyes? There is more hope for a fool than for them.

Proverbs 27:1–2, 21

1 Do not boast about tomorrow, for you do not know what a day may bring. 2 Let someone else praise you, and not your own mouth; an outsider, and not your own lips.

21 The crucible for silver and the furnace for gold, but people are tested by their praise.

Proverbs 28:13

13 Whoever conceals their sins does not prosper, but the one who confesses and renounces them finds mercy.

Proverbs 29:1, 23

1 Whoever remains stiff-necked after many rebukes will suddenly be destroyed—without remedy.

23 Pride brings a person low, but the lowly in spirit gain honor.

Proverbs 30:21–28

21 "Under three things the earth trembles, under four it cannot bear up: 22 a servant who becomes king, a godless fool who gets plenty to eat, 23 a contemptible woman who gets married, and a servant who displaces her mistress. 24 "Four things on earth are small, yet they are extremely wise: 25 Ants are creatures of little strength, yet they store

up their food in the summer; 26 hyraxes are creatures of little power, yet they make their home in the crags; 27 locusts have no king, yet they advance together in ranks; 28 a lizard can be caught with the hand, yet it is found in kings' palaces.

Chapter 24: Laziness vs Hard Work
Ecclesiastes 10:18
If a man is lazy, the rafters sag: if his hands are idle, the house leaks.

Proverbs 6:6–11
6 Go to the ant, you sluggard; consider its ways and be wise! 7 It has no commander, no overseer or ruler, 8 yet it stores its provisions in summer and gathers its food at harvest. 9 How long will you lie there, you sluggard? When will you get up from your sleep? 10 A little sleep, a little slumber, a little folding of the hands to rest—11 and poverty will come on you like a thief and scarcity like an armed man.

Proverbs: 10:4–5, 26
4 Lazy hands make for poverty, but diligent hands bring wealth. 5 He who gathers crops in summer is a prudent son, but he who sleeps during harvest is a disgraceful son.
26 As vinegar to the teeth and smoke to the eyes, so are sluggards to those who send them.

Proverbs: 12:11, 24, 27
11 Those who work their land will have abundant food, but those who chase fantasies have no sense.
24 Diligent hands will rule, but laziness ends in forced labor.
27 The lazy do not roast any game, but the diligent feed on the riches of the hunt.

Proverbs: 13:4
4 A sluggard's appetite is never filled, but the desires of the diligent are fully satisfied.

Proverbs: 14:23
23 All hard work brings a profit, but mere talk leads only to poverty.

Proverbs: 15:19
19 The way of the sluggard is blocked with thorns, but the path of the upright is a highway.

Proverbs: 16:26
26 The laborer's appetite works for him; his hunger drives him on.

Proverbs: 18:9
9 One who is slack in his work is brother to one who destroys.

Proverbs: 19:15, 24
15 Laziness brings on deep sleep, and the shiftless go hungry.
24 A sluggard buries his hand in the dish; he will not even bring it back to his mouth!

Proverbs: 20:4,13
4 Sluggards do not plow in season; so at harvest time they look but find nothing.
13 Do not love sleep or you will grow poor; stay awake and you will have food to spare.

Proverbs: 21:25–26
25 The craving of a sluggard will be the death of him, because his hands refuse to work. 26 All day long he craves for more, but the righteous give without sparing.

Proverbs: 22:13
13 The sluggard says, "There's a lion outside! I'll be killed in the public square!"

Proverbs: 24:30–34
30 I went past the field of a sluggard, past the vineyard of someone who has no sense; 31 thorns had come up everywhere, the ground was covered with weeds, and the stone wall was in ruins. 32 I applied my heart to what I observed and learned a lesson from what I saw: 33 A little sleep, a little slumber, a little folding of the hands to rest—34 and poverty will come on you like a thief and scarcity like an armed man.

Proverbs: 26:13–16
13 A sluggard says, "There's a lion in the road, a fierce lion roaming the streets!" 14 As a door turns on its hinges, so a sluggard turns on his bed. 15 A sluggard buries his hand in the dish; he is too lazy to bring it back to his mouth. 16 A sluggard is wiser in his own eyes than seven people who answer discreetly.

Proverbs: 27:18
18 The one who guards a fig tree will eat its fruit, and whoever protects their master will be honored.

Proverbs: 28:19
19 Those who work their land will have abundant food, but those who chase fantasies will have their fill of poverty.

PART 6: YOUR TONGUE IS ON FIRE
James 3:4–6
4 Or take ships as an example. Although they are so large and are driven by strong winds, they are steered by a very small rudder wherever the pilot wants to go. 5 Likewise, the tongue is a small part of the body, but it makes great boasts. Consider what a great forest is set on fire by a small spark. 6 The tongue also is a fire, a world of evil among the parts of the body. It corrupts the whole body, sets the whole course of one's life on fire, and is itself set on fire by hell.

Chapter 25: Good Tongue Bad Tongue

Proverbs 4:24

24 Keep your mouth free of perversity; keep corrupt talk far from your lips.

Proverbs 10:8, 10, 14, 18–19

8 The wise in heart accept commands, but a chattering fool comes to ruin.

10 Whoever winks maliciously causes grief, and a chattering fool comes to ruin.

14 The wise store up knowledge, but the mouth of a fool invites ruin.

18 Whoever conceals hatred with lying lips and spreads slander is a fool. 19 Sin is not ended by multiplying words, but the prudent hold their tongues.

Proverbs 11:12–13

12 Whoever derides their neighbor has no sense, but the one who has understanding holds their tongue. 13 A gossip betrays a confidence, but a trustworthy person keeps a secret.

Proverbs 12:6, 14, 18–19, 22, 25

6 The words of the wicked lie in wait for blood, but the speech of the upright rescues them.

14 From the fruit of their lips people are filled with good things, and the work of their hands brings them reward.

18 The words of the reckless pierce like swords, but the tongue of the wise brings healing. 19 Truthful lips endure forever, but a lying tongue lasts only a moment.

22 The LORD detests lying lips, but he delights in people who are trustworthy. 25 Anxiety weighs down the heart, but a kind word cheers it up.

Proverbs 13:2–3

2 From the fruit of their lips people enjoy good things, but the unfaithful have an appetite for violence. 3 Those who guard their lips preserve their lives, but those who speak rashly will come to ruin.

Proverbs 14:3, 25

3 A fool's mouth lashes out with pride, but the lips of the wise protect them.

25 A truthful witness saves lives, but a false witness is deceitful.

Proverbs 15:1–2, 4, 7, 23

1 A gentle answer turns away wrath, but a harsh word stirs up anger. 2 The tongue of the wise adorns knowledge, but the mouth of the fool gushes folly.

4 The soothing tongue is a tree of life, but a perverse tongue crushes the spirit.

7 The lips of the wise spread knowledge, but the hearts of fools are not upright.

23 A person finds joy in giving an apt reply— and how good is a timely word!

Proverbs 16:13, 23–24, 27–28

13 Kings take pleasure in honest lips; they value the one who speaks what is right.

23 The hearts of the wise make their mouths prudent, and their lips promote instruction. 24 Gracious words are a honeycomb, sweet to the soul and healing to the bones.

27 A scoundrel plots evil, and on their lips it is like a scorching fire. 28 A perverse person stirs up conflict, and a gossip separates close friends.

Proverbs 17:4, 7, 9, 20, 27–28

4 A wicked person listens to deceitful lips; a liar pays attention to a destructive tongue.

7 Eloquent lips are unsuited to a godless fool—how much worse lying lips to a ruler!
9 Whoever would foster love covers over an offense, but whoever repeats the matter separates close friends.
20 One whose heart is corrupt does not prosper; one whose tongue is perverse falls into trouble.
27 The one who has knowledge uses words with restraint, and whoever has understanding is even-tempered. 28 Even fools are thought wise if they keep silent, and discerning if they hold their tongues.

Proverbs 18:4, 6–8, 20–21
4 The words of the mouth are deep waters, but the fountain of wisdom is a rushing stream.
6 The lips of fools bring them strife, and their mouths invite a beating. 7 The mouths of fools are their undoing, and their lips are a snare to their very lives. 8 The words of a gossip are like choice morsels; they go down to the inmost parts.
20 From the fruit of their mouth a person's stomach is filled; with the harvest of their lips they are satisfied. 21 The tongue has the power of life and death, and those who love it will eat its fruit.

Proverbs 20:15, 19
15 Gold there is, and rubies in abundance, but lips that speak knowledge are a rare jewel.
19 A gossip betrays a confidence; so avoid a man who talks too much.

Proverbs 21:6, 23
6 A fortune made by a lying tongue is a fleeting vapor and a deadly snare.
23 Those who guard their mouths and their tongues keep themselves from calamity.

Proverbs 25:9–10, 15, 20, 23, 25

9 If you take your neighbor to court, do not betray another's confidence, 10 or the one who hears it may shame you and the charge against you will stand.

15 Through patience a ruler can be persuaded, and a gentle tongue can break a bone.

20 Like one who takes away a garment on a cold day, or like vinegar poured on a wound, is one who sings songs to a heavy heart.

23 Like a north wind that brings unexpected rain is a sly tongue—which provokes a horrified look.

25 Like cold water to a weary soul is good news from a distant land.

Proverbs 26:2, 18–19, 20–26, 28

2 Like a fluttering sparrow or a darting swallow, an undeserved curse does not come to rest.

18 Like a maniac shooting flaming arrows of death 19 is one who deceives their neighbor and says, "I was only joking!"

20 Without wood a fire goes out; without a gossip a quarrel dies down. 21 As charcoal to embers and as wood to fire, so is a quarrelsome person for kindling strife. 22 The words of a gossip are like choice morsels; they go down to the inmost parts. 23 Like a coating of silver dross on earthenware are fervent lips with an evil heart. 24 Enemies disguise themselves with their lips, but in their hearts they harbor deceit. 25 Though their speech is charming, do not believe them, for seven abominations fill their hearts. 26 Their malice may be concealed by deception, but their wickedness will be exposed in the assembly.

28 A lying tongue hates those it hurts, and a flattering mouth works ruin.

Proverbs 27:5

5 Better is open rebuke than hidden love.

Proverbs 28:23

23 Whoever rebukes a person will in the end gain favor rather than one who has a flattering tongue.

Proverbs 29:5, 20

5 Those who flatter their neighbors are spreading nets for their feet.

20 Do you see someone who speaks in haste? There is more hope for a fool than for them.

Proverbs 30:10–14, 32–33

10 "Do not slander a servant to their master, or they will curse you, and you will pay for it. 11 "There are those who curse their fathers and do not bless their mothers; 12 those who are pure in their own eyes and yet are not cleansed of their filth; 13 those whose eyes are ever so haughty, whose glances are so disdainful; 14 those whose teeth are swords and whose jaws are set with knives to devour the poor from the earth and the needy from among mankind.

32 If you play the fool and exalt yourself, or if you plan evil, clap your hand over your mouth! 33 For as churning cream produces butter, and as twisting the nose produces blood, so stirring up anger produces strife.

Chapter 26: Know When to Shut Up

James 1:19

My dear brothers and sisters, take note of this: Everyone should be quick to listen, slow to speak, and slow to become angry.

Proverbs 18:13, 15, 17

13 He who answers before listening—that is his folly and shame.

15 The heart of the discerning acquires knowledge, for the ears of the wise seek it out.

17 In a lawsuit the first to speak seems right, until someone comes forward and questions him.

Chapter 27: Discipline for the Student

Hebrews 12:11

11 No discipline seems pleasant at the time, but painful. Later on, however, it produces a harvest of righteousness and peace for those who have been trained by it.

Proverbs 3:11–12
11 My son, do not despise the LORD's discipline, and do not resent his rebuke, 12 because the LORD disciplines those he loves, as a father the son he delights in.

Proverbs 5:11–14
11 At the end of your life you will groan, when your flesh and body are spent. 12 You will say, "How I hated discipline! How my heart spurned correction! 13 I would not obey my teachers or turn my ear to my instructors. 14 And I was soon in serious trouble in the assembly of God's people."

Proverbs 5:21–23
21 For your ways are in full view of the LORD, and he examines all your paths. 22 The evil deeds of the wicked ensnare them; the cords of their sins hold them fast. 23 For lack of discipline they will die, led astray by their own great folly.

Proverbs 10:17
17 Whoever heeds discipline shows the way to life, but whoever ignores correction leads others astray.

Proverbs 12:1
1 Whoever loves discipline loves knowledge, but whoever hates correction is stupid.

Proverbs 13:18
18 Whoever disregards discipline comes to poverty and shame, but whoever heeds correction is honored.

Proverbs 13:13

13 Whoever scorns instruction will pay for it, but whoever respects a command is rewarded.

Proverbs 15:5, 10, 12, 31–32

5 A fool spurns a parent's discipline, but whoever heeds correction shows prudence.

10 Stern discipline awaits anyone who leaves the path; the one who hates correction will die.

12 Mockers resent correction, so they avoid the wise.

31 Whoever heeds life-giving correction will be at home among the wise. 32 Those who disregard discipline despise themselves, but the one who heeds correction gains understanding.

Proverbs 16:20

20 Whoever gives heed to instruction prospers, and blessed is the one who trusts in the LORD.

Proverbs 20:30

30 Blows and wounds scrub away evil, and beatings purge the inmost being.

Proverbs 19:16, 27

16 Whoever obeys instructions guards their life, but whoever shows contempt for their ways will die.

27 Stop listening to instruction, my son, and you will stray from the words of knowledge.

Proverbs 21:11

11 When a mocker is punished, the simple gain wisdom; when a wise man is instructed; he gets knowledge.

Proverbs 23:12

12 Apply your heart to instruction and your ears to words of knowledge.

Proverbs 25:11–12

11Like apples of gold in settings of silver is a ruling rightly given. 12 Like an earring of gold or an ornament of fine gold is the rebuke of a wise judge to a listening ear.

Chapter 28: Discipline for the Teacher

Proverbs 9:7–9

7 Whoever corrects a mocker invites insults; whoever rebukes the wicked incurs abuse. 8 Do not rebuke mockers or they will hate you; rebuke the wise and they will love you. 9 Instruct the wise and they will be wiser still; teach the righteous and they will add to their learning.

Proverbs 13:24

24 Whoever spares the rod hates their children, but the one who loves their children is careful to discipline them.

Proverbs 19:18, 25, 29

18 Discipline your children, for in that there is hope; do not be a willing party to their death.

25 Flog a mocker, and the simple will learn prudence; rebuke the discerning, and they will gain knowledge.

29 Penalties are prepared for mockers, and beatings for the backs of fools.

Proverbs 22:6, 15

6 Start children off on the way they should go, and even when they are old they will not turn from it.

15 Folly is bound up in the heart of a child, but the rod of discipline will drive it far away.

Proverbs 23:13–14

13 Do not withhold discipline from a child; if you punish them with the rod, they will not die. 14 Punish them with the rod and save them from death.

Proverbs 29:15, 17

15 A rod and a reprimand impart wisdom, but a child left undisciplined disgraces its mother.

17 Discipline your children, and they will give you peace; they will bring you the delights you desire.

Proverbs 26:3

3 A whip for the horse, a bridle for the donkey, and a rod for the backs of fools!

Proverbs 24:10–12

10 If you falter in a time of trouble, how small is your strength! 11 Rescue those being led away to death; hold back those staggering toward slaughter. 12 If you say, "But we knew nothing about this," does not he who weighs the heart perceive it? Does not he who guards your life know it? Will he not repay everyone according to what they have done?

Proverbs 25:11–12

11 Like apples of gold in settings of silver is a ruling rightly given. 12 Like an earring of gold or an ornament of fine gold is the rebuke of a wise judge to a listening ear.

Proverbs 28:17

17 Anyone tormented by the guilt of murder will seek refuge in the grave; let no one hold them back.

Proverbs 29:15, 17–19, 21

15 A rod and a reprimand impart wisdom, but a child left undisciplined disgraces its mother.

17 Discipline your children, and they will give you peace; they will bring you the delights you desire. 18 Where there is no revelation, people cast off restraint; but blessed is the one who heeds wisdom's instruction. 19 Servants cannot be corrected by mere words; though they understand, they will not respond.

21 A servant pampered from youth will turn out to be insolent.

PART 7: DON'T BE EVIL (OR STUPID)

Proverbs 22:1

A good name is more desirable than great riches; to be esteemed is better than silver or gold.

Chapter 29: Integrity

Philippians 1:9–10

9 And this is my prayer: That your love may abound more and more in knowledge and depth of insight, 10 so that you may be able to discern what is best and may be pure and blameless until the day of Christ.

Proverbs 3:27–32

27 Do not withhold good from those to whom it is due, when it is in your power to act. 28 Do not say to your neighbor, "Come back tomorrow and I'll give it to you"—when you already have it with you. 29 Do not plot harm against your neighbor, who lives trustfully near you. 30 Do not accuse anyone for no reason—when they have done you no harm. 31 Do not envy the violent or choose any of their ways. 32 For the LORD detests the perverse but takes the upright into his confidence.

Proverbs 4:14–19

14 Do not set foot on the path of the wicked or walk in the way of evildoers. 15 Avoid it, do not travel on it; turn from it and go on your way. 16 For they cannot rest until they do evil; they are robbed of sleep till they make someone stumble. 17 They eat the bread of wickedness and drink the wine of violence. 18 The path of the righteous is like the morning sun, shining ever brighter till the full light of day. 19 But the way of the wicked is like deep darkness; they do not know what makes them stumble.

Proverbs 6:12–19

12 A troublemaker and a villain, who goes about with a corrupt mouth, 13 who winks maliciously with his eye, signals with his feet and motions with his fingers, 14 who plots evil with deceit in his heart— he always stirs up conflict. 15 Therefore disaster will overtake him in an instant; he will suddenly be destroyed—without remedy. 16 There are six things the LORD hates, seven that are detestable to him: 17 haughty eyes, a lying tongue, hands that shed innocent blood, 18 a heart that devises wicked schemes, feet that are quick to rush into evil, 19 a false witness who pours out lies and a person who stirs up conflict in the community.

Proverbs 10:9, 22

9 Whoever walks in integrity walks securely, but whoever takes crooked paths will be found out.
22 The blessing of the LORD brings wealth, without painful toil for it.

Proverbs 11:1, 3

1 The LORD detests dishonest scales, but accurate weights find favor with him.
3 The integrity of the upright guides them, but the unfaithful are destroyed by their duplicity.

Proverbs 12:17, 20

17 An honest witness tells the truth, but a false witness tells lies.
20 Deceit is in the hearts of those who plot evil, but those who promote peace have joy.

Proverbs 13:17

17 A wicked messenger falls into trouble, but a trustworthy envoy brings healing.

Proverbs 14:5, 11, 14, 22

5 An honest witness does not deceive, but a false witness pours out lies.

11 The house of the wicked will be destroyed, but the tent of the upright will flourish.

14 The faithless will be fully repaid for their ways, and the good rewarded for theirs.

22 Do not those who plot evil go astray? But those who plan what is good find love and faithfulness.

Proverbs 15:27
27 The greedy bring ruin to their households, but the one who hates bribes will live.

Proverbs 16:11, 30
11 Honest scales and balances belong to the LORD; all the weights in the bag are of his making.

30 Whoever winks with their eye is plotting perversity; whoever purses their lips is bent on evil.

Proverbs 17:8, 15, 23, 26
8 A bribe is seen as a charm by the one who gives it; they think success will come at every turn.

15 Acquitting the guilty and condemning the innocent— the LORD detests them both.

23 The wicked accept bribes in secret to pervert the course of justice.

26 If imposing a fine on the innocent is not good, surely to flog honest officials is not right.

Proverbs 19:5, 9
5 A false witness will not go unpunished, and whoever pours out lies will not go free.

9 A false witness will not go unpunished, and whoever pours out lies will perish.

Proverbs 20:10, 17, 23

10 Differing weights and differing measures—the LORD detests them both.

14 "It's no good, it's no good!" says the buyer—then goes off and boasts about the purchase.

17 Food gained by fraud tastes sweet, but one ends up with a mouth full of gravel.

23 The LORD detests differing weights, and dishonest scales do not please him.

Proverbs 21:3, 8, 28–29

3 To do what is right and just is more acceptable to the LORD than sacrifice.

8 The way of the guilty is devious, but the conduct of the innocent is upright.

28 A false witness will perish, but a careful listener will testify successfully. 29 The wicked put up a bold front, but the upright give thought to their ways.

Proverbs 22:1, 28

1 A good name is more desirable than great riches; to be esteemed is better than silver or gold.

28 Do not move an ancient boundary stone set up by your ancestors.

Proverbs 23:1–3, 10–11

1 When you sit to dine with a ruler, note well what is before you, 2 and put a knife to your throat if you are given to gluttony. 3 Do not crave his delicacies, for that food is deceptive.

10 Do not move an ancient boundary stone or encroach on the fields of the fatherless, 11 for their Defender is strong; he will take up their case against you.

Proverbs 24:23–26

23 These also are sayings of the wise: To show partiality in judging is not good: 24 Whoever says to the guilty, "You are innocent," will be cursed by peoples and denounced by nations. 25 But it will go well with those who convict the guilty, and rich blessing will come on them. 26 An honest answer is like a kiss on the lips.

Proverbs 25:18

18 Like a club or a sword or a sharp arrow is one who gives false testimony against a neighbor.

Proverbs 28:18, 21

18 The one whose walk is blameless is kept safe, but the one whose ways are perverse will fall into the pit.
21 To show partiality is not good—yet a person will do wrong for a piece of bread.

Proverbs 29:10, 24

10 The bloodthirsty hate a person of integrity and seek to kill the upright.
24 The accomplices of thieves are their own enemies; they are put under oath and dare not testify.

Chapter 30: Evil (and Stupid?)
John 3:20

20 Everyone who does evil hates the light, and will not come into the light for fear that their deeds will be exposed.

Proverbs 3:25–26

25 Have no fear of sudden disaster or of the ruin that overtakes the wicked, 26 for the LORD will be at your side and will keep your foot from being snared.

Proverbs 11:7

7 When a wicked man dies, his hope perishes; all he expected from his power comes to nothing.

Proverbs 17:11, 13

11 Evildoers foster rebellion against God; the messenger of death will be sent against them.

13 Evil will never leave the house of one who pays back evil for good.

Proverbs 18:3

3 When wickedness comes, so does contempt, and with shame comes reproach.

Proverbs 19 28

28 A corrupt witness mocks at justice, and the mouth of the wicked gulps down evil.

Proverbs 21:7, 10, 27

7 The violence of the wicked will drag them away, for they refuse to do what is right.

10 The wicked crave evil; their neighbors get no mercy from them.

27 The sacrifice of the wicked is detestable—how much more so when brought with evil intent!

Proverbs 22:8

8 Whoever sows injustice reaps calamity, and the rod they wield in fury will be broken.

Proverbs 24:8–9, 15–16, 19–20

8 Whoever plots evil will be known as a schemer. 9 The schemes of folly are sin, and people detest a mocker.

15 Do not lurk like a thief near the house of the righteous, do not plunder their dwelling place; 16 for though the righteous fall seven times, they rise again, but the wicked stumble when calamity strikes.

19 Do not fret because of evildoers or be envious of the wicked, 20 for the evildoer has no future hope, and the lamp of the wicked will be snuffed out.

Proverbs 26:27
27 If a man digs a pit, he will fall into it; if a man rolls a stone, it will roll back on him.

Proverbs 28:4
4 Those who forsake instruction praise the wicked, but those who heed it resist them.
Zacchaeus the Tax Collector

Luke 19:1–10
1 Jesus entered Jericho and was passing through. 2 A man was there by the name of Zacchaeus; he was a chief tax collector and was wealthy. 3 He wanted to see who Jesus was, but because he was short he could not see over the crowd. 4 So he ran ahead and climbed a sycamore-fig tree to see him, since Jesus was coming that way. 5 When Jesus reached the spot, he looked up and said to him, "Zacchaeus, come down immediately. I must stay at your house today." 6 So he came down at once and welcomed him gladly. 7 All the people saw this and began to mutter, "He has gone to be the guest of a sinner." 8 But Zacchaeus stood up and said to the Lord, "Look, Lord! Here and now I give half of my possessions to the poor, and if I have cheated anybody out of anything, I will pay back four times the amount." 9 Jesus said to him, "Today salvation has come to this house, because this man, too, is a son of Abraham. 10 For the Son of Man came to seek and to save the lost."

Chapter 31: Injustice
James 2:14–17
14 What good is it, my brothers and sisters, if someone claims to have faith but has no deeds? Can such faith save them? 15 Suppose a brother or a sister is without clothes and daily food. 16 If one of you says to

them, "Go in peace; keep warm and well fed," but does nothing about their physical needs, what good is it? 17 In the same way, faith by itself, if it is not accompanied by action, is dead.

Proverbs 10:15
15 The wealth of the rich is their fortified city, but poverty is the ruin of the poor.

Proverbs 13:23
23 A poor man's field may produce abundant food, but injustice sweeps it away.

Proverbs 14:20
20 The poor are shunned even by their neighbors, but the rich have many friends.

Proverbs 17:5
5 Whoever mocks the poor shows contempt for their Maker; whoever gloats over disaster will not go unpunished.

Proverbs 18:5, 23
5 It is not good to be partial to the wicked and so deprive the innocent of justice.
23 The poor plead for mercy, but the rich answer harshly.

Proverbs 19:4, 7
4 Wealth attracts many friends, but even the closest friend of the poor person deserts them.
7 The poor are shunned by all their relatives—how much more do their friends avoid them! Though the poor pursue them with pleading, they are nowhere to be found.

Proverbs 21:13

13 Whoever shuts their ears to the cry of the poor will also cry out and not be answered.

Proverbs 22:22–23

22 Do not exploit the poor because they are poor and do not crush the needy in court, 23 for the LORD will take up their case and will exact life for life.

Proverbs 27:7

7 One who is full loathes honey from the comb, but to the hungry even what is bitter tastes sweet.

Proverbs 31:8–9

8 Speak up for those who cannot speak for themselves, for the rights of all who are destitute. 9 Speak up and judge fairly; defend the rights of the poor and needy.

PART 8: BARRIERS TO SUCCESS

Chapter 32: Anger and Temper

Proverbs 10:12

12 Hatred stirs up conflict, but love covers over all wrongs.

Proverbs 14:16–17

16 The wise fear the LORD and shun evil, but a fool is hotheaded and yet feels secure. 17 A quick-tempered person does foolish things, and the one who devises evil schemes is hated.

Proverbs 15:18, 20

18 A hot-tempered person stirs up conflict, but the one who is patient calms a quarrel.

20 A wise son brings joy to his father, but a foolish man despises his mother.

Proverbs 16:29, 32

29 A violent person entices their neighbor and leads them down a path that is not good.

32 Better a patient person than a warrior, one with self-control than one who takes a city.

Proverbs 17:14, 19

14 Starting a quarrel is like breaching a dam; so drop the matter before a dispute breaks out.

19 Whoever loves a quarrel loves sin; whoever builds a high gate invites destruction.

Proverbs 18:1, 18–19

1 An unfriendly person pursues selfish ends and against all sound judgment starts quarrels.

18 Casting the lot settles disputes and keeps strong opponents apart.

19 A brother wronged is more unyielding than a fortified city; disputes are like the barred gates of a citadel.

Proverbs 19:3, 19

3 A person's own folly leads to their ruin, yet their heart rages against the LORD.

19 A hot-tempered person must pay the penalty; rescue them, and you will have to do it again.

Proverbs 20:3

3 It is to one's honor to avoid strife, but every fool is quick to quarrel.

Proverbs 21:14

14 A gift given in secret soothes anger, and a bribe concealed in the cloak pacifies great wrath.

Proverbs 22:10, 24–25

10 Drive out the mocker, and out goes strife; quarrels and insults are ended. 24 Do not make friends with a hot-tempered person, do not associate with one easily angered, 25 or you may learn their ways and get yourself ensnared.

Proverbs 27:4

4 Anger is cruel and fury overwhelming, but who can stand before jealousy?

Proverbs 29:22

22 An angry person stirs up conflict, and a hot-tempered person commits many sins.

James 1:2–3

2 Consider it pure joy, my brothers and sisters, a whenever you face trials of many kinds, 3 because you know that the testing of your faith produces perseverance.

Chapter 33: You Killed My Father, Prepare to Die (Revenge)

Proverbs 20: 22

22 Do not say, "I'll pay you back for this wrong!" Wait for the LORD, and he will deliver you.

Proverbs 24:28–29

28 Do not testify against your neighbor without cause— would you use your lips to mislead? 29 Do not say, "I'll do to them as they have done to me; I'll pay them back for what they did."

Proverbs 24:21–22

21 If your enemy is hungry, give him food to eat; if he is thirsty, give him water to drink. 22 In doing this, you will heap burning coals on his head, and the LORD will reward you.

Proverbs 29:26

26 Many seek an audience with a ruler, but it is from the LORD that one gets justice.

Romans 12:17–21

17 Do not repay anyone evil for evil. Be careful to do what is right in the eyes of everyone. 18 If it is possible, as far as it depends on you, live at peace with everyone. 19 Do not take revenge, my dear friends, but leave room for God's wrath, for it is written: "It is mine to avenge; I will repay," says the Lord. 20 On the contrary:

"If your enemy is hungry, feed him; if he is thirsty, give him something to drink. In doing this, you will heap burning coals on his head."

21 Do not be overcome by evil, but overcome evil with good.

Chapter 34: Envy

Exodus 20:17

You shall not covet your neighbor's house. You shall not covet your neighbor's wife, or his male or female servant, his ox or donkey, or anything that belongs to your neighbor.

Proverbs 23:17–18

17 Do not let your heart envy sinners, but always be zealous for the fear of the LORD. 18 There is surely a future hope for you, and your hope will not be cut off.

Proverbs 24:1–2

1 Do not envy the wicked, do not desire their company; 2 for their hearts plot violence, and their lips talk about making trouble.

Chapter 35: Hedonism Overboard

Proverbs 21:17

17 Whoever loves pleasure will become poor; whoever loves wine and olive oil will never be rich.

Proverbs 23:19–21, 29–35

19 Listen, my son, and be wise, and set your heart on the right path: 20 Do not join those who drink too much wine or gorge themselves on meat, 21 for drunkards and gluttons become poor, and drowsiness clothes them in rags.

29 Who has woe? Who has sorrow? Who has strife? Who has complaints? Who has needless bruises? Who has bloodshot eyes? 30 Those who linger over wine, who go to sample bowls of mixed wine. 31 Do not gaze at wine when it is red, when it sparkles in the cup, when it goes down smoothly! 32 In the end it bites like a snake and poisons like a viper. 33 Your eyes will see strange sights, and your mind will imagine confusing things. 34 You will be like one sleeping on the high seas, lying on top of the rigging. 35 "They hit me," you will say, "but I'm not hurt! They beat me, but I don't feel it! When will I wake up so I can find another drink?"

Proverbs 25:16–17, 28

16 If you find honey, eat just enough—too much of it, and you will vomit. 17 Seldom set foot in your neighbor's house—too much of you, and they will hate you.

Proverbs 27:20

20 Death and Destruction are never satisfied, and neither are the eyes of man.

Proverbs 30:15–16

15 The leech has two daughters. "Give! Give!" they cry. There are three things that are never satisfied, four that never say, "Enough!": 16 the grave, the barren womb, land, which is never satisfied with water, and fire, which never says, "Enough!"

Chapter 36: Temptation
Proverbs 1:10–19

10 My son, if sinful men entice you, do not give in to them. 11 If they say, "Come along with us; let's lie in wait for innocent blood, let's ambush some harmless soul; 12 let's swallow them alive, like the grave, and whole, like those who go down to the pit; 13 we will get all sorts of valuable things and fill our houses with plunder; 14 cast lots with us; we will all share the loot"—15 my son, do not go along with them, do not set foot on their paths; 16 for their feet rush into evil, they are swift to shed blood. 17 How useless to spread a net where every bird can see it! 18 These men lie in wait for their own blood; they ambush only themselves! 19 Such are the paths of all who go after ill-gotten gain; it takes away the life of those who get it.

Proverbs 4:25–27

25 Let your eyes look straight ahead; fix your gaze directly before you. 26 Give careful thought to the paths for your feet and be steadfast in all your ways. 27 Do not turn to the right or the left; keep your foot from evil.

Proverbs 20:1

1 Wine is a mocker and beer a brawler; whoever is led astray by them is not wise.

Proverbs 25:28

28 Like a city whose walls are broken through is a person who lacks self-control.

Proverbs 31:1–7

1 The sayings of King Lemuel—an inspired utterance his mother taught him. 2 Listen, my son! Listen, son of my womb! Listen, my son, the answer to my prayers! 3 Do not spend your strength on women, your vigor on those who ruin kings. 4 It is not for kings, Lemuel—it is not for kings to drink wine, not for rulers to crave beer, 5 lest they drink

and forget what has been decreed, and deprive all the oppressed of their rights. 6 Let beer be for those who are perishing, wine for those who are in anguish! 7 Let them drink and forget their poverty and remember their misery no more.

PART 9: ME MANAGEMENT
Chapter 37: Joy
Proverbs 13:12, 19
12 Hope deferred makes the heart sick, but a longing fulfilled is a tree of life.
19 A longing fulfilled is sweet to the soul, but fools detest turning from evil.

Proverbs 14:30
30 A heart at peace gives life to the body, but envy rots the bones.

Proverbs 15:13, 15, 30
13 A happy heart makes the face cheerful, but heartache crushes the spirit. 15 All the days of the oppressed are wretched, but the cheerful heart has a continual feast.
30 Light in a messenger's eyes brings joy to the heart, and good news gives health to the bones.

Proverbs 17:22
22 A cheerful heart is good medicine, but a crushed spirit dries up the bones.

Chapter 38: Faith
Proverbs 3:3–6
3 Let love and faithfulness never leave you; bind them around your neck, write them on the tablet of your heart. 4 Then you will win favor and a good name in the sight of God and man. 5 Trust in the LORD with all your heart and lean not on your own understanding;
6 in all your ways submit to him, and he will make your paths straight.

Proverbs 25:19

19 Like a broken tooth or a lame foot is reliance on the unfaithful in a time of trouble.

Chapter 39: Patience

Proverbs 14:29

29 Whoever is patient has great understanding, but one who is quick-tempered displays folly.

Proverbs 16:32

32 Better a patient person than a warrior, one with self-control than one who takes a city.

Proverbs 19:2, 11

2 Desire without knowledge is not good—how much more will hasty feet miss the way!

11 A person's wisdom yields patience; it is to one's glory to overlook an offense.

Proverbs 20:25

25 It is a trap to dedicate something rashly and only later to consider one's vows.

Proverbs 21:5

5 The plans of the diligent lead to profit as surely as haste leads to poverty.

Chapter 40: RIGHTEOUSNESS: The Output of Wisdom

Matthew 1:18–21

18 This is how the birth of Jesus Christ came about: His mother Mary was pledged to be married to Joseph, but before they came together, she was found to be with child through the Holy Spirit. 19 Because Joseph her husband was a righteous man and did not want to expose her to public disgrace, he had in mind to divorce her quietly. 20 But

after he had considered this, an angel of the Lord appeared to him in a dream and said, "Joseph son of David, do not be afraid to take Mary home as your wife, because what is conceived in her is from the Holy Spirit. 21 She will give birth to a son, and you are to give him the name Jesus, because he will save his people from their sins.

James 3:17–18
17 But the wisdom that comes from heaven is first of all pure, then peace-loving, considerate, submissive, full of mercy, and good fruit, impartial and sincere. 18 Peacemakers who sow in peace raise a harvest of righteousness.

Proverbs 3:33–35
33 The LORD's curse is on the house of the wicked, but he blesses the home of the righteous. 34 He mocks proud mockers but shows favor to the humble and oppressed. 35 The wise inherit honor, but fools get only shame.

Proverbs 10:2–3,6–7,11,16, 20–21, 24–25, 28–32
2 Ill-gotten treasures have no lasting value, but righteousness delivers from death. 3 The LORD does not let the righteous go hungry, but he thwarts the craving of the wicked.
6 Blessings crown the head of the righteous, but violence overwhelms the mouth of the wicked 7 The name of the righteous is used in blessings, but the name of the wicked will rot.
11 The mouth of the righteous is a fountain of life, but the mouth of the wicked conceals violence.
16 The wages of the righteous is life, but the earnings of the wicked are sin and death.
20 The tongue of the righteous is choice silver, but the heart of the wicked is of little value. 21 The lips of the righteous nourish many, but fools die for lack of sense.

24 What the wicked dread will overtake them; what the righteous desire will be granted. 25 When the storm has swept by, the wicked are gone, but the righteous stand firm forever.

28 The prospect of the righteous is joy, but the hopes of the wicked come to nothing. 29 The way of the LORD is a refuge for the blameless, but it is the ruin of those who do evil. 30 The righteous will never be uprooted, but the wicked will not remain in the land. 31 From the mouth of the righteous comes the fruit of wisdom, but a perverse tongue will be silenced. 32 The lips of the righteous know what finds favor, but the mouth of the wicked only what is perverse.

Proverbs 11:4–6, 8–11, 16–21, 23, 27–31

4 Wealth is worthless in the day of wrath, but righteousness delivers from death. 5 The righteousness of the blameless makes their paths straight, but the wicked are brought down by their own wickedness. 6 The righteousness of the upright delivers them, but the unfaithful are trapped by evil desires.

8 The righteous person is rescued from trouble, and it falls on the wicked instead. 9 With their mouths the godless destroy their neighbors, but through knowledge the righteous escape. 10 When the righteous prosper, the city rejoices; when the wicked perish, there are shouts of joy. 11 Through the blessing of the upright a city is exalted, but by the mouth of the wicked it is destroyed.

16 A kindhearted woman gains honor, but ruthless men gain only wealth. 17 Those who are kind benefit themselves, but the cruel bring ruin on themselves. 18 A wicked person earns deceptive wages, but the one who sows righteousness reaps a sure reward. 19 Truly the righteous attain life, but whoever pursues evil finds death. 20 The LORD detests those whose hearts are perverse, but he delights in those whose ways are blameless. 21 Be sure of this: The wicked will not go unpunished, but those who are righteous will go free.

23 The desire of the righteous ends only in good, but the hope of the wicked only in wrath.

27 Whoever seeks good finds favor, but evil comes to one who searches for it. 28 Those who trust in their riches will fall, but the righteous will thrive like a green leaf. 29 Whoever brings ruin on their family will inherit only wind, and the fool will be servant to the wise. 30 The fruit of the righteous is a tree of life, and the one who is wise saves lives. 31 If the righteous receive their due on earth, how much more the ungodly and the sinner!

Proverbs 12:3, 5, 7, 10, 12–13, 21, 26, 28
3 No one can be established through wickedness, but the righteous cannot be uprooted.
5 The plans of the righteous are just, but the advice of the wicked is deceitful.
7 The wicked are overthrown and are no more, but the house of the righteous stands firm.
10 The righteous care for the needs of their animals, but the kindest acts of the wicked are cruel.
12 The wicked desire the stronghold of evildoers, but the root of the righteous endures. 13 Evildoers are trapped by their sinful talk, but a righteous man escape trouble.
21 No harm overtakes the righteous, but the wicked have their fill of trouble.
26The righteous choose their friends carefully, but the way of the wicked leads them astray.
28 In the way of righteousness there is life; along that path is immortality.

Proverbs 13:5–6, 9, 21, 25
5 The righteous hate what is false, but the wicked make themselves a stench and bring shame on themselves. 6 Righteousness guards the person of integrity, but wickedness overthrows the sinner.
9 The light of the righteous shines brightly, but the lamp of the wicked is snuffed out.

21 Trouble pursues the sinner, but the righteous are rewarded with good things.

25 The righteous eat to their hearts' content, but the stomach of the wicked goes hungry.

Proverbs 14:2, 4, 19, 32, 34

2 Whoever fears the LORD walks uprightly, but those who despise him are devious in their ways.

4 Where there are no oxen, the manger is empty, but from the strength of an ox come abundant harvests.

19 Evildoers will bow down in the presence of the good, and the wicked at the gates of the righteous.

32 When calamity comes, the wicked are brought down, but even in death the righteous seek refuge in God.

34 Righteousness exalts a nation, but sin condemns any people.

Proverbs 15:3, 6, 9, 28, 29

3 The eyes of the LORD are everywhere, keeping watch on the wicked and the good.

6 The house of the righteous contains great treasure, but the income of the wicked brings ruin.

8 The LORD detests the sacrifice of the wicked, but the prayer of the upright pleases him.

9 The LORD detests the way of the wicked, but he loves those who pursue righteousness.

28 The heart of the righteous weighs its answers, but the mouth of the wicked gushes evil. 29 The LORD is far from the wicked, but he hears the prayer of the righteous.

Proverbs 16:12, 17, 31

12 Kings detest wrongdoing, for a throne is established through righteousness.

17 The highway of the upright avoids evil; those who guard their ways preserve their lives.

31 Gray hair is a crown of splendor; it is attained in the way of righteousness.

Proverbs 18:10
10 The name of the LORD is a fortified tower; the righteous run to it and are safe.

Proverbs 20:7
7 The righteous lead blameless lives; blessed are their children after them.

Proverbs 21:12, 15, 21
12 The Righteous One takes note of the house of the wicked and brings the wicked to ruin.
15 When justice is done, it brings joy to the righteous but terror to evildoers.
18 The wicked become a ransom for the righteous, and the unfaithful for the upright.
21Whoever pursues righteousness and love finds life, prosperity and honor.

Proverbs 22:5, 11, 12
5 In the paths of the wicked lie thorns and snares, but he who guards his soul stays far from them.
11 One who loves a pure heart and who speaks with grace will have the king for a friend. 12 The eyes of the LORD keep watch over knowledge, but he frustrates the words of the unfaithful.

Proverbs 23:15–16
15 My son, if your heart is wise, then my heart will be glad indeed;16 my inmost being will rejoice when your lips speak what is right.

Proverbs 25:4–5, 26

4 Remove the dross from the silver, and a silversmith can produce a vessel; 5 remove wicked officials from the king's presence, and his throne will be established through righteousness.

26 Like a muddied spring or a polluted well are the righteous who give way to the wicked.

Proverbs 28:1

1 The wicked flee though no one pursues, but the righteous are as bold as a lion.

Proverbs 29:6, 7, 16, 27

6 Evildoers are snared by their own sin, but the righteous shout for joy and are glad. 7 The righteous care about justice for the poor, but the wicked have no such concern.

16 When the wicked thrive, so does sin, but the righteous will see their downfall.

27 The righteous detest the dishonest; the wicked detest the upright.

James 1:23–24

23 Anyone who listens to the word but does not do what it says is like someone who looks at his face in a mirror 24 and, after looking at himself, goes away and immediately forgets what he looks like.

1 Kings 3:9

9 So give your servant a discerning heart to govern your people and to distinguish between right and wrong. For who is able to govern this great people of yours?"

Chapter 41: GOTCHAS and WARNINGS

Ecclesiastes 7:16–18

16 Do not be overrighteous, neither be overwise— why destroy yourself? 17 Do not be overwicked and do not be a fool— why die before your time? 18 It is good to grasp the one and not let go of the other. Whoever fears God will avoid all extremes.

Matthew 7:13–14

13 "Enter through the narrow gate. For wide is the gate and broad is the road that leads to destruction, and many enter through it. 14 But small is the gate and narrow the road that leads to life, and only a few find it.

One More Thing:

Romans 10:9

9 If you declare with your mouth, "Jesus is Lord," and believe in your heart that God raised him from the dead, you will be saved. 10 For it is with your heart that you believe and are justified, and it is with your mouth that you profess your faith and are saved.

Acumen is an engaging community of CEOs and business owners who want more—personally and professionally.

With a proven framework to grow your business, we challenge and guide you as a leader. (Is this what you've been missing?")

Sharpen *Your* Edge

Acumen's purpose is to Ignite a Higher Standard of CEO influence and Business Impact.

We do this by building accelerator communities that sharpen, challenge, and inspire CEOs and Owners.

Want to get stay connected, improve performance, and accelerate growth?

- Join our email list and receive more tools and encouragement: www.AcumenImpact.com
- Learn more about joining a CEO and Owner team: email sharpen@AcumenImpact.com

CPSIA information can be obtained
at www.ICGtesting.com
Printed in the USA
LVHW021000081019
633522LV00011B/493/P